INTERNATIONAL ISLAMIC CONFERENCE

Dawa and Development of the Muslim World

The Future Perspective

17–21 Safar 1408/11–15 October 1987

Makkah Al Mukarramah/Muslim World League

بِسْمِ اللّهِ الرَّحْمٰنِ الرَّحِيمِ

And that there might grow out of you a community (of people) who invite unto all that is good and enjoin the doing of what is right and forbid the doing of what is wrong. And it is they, they who shall attain to a happy state!

The Quran 3:104

Beyond Frontiers

Islam and Contemporary Needs

Edited by *Merryl Wyn Davies*
and *Adnan Khalil Pasha*

MANSELL

LONDON AND NEW YORK

First published 1989 by **Mansell Publishing Limited**
A Cassell imprint
Artillery House, Artillery Row, London SW1P 1RT, England
125 East 23rd Street, Suite 300, New York 10010, U.S.A.

© Merryl Davies, Adnan Khalil Pasha and the contributors 1989

British Library Cataloguing in Publication Data

Beyond frontiers: Islam and contemporary needs.
  1. Islam
  I. Davies, Merryl Wyn   II. Pasha, Adnan Khalil
  297
  ISBN 0–7201–2039–X

Library of Congress Cataloging in Publication Data

Beyond frontiers: Islam and contemporary needs / edited by Merryl Wyn
  Davies and Adnan Khalil Pasha.
    p.   cm.
  Includes index.
  ISBN 0–7201–2039–X
  1. Dawah (Islam) I. Davies, Merryl Wyn.   II. Pasha,
  Adnan Khalil.
  BP170.85.B48   1989
  297'.7—dc20   89–12316
                                                                      CIP

This book has been printed and bound in Great Britain: typeset by
Colset (Private) Ltd., Singapore, and printed and bound by Biddles Ltd.,
Guildford, on Onslow Book Wove paper.

Contents

Contributors

Aslam Abdullah, a freelance journalist, was until recently Associate Editor of *Arabia: Islamic World Review*.

Syed Z. Abedin is Director of the Insitute of Muslim Minority Affairs and Editor of its bi-annual *Journal*.

M. Manazir Ahsan is Director of the Islamic Foundation, Leicester, author of *Social Life Under the Abbasids*, 1979, and Editor of the quarterly journal, *Muslim World Book Review*.

Ayman Ahwal, a freelance journalist, has spent much of his life helping refugees in the Sudan, Eritrea, Pakistan and other parts of the world.

Mir Qasim Ali is Director of the Bangladesh Office of the Muslim World League, and is involved in a number of projects aimed at eradicating poverty.

Merryl Wyn Davies, writer and television producer, is the author of *Knowing One Another: Shaping an Islamic Anthropology*, 1988, and the producer of *Faces of Islam* (a series of twelve half-hour discussion programmes on the central ideas and concepts of Islam).

Abdul Wahid Hamid is Director of Muslim Educational and Literary Services (MELS), London, and the author of *Islam: the Natural Way*, 1989, and a number of secondary school textbooks.

Kamal Hasan, Shaikh of the Centre for Fundamental Studies, International Islamic University, Malaysia, is the author of *Muslim Intellectual Responses to 'New Order' Modernization in Indonesia*, 1982.

Aisha Lemu, Secretary of the Islamic Education Trust of Nigeria and Amira of the Federation of Muslim Women's Associations of Nigeria (FOMWAN), is the author of a number of junior and secondary school textbooks.

Ayyub Malik is a senior partner in the architectural firm, Chapman, Taylor and Partners, of London.

Abdullah Omar Naseef, Secretary-General of the Muslim World League, Makkah, is co-editor of *Social and Natural Sciences: The Islamic Perspective*, 1981, and Editor of *Today's Problems, Tomorrow's Solutions*, 1988.

Adnan Khalil Pasha is Assistant Secretary-General for Education and Culture, Muslim World League, Makkah.

Fadlullah Wilmot was, until recently, Director of Information for the Regional Islamic Dawa Council of South East Asia and the Pacific (RISEAP) and Editor of their journal, *Al-Nahdah*. He is the author of *A Layman's Guide to Islam*, 1989.

Introduction
Dawa and Development: The Future Dimension

Adnan Khalil Pasha

The message of Islam is universal and addressed to the whole of mankind. Muslims therefore have the obligation to ensure that it reaches all peoples at all times in human history. The message remains the same but conventions of communication and relevant issues are determined by the ever-changing circumstances. Repeating the communicative formulaes of a bygone era, couching our ideas in topics of no immediate relevance to today or evading major contemporary predicaments in order to hold to a narrow focus of primary moral teachings diminishes the stature and import of the message of Islam. *Dawa*, communicating the message of Islam, is an obligation that cannot be shirked by Muslims, neither can it be fulfilled by anything less than our greatest exertions. The status and means of *dawa* are an indication of the health and vibrancy of Muslim civilization, its ability to keep pace with the challenge of history and express itself as a total way of life, harnessing and utilizing all the potential of the time according to its timeless ethic. By evaluating how we undertake *dawa*, we can discern how we as Muslims are fitting ourselves for the future.

Dawa first has to be directed towards Muslims. Here, *dawa* must go beyond the simple sermonizing about Islam. Apart from concentrating our minds on spiritual matters, *dawa* must tackle the basic problems of Muslim communities, must promote self-sufficiency and self-reliance. There are some major questions to be addressed. How can *dawa* become a major tool of community development? How can *dawa* be used to tackle the basic ills of Muslim society, from poverty and illiteracy to parochialism and sectarianism that so deform Muslim societies? What can be done to wean Muslims away from religious factionalism? How can we emphasize the rich diversity of Islam? What contributions can Muslims make to multicultural societies and what should be the position of multiculturalism in Muslim societies? What are the dynamics of 'unity in diversity'? Should minority Muslim populations isolate themselves from the concerns of non-Muslim majorities? What is the future of Muslim minorities across the globe? What can be done to promote ethnic and linguistic unity in the Muslim world? How can we make ethnicity and the diversity of Muslim culture a source of strength for Muslim people? What can we do to promote self-confidence in indigenous traditions and cultures?

When answers to such questions are sought with reference to *dawa*, a whole new perspective emerges. From the dawn of time the challenge of Islam has always been the same. Islam summons all men and women to acknowledge their submission before Allah, the Creator, the Beneficent, the Merciful, the First and the Last. This acknowledgement requires those who submit to the will of Allah to follow the Straight Path, the Path of Islam, as revealed in the Quran and taught by the Prophet Muhammad, by his practice and examples. The guidance the Quran provides, which was given a practical shape by the Prophet, is valid for all time and all places. Those who follow this guidance will prosper, both in this world and the next.

However, the eternal values of Islam have to be lived in the realities of a changing world. At a time when the pace of change is increasing, when science and technology are rapidly transforming society, the question confronting believers is not one of arresting or standing against change. The central question is how to express the eternal teachings and values of Islam, in the best possible way, in the face of rapid change.

There are nearly one billion Muslims spread around the globe, a community of believers united in the common worship of Allah. The bond of faith is symbolized each day when, no matter where we are, all Muslims turn towards Makkah to offer daily prayers. Indeed, Muslims are an *ummah*, an international community united in its values and goals, in its aspirations and practice of Islam. But today there is another force which binds the *ummah* together: the force of rapid change. Muslims everywhere face the challenge of clarifying the meaning of faith and of finding the best possible expression of Islamic values in the face of the diversity of change which we all meet in our daily lives.

However, change is not only affecting Muslim societies, but is also

having a major effect on Western civilization. In recent times, Western
societies have gone through numerous transformations, some positive,
some destructive. There is no doubt that Muslims can learn a great deal
from the West, for Western and Muslim civilizations have a great deal in
common and share a number of basic human values. But the frames of
reference of the two civilizations are not the same: Western civilization
has its roots in a secular tradition which has done considerable harm to
the social and ecological fabric of our planet. Indeed, the secular
approach has harmed all societies, traditional and modern, throughout
the world. While the two civilizations share many of their goals and
aspirations, their paths are not the same.

The most profound challenge that faces Muslim societies is to map
out a clear path to the future. Muslims must find new ways of expressing
and communicating our belief in Islam, both to solve ever-increasing
problems and to provide an example so that other societies might appre-
ciate the nobility of Islam and follow the path of the believers; the best
possible way of practising *dawa* is by example, both individually and
through the community.

The 'Dawa and Development' Conference tried to focus the minds of
the participating thinkers, scholars and community workers on mapping
out directions for future thought and action. The result of the deliberations appear in three volumes, the first two being *Today's Problems and
Tomorrow's Solutions: the Future Structure of Muslim Societies* and *An
Early Crescent: the Future of Knowledge and Environment in Islam*. While
the earlier volumes focused on the Shariah and Islamization, economy
and family life, thought and epistemology, science and environment, the
present book concerns itself with the practical dimensions of *dawa*.
Beyond Frontiers develops a fresh perspective on *dawa* and relates *dawa*
specifically to community development and the evolution of contemporary (both traditional and modern) modes of communicating Islam.

Dawa, as M. Manazir Ahsan points out in 'Dawa and its significance
for the future', literally means 'call' and in Islamic terminology 'an
invitation to Islam'. For him Islam means *dawa*, or *dawa* is essentially
the fulfilment of Islam. This call is directed towards Muslims as well as
non-Muslims. It is a continuous process, 'a perpetual endeavour aimed
at inviting one's own self, every Muslim and all those who are not yet
Muslims to embrace Islam willingly and completely'. It is not 'an occupation to be undertaken by a professional group, neither is it a contingent, part-time activity nor one undertaken in reaction to Christian or
communist onslaught'. The textbook of *dawa* is the Sunnah, the example of the Prophet. But Ahsan does not regard *dawa* simply as a process;

he also envisages it as a critique. He states categorically that 'a thorough critique of Western civilization is part of *dawa*: on all issues, whether it is the theory of knowledge, problems of race and colour, sexual politics or AIDS, disintegration of the family, economy or politics, war or peace, Muslims have to present appropriate solutions derived from the Quran and Sunnah and make known the merits of these solutions using the appropriate language, medium and technology'.

Fadlullah Wilmot extends that critique to Muslims themselves. The basic problem of *dawa*, he states in his 'Dawa, a practical approach for the future', is that those engaged in it are not the best specimens of Islamic ideals and aspirations. *Dawa* must thus start with self-criticism. For example, 'much of contemporary *dawa* has a negative view of culture and some *dawa* movements are actively opposed to the burning needs of men and women for the aesthetic and the beautiful. For *dawa* movements culture has come to be equated with ritual; and expressions of art, music and literature are sacrificed at the altar of 'minimal Islam'. Wilmot argues that *dawa* is a gradual process and does not offer instant, palliatives; it 'does not seek one-dimensional simplistic solutions'. He argues that the emphasis of *dawa* should be on solving the pressing problems of Muslims: eradication of poverty, provision of nutrition and education to the young, empowering the powerless, delivering the rights of the marginalized, securing justice for the oppressed and providing basic necessities for the vast majority of mankind'. Such a perspective on *dawa* is the prime focus for reconstructing Muslim civilization. What Ahsan and Wilmot are saying is that without a thriving, dynamic Muslim civilization that personifies the best in human thought and behaviour, *dawa* cannot be fully realized.

Given the fact *dawa* is a religious duty of every Muslim, is it possible for Muslims to engage in dialogue with believers of other faiths without proselytizing? Is it possible, asks Syed Z. Abedin in his 'Dawa and dialogue, believers and promotion of mutual trust', for the followers Islam and Christianity to come together to promote trust and community? Can Christian–Muslim dialogues achieve this goal? Both on the basis of textual evidence and reasoned arguments, Abedin concludes that in the promotion of 'righteousness and piety' Muslims as believers can co-operate in any effort towards that goal with any group. Indeed, given the present conditions of mankind, he thinks that it is imperative for the followers of the two faiths to co-operate in ensuring the survival of mankind, attainment of peace and harmony and the enrichment of the quality of life. But this coming together must be on the basis of equality and dignity. *Dawa* should not be equated with conversion. Abedin also convincingly argues that while *dawa* belongs to the realm of man, conversion — change of heart — belongs to the domain of God. Thus *dawa* does not aim at conversion, 'a body count'; it aims at promoting good in general and communicating the message of Islam in particular; *dawa* can, therefore, continue *ad infinitum* without saving 'a single soul'.

Abedin sees 'promoting good' in its widest possible sense. Part Two of this volume spells out more specifically what 'promoting good' can mean for Muslims. For Kamal Hasan, the ideals of *dawa* are not much different from the goals of community development. As he writes in 'The nature of our community, the tasks ahead', '*Dawa* aimed at community development requires that we understand the nature of communities with which we are dealing'. He examines the major characteristics and trends of Muslim societies and identifies rapid population growth, unemployment, rural migrations, illiteracy and many other factors as urgently needing attention. On the positive side appear the phenomena of 'revivalism' or 'resurgence', the growth of Islamic financial, social and educational institutions. All these areas must become the focus of *dawa*; Hasan himself tackles the educational aspects of community development and the particular problems of Muslim minorities and concludes with some specific suggestions for improving the conditions of the global Muslim community, the *ummah*.

The theme of community development is continued by Ayyub Malik, who considers it to be the basic component of Muslim cities and society. As he reflects on the creation of a post-modern world in his 'Places, people and poverty, the challenge of change', Malik suggests that Muslims must prepare to contribute the social, moral and ideological concepts of their own system of values if they are to play an active part in the next cycle of world history. Unconscious and uncritical imitation of modernity is the root cause for the present degradation of Muslim people. Muslim thought and development activities have up-to-now been based solely on an alien and borrowed modernity — this is why 'despite the modernizing policies and efforts of the last few decades, the living conditions, the experience and emotion of the fast-growing Muslim cities remain evident only in their social and cultural irrelevance, their environmental decay and despair and their unremitting ugliness'. Malik asserts that every age has to confront its own change and define its own modernity. 'Human and social ideals, visions, and worldviews need all to be spelt out in some detail by every society at each level of its reality and each stage of its history'. An equitable future for Muslim people can be shaped if the community becomes intrinsically involved in building its own environment, where imams, *ulamas* and the people come together to shape a community, their built and natural environments.

Mir Qasim Ali explores how *dawa* can be used for community development by examining the *dawa* programmes in Bangladesh. Poverty must be attacked from an integrated framework, he argues in his 'Meeting basic needs, the example of Bangladesh'; *dawa* thus has to go beyond the provision of food. He describes the Comprehensive Integrated Development Programme, a long-range endeavour that aims to promote self-sufficiency and self-reliance among the rural population by providing a string of economic and social service packages to tackle poverty, ill health, illiteracy and social malaise. The cornerstone of the plan is community participation in planning, implementation, monitoring and evaluation of the programme.

Hasan, Malik and Ali see community consensus and participation as the key to development; in their analyses, *dawa* must go hand-in-hand with open dialogue in which all segments of the community freely participate. The next two papers in this section deal with two minorities which are almost always excluded from dialogue, often marginalized and suppressed. Aisha Lemu argues forcefully that women cannot be excluded either from *dawa* or, what amounts to the same thing in the context of this book, from development. In 'Educating the other half, no half measures', she argues that women's education should be a major priority for *dawa* work. Even in their conventional roles, women are accepted as the guardians of our future. How then can uneducated women lay the foundations of a dynamic, thriving Islamic civilization of the future? 'An uneducated woman can do little to promote her children's education. She cannot teach what she does not know. She cannot supervise her children's homework, or give them useful guidance or counselling in their school affairs or choice of careers. She may even have a negative effect on the education of daughters in particular, discouraging them because she feels inferior or left behind, or because she sees them departing from what is traditionally expected of females, and cannot see the need for their having more than the bare minimum of education.' Lemu is in favour of women's education in an holistic framework where women are exposed to the full range of subjects at higher levels, as well as the appropriate preparation for such subjects. She offers some practical suggestions based on her own experience in Nigeria.

Ayman Ahwal describes the plight of the other, almost forgotten, minority — the refugees. In 'A nation in exile, tackling the problem of refugees', he tells us that of the over twelve million refugees in the world, most are Muslims. Huge numbers of refugees from Afghanistan,

Ethiopia, Palestine, Kurdistan, Iran, Iraq, Chad, Uganda, Mozambique and Somalia live in the squalor of refugee camps. Having fled their countries to escape war, famine, oppression and natural disasters, they are to be found living in sprawling communities near the border of the first country of sanctuary they have reached. 'The Prophet himself was a refugee and a migrant, that the Muslim calendar is dated from his *hijra*, migration, to a place of refuge, and that those who migrated with him, the *muhijirin*, became the core and inspiration of the Medina state. This prototype Muslim nation of refugees is to this day the example of all Muslim life, secular and spiritual. Thus the very condition of being a refugee can be seen as being sanctified, the evolution of such a society as having the best possible exemplary model, and its aspirations and outcomes as having the most momentous possibilities'. Yet, the situation of refugees and the esteem in which they are held today is very different. 'Their very existence is a cause for collective shame on the part of the world community'. The refugees often end up totally dependent for their existence on aid agencies, which can often be tyrannical, their influence often wielded in far from diplomatic ways. He charts the rise of Muslim aid agencies and offers some practical suggestions for alleviating the plight of the refugees.

The malaise of contemporary Muslim societies and their suffocation in poverty and degradation is partly a product of their history, partly an outcome of the unjust structures of the modern world, and partly due to their own neglect of the teachings and ideals of Islam. Many contemporary Muslim scholars have argued that Muslim masses have become totally divorced from Islam, that their knowledge of Islam is often half-baked, based more on superstitions and folklore than on the true teachings of Islam. If this is true, the fault must lie in how Islam is being communicated. The third part of this volume, therefore, focuses on improving the communication of Islam in our time.

Aslam Abdullah offers a comprehensive survey of the Muslim print media. He describes a society dominated by mental and physical poverty. In 'Muslim Print media, present status and future directions'. The existing print media in the Muslim world is largely controlled both by national agencies and outside powers, and is of extremely poor quality. It is produced by the elite for the elite; issues of importance to rural population, women and other marginalized segments of society are totally ignored. It follows the news values of the West and is heavily dependent on a handful of Western news agencies. He makes a number of suggestions to improve the situation, from undertaking certain basic studies to establishing essential services — such as national press archives, photographic libraries, media monitoring groups — all of which need urgent and serious attention from Muslim quarters.

Abdul Wahid Hamid, in 'Urban grapevines, establishing community newspapers', suggests that the isolation and alienation of both urban and rural populations can be ameliorated by setting up community newspapers. He lists a number of important roles such newspapers can play, from providing basic civic and community information to campaigning for local issues, from promoting businesses and entrepreneurs to acting as watchdogs. He discusses some of the basic requirements for launching such papers.

Radio and television, the broadcast media are the most pervasive means of communication in the modern world. Merryl Wyn Davies seeks to develop a set of Islamic principles that would distinguish a distinctive Muslim public-service broadcasting. She begins by making an arresting analysis of the Islamic conception of existence and community which leads her to conclude there should be a natural affinity between Muslims and the broadcast media and that Muslims should see broadcasting as an opportunity for serving the objectives of Islam.

Davies discusses how Muslim broadcasting should derive moral and ethical guidelines from Islam to develop its own culture of broadcasting instead of remaining dependent upon the conventions of broadcasting imported with the technology from Western civilization. The ending of what she terms 'imitative inertia' by Muslims would create a public-service broadcasting system that would itself be a contemporary testimony to *dawa*, a channel of communication for *dawa* and would provide a forum in which the issues raised by other writers in this volume as the substance of *dawa* would be addressed by educational and informational programming. Davies argues that unless Muslims are prepared to allocate financial backing to such broadcasting endeavours, the full potentiality of an integrated service will never be developed.

Abdullah Omar Naseef brings *Beyond Frontiers* to a fitting close by arguing that *dawa* should be the cornerstone for planning for the Muslim *ummah*. He says that planning 'defines a course along which we wish to proceed, in practical terms of policies and programmes that can be undertaken'. The Muslim *ummah* is beset with disasters from floods to famine, from poverty to environmental pollution; we are thus continuously engaged in crisis management. It is because we see these events as disasters that we feel so helpless, so overwhelmed. We must learn to turn them into hurdles, which are surmountable. Disasters become hurdles when we anticipate them, when we involve ourselves in risk management. Thus, the outlook of risk assessment needs to be part of the planning and thinking of Muslims in a wide-ranging and inclusive way. 'Risk assessment is the implementation of the duties and obligations of the *khilafah*, the action of the prudent steward. It is the operation of the central teachings of Islam in the conditions and opportunities of the modern world.' 'The objective of *dawa* is a gradual reformation of society, a continual transformation of people and communities to bring them closer to the Straight Path and maintain them along this Straight Path. Islamic risk assessment as part of every activity is the mental awareness necessary for this inescapable task'. His conclusion should shape the thoughts and actions of all those who have taken it upon themselves to invite others to all that is good. '*Dawa* today is about planning to change things, to transmute the potential and real disasters of our times into surmountable hurdles. It is the only training available to Muslims to prepare ourselves to inhabit a viable Islamic future'.

Time, change and the frailties of mankind have carried Muslims along many diverse paths. Yet our worldview forces us to think about the common well-being of the *ummah*, to strive to co-operate, despite the differences of our circumstances, and to place our common endeavour in the service of improving the state of all mankind. The challenge of *dawa* today is to ensure that Muslims throughout the world evolve a lifestyle based on self-reliance and self-sufficiency, cultural authenticity and social justice, creativity and innovative problem-solving. *Dawa* demands that we seriously reflect on a wide range of questions. How can we exert our best efforts to enable the sublime trust of Allah, our terrestrial home, the earth, to flourish in the face of the inevitable rapid and wide-ranging change? How can we hold strongly to the spirit and essence of Islam? What does it mean today to seek Allah's pleasure amid the profusion of choices and opportunities that are available to mankind? How can Muslims, despite their differences, be united and work, think and tackle their problems together? How can Muslims offer each other practical aid, support and mutual understanding derived from their faith when they live in so many different nations, in differing conditions, facing different demands? How can we draw upon the common legacy of our history to help us identify the Straight Path which we must walk through the changing times of the fifteenth *hijra* century? The true contemporary significance of *dawa* will begin with practical and pragmatic answers to these questions.

Part One

*The Meaning and
Significance of Dawa*

Dawa and Its Significance for the Future

M. Manazir Ahsan

Thomas Arnold records that a Muslim juriconsult who came to Eastern Europe at the beginning of the eleventh century, not in freedom but in chains, was instrumental in bringing thousands of Europeans to Islam. One wonders how this man, most probably not knowing the language of the people, not familiar with their customs and traditions and not able to move about freely, was able to accomplish what millions of Muslims living freely in the West in comfort and affluence, with freedom and opportunities, cannot perform these days. It is an indictment to one billion Muslims all over the world that in spite of all their facilities of freedom and publicity, they cannot achieve what a prisoner did centuries ago. In fact, what this Muslim prisoner accomplished is not unusual; the early history of Islam is replete with instances of individual Muslim savants, *ulama* and *sufia*, illuminating the hearts of people with the light of *iman*, faith, and spreading the message of Islam far and wide.

The word *dawa* has been so used, misused and abused by Muslim and non-Muslim writers and polemicists that in the maze of discussion and counter-discussion, it has lost many of the dimensions of its true meaning. Unless the true nature, scope and significance of *dawa* is understood with all its implications and dimensions, it is not possible to chart any future plan for this noble calling.

Dawa literally means 'call' and in Islamic terminology 'an invitation to Islam', and it is the *raison d'etre* of the existence of the Muslim *ummah*, both at the micro and macro level. It would not be incorrect to say that Islam means *dawa* — for *dawa* is essentially the fulfillment of Islam. One can become a Muslim by declaring the Shahadah: 'I bear witness there is no god but Allah and Muhammad is His Servant and Messenger'. But the true Shahadah, that is witness, cannot mature, flower and bear fruit unless the private confession assumes the form of a public proclammation of the truth. This is what *dawa* means.

Witnessing by word, *Shahadah bil qaul*, and reinforcing it by action *Shahadah bil Amal*, are two sides of the same coin — both are complementary and necessary to the other. Muslims cannot offer their lives as testimonies to Islam, and thereby fulfill the demands of *dawa*, unless both aspects of the testimony, words and actions, are properly synchronized and present in their lives. To acquire only one aspect is not only discouraged by the whole body of teaching and ethos of Islam but runs the risk of becoming hypocritical.

It is wrong to assume that *dawa* is aimed only at non-Muslims and that Muslims, by virtue of their birth in a Muslim family or be declaring the *Kalimah as Shahadah*, the declaration of faith, at the time of entering the fold of Islam, have been absolved of this responsibility for life. Islam is not a once-in-a-lifetime decision, but a process, a lifelong pursuit. Islam is not a status conferred by the declaration of faith, it is a dynamic state of becoming affirmed by constant activity throughout the course of life — the mechanism of affirmation is *dawa*. So *dawa* must begin with the conscious action of the individual Muslim's lifestyle, to be expressed in the organization of the community to offer an example and invite others to the path of Islam as a complete way of life. To be a Muslim means continually to strive to become Muslim. 'You who believe enter into the fold of Islam completely' (Quran 2:208) and 'Do not embrace death unless you are in a state of Islam' (Quran 3:101).

Dawa is, therefore, a continuous process, a perpetual endeavour aimed at inviting one's own self, every Muslim and all those who are not yet Muslims to embrace Islam willingly and completely. Similarly, *dawa* is not an occupation to be undertaken by any professional group, neither is it a contingent or part-time activity nor one undertaken in reaction to Christian missions or communist onslaughts. *Dawa* is the responsibility of every Muslim, whether a ruler or ruled, a leader or follower, a scholar or student, a Sufi or soldier, a trader or farmer, wealthy or poor, a man or a woman, living in the East or the West, North or the South. No one has a greater or lesser responsibility among *Daiya*, those who undertake *dawa*, and no one can shirk, postpone or evade this responsibility under any circumstances.

Dawa is by no means an easy task; neither is there a mechanical or uniform way of performing it, for no two people perform *dawa* in exactly the same way. Each section of society must accomplish this task in its own way with whatever faculties Allah has endowed them and with whatever wisdom and skill they can muster. The scholars and intellectuals of Islam will have their own methods and techniques of *dawa*, as will soldiers, diplomats, students and people in other walks of life.

Dawa is an essential part of the Sunnah, the way of the Prophet. Indeed, the very nature of the Sunnah, the record of the words and deeds of the Prophet Muhammad, is to be the textbook of *dawa*, a summation of its dimensions. *Dawa* must be undertaken in recognition of the mission of *Shahadah* and *gist*, or witnessing to the truth and justice. Moreover, *dawa* cannot be done correctly and fruitfully unless it is put in its proper place in the total framework of Islam. Similarly, the concepts, approaches and methods of *dawa* cannot be derived from sources other than the Quran and Sunnah of the Prophet Muhammad and the lives of other messengers. Ideally, *dawa* should be done at the macro, intermediate and micro levels of society. If, for various reasons, it is not possible to achieve this in modern times at least it must be done at some intermediate and micro levels.

Since *dawa* is essentially a call for change from sickness to health and the *daiyah* is not merely a transmitter of a message, it is essential that a rapport be established between the proponent and the listener. *Dawa* cannot be a unilateral, one-way process. It must involve a meaningful dialogue to be pursued with care, wisdom and patience. Unless the audience is psychologically attuned to be receptive, the message will not find its way to the heart. This is why all methods of compulsion, exploitation, inciting combative reaction or provoking prejudiced retaliation are strictly forbidden in Islam. *Dawa* has to be achieved with understanding, compassion, *sabr*, and above all, with great wisdom. This is also why the quality of the Prophet's benevolent disposition has been commended as the reason for his successful mission (Quran 3:159).

Dawa should be a gradual process with fixed priorities. Fundamentals must take precedence over details and obligatory duties should come before non-obligatory ones. Faith, *iman*, should be the cornerstone of all *dawa*, through the attainment of which the road to an Islamic life can be followed. Everything cannot be achieved at once. Was not the Quran revealed piecemeal over a period of twenty-three years so that people and society could adopt Islam step-by-step and become firmly rooted in it through a gradual process? Moreover, *dawa* entails the evolution of a system of moral training and spiritual purification, *tarbiyyah* and *tazkiyyah*, so that the mechanism for absorption and consolidation operates along with the machinery for contact and expansion.

The numerical strength of Islam has never been as great as it is today. Yet Muslims as a whole have little, if any, impact on the global scene, neither in economy nor politics nor in intellectual and scientific pursuits. The image of Islam portrayed both in the East and West is mostly negative, truncated, a partial view. There may be some external contributory factors, such as a long spell of colonialism in Muslim lands, but no one except Muslims can be blamed for their dismal failure to make an impact on the world scene. Any perceptive analyst will discern that the Muslim *ummah*, the international community of believers, despite being designated as 'the best' and 'middle most community' in the Quran, have on the whole failed in their duty to carry the message of Islam to mankind at large. The laurels announced for Muslims to be 'the best among nations' (Quran 3:110) are not without responsibility. It is conditional on their will to bid what is proper and forbid what is improper and believe in God. The responsibility of *Amr bil Maruf was an Nahi anil Munkar* is not only confined to the Muslim masses; it is designed to address the whole of mankind, *Ukhrijat lin Nas*, irrespective of creed, language, territory and colour. Muslims are therefore witnesses to the whole of mankind, to whom they are supposed to present through their lives a complete model of Islam.

The theoretical framework of *dawa* being such, the contemporary situation of the Muslim *ummah* does not inspire much hope for we are performing almost no *dawa*. Very little, if any, portion of national resources are spent on this vital duty. Moreover, Muslims living within non-Muslim countries by-and-large are indifferent to this immensely important task. With rare exceptions, *dawa* among non-Muslims commands little of their attention, time and resources, and for the most part the comprehensive nature of *dawa*, its scope and dimensions are not fully comprehended, let alone appreciated. Whether because of unawareness, indifference or neglect, the state of the Muslim mind and attitude, both individual and collective, towards *dawa* is pathetic. The contemporary Muslim *Shahadah*, witness to Islam, in both words and actions does not correspond with the reality of Islam. The gap between ideal and practice is overwhelming and contradictions between Islam as it ought to be and Islam as reflected in Muslim life are pronounced.

The entire Muslim world, with rare exceptions, is in the grip of Western domination, a domination so overpowering and all pervading that there is hardly any layer where the influence of Western culture has not penetrated. Although at village level some Islamic institutions still survive, in the metropolis and urban areas almost all the social, economic, administrative and political institutions of traditional Muslim societies have been replaced by Western-style institutions. These are run mostly by people who have been educated or trained in the West or in Western-style universities in their own countries. This minority administrative cadre, sometimes hand-in-hand with army elites to whom Western values are dearer than Islamic and whose life patterns show all the trappings of Western values, directly or indirectly dominate the entire Muslim *ummah*.

Any analysis of the contemporary Muslim situation has to take into consideration the limitations and obstacles imposed upon the work of *dawa* by internal and external factors. The legacy of hostility between the West and Islam, branching out into misconception and misrepresentation, mistrust and prejudice is not the only obstacle. The limitations of *dawa* at the level of the *ummah*, in Muslim societies and states, as well as at the level of very large groups, institutions and structures such as mosques and schools, which Khuram Murrad calls the 'macro' and the 'intermediate' levels are no less problematic. They are mostly beyond the reach and competence of ordinary Muslims to do anything effective.

This does not mean that efforts are not afoot to Islamize Muslim societies and establish a collective system of Islam to bring about the metamorphosis desired by Islam at macro and intermediate levels. There have always been such efforts in Muslim history and they should certainly be intensified with the aim of eliminating all vestiges of *jahili* culture and domination in the private and public life of the Muslim *ummah*, so that a true living Islamic model is presented to the world. The movement to Islamization whether it be of state institutions or in the intellectual endeavours of Muslim thinkers can all be encompassed within the framework of *dawa* and are the meaning and content of *dawa*. *Dawa* at the micro level is mostly being performed by individuals and small organizations and groups. Even at that level the situation leaves much to be desired: the work of *dawa* is often carried out with limited knowledge and an incomplete vision of Islam and, consequently, is not very effective.

As the whole Muslim world is under the spell of Western secular and materialistic culture, represented by the superpowers and their client states, the furtherance of the practice of *dawa* has to be tackled with great care and propriety. Any superficial analysis without going deeply into the makeup of western *jahili* civilization will only result in superficial solutions. Although, symbolically, religion is apparent in individual and private lives, it has no place at the centre of power and places of policy formulation. The godless, rather than anti-God, culture and man-made contours of Western civilization have played havoc with the individual and collective life of the people. The disintegration of the family, rising rates of crime, juvenile delinquency, use of alcohol and drugs resulting in increasing rates of crime, frustration and suicide, perversions in sex life with rape of minors and women, incest and abuse of children are all manifestions of the predicament of Western culture. The economic life dominated by usury, consumerism and maximization of pleasure at the cost of justice and equity have created mountains of food and wealth in some parts of the world, while in other areas millions of people are starving to death or at best receiving meagre handouts in the name of aid and charity. The concept of racial superiority has already condemned millions of humans to servitude and extinction. The arms race in war technology and nuclear power has made the whole world a hostage, the present stockpile of weapons being enough to destroy the earth completely many times over. The economic cost of deadly chemical and nuclear weaponry is staggering. Global military expenditure is estimated to be in the region of one million million dollars a year or two million dollars a minute — a mere one-fifth of which would be sufficient to elimate hunger and poverty from the world!

Western culture is not limited to the territories of the West; many Muslim countries, being direct or indirect recipients, are suffering the same fate. Muslims as an *ummah* must face the situation squarely and boldly at all levels. Although every Muslim, whether a scholar or unlettered, has the responsibility of rectifying the situation; the people with knowledge and wisdom have more responsibility than anyone else. The demands of *dawa* will not be fulfilled if instead of analysing the situation and rectifying the disease at every level, Muslims curse, hurl abuse and neglect to share the blessings they possess. Is it conceivable that Muslims, occupying the position of 'doctor', as it were, can pass through the areas infested with disease, yet remain indifferent, unconcerned and unmoved? Is it possible for a doctor to remain unaffected if he finds a patient dying of some curable disease? Or, to put it in a different way, is it possible that there can be fire in the hearts of Muslims and yet its warmth and glow not reach those in its vicinity? How long will Muslims lament the situation and yet not do anything positive to rectify it? The challenge of the *jahili* culture has to be faced at all levels without being modest or apologetic. The disease of Western civilization has to be cured with a doctor's skill, understanding, wisdom and care. The adversary has to be faced on its own ground and overwhelmed with superior argument and examples as taught by God and His Prophets. The legacy of misgivings and misunderstandings, whether genuine or ill-founded, whether deliberately believed or falsely implanted has to be weeded out. Though some negative impressions of Islam may be products of Muslims' failure and follies, others are the result of obduracy born of general arrogance, greed and anger, some perpetuated from the days of early Islam, some the after-effects of Western colonization of the recent past. *Dawa* must be made effectively and relentlessly to overcome all manifestations of ignorance, prejudice and hostility. But this has to be done according to the Quranic terminology 'with wisdom and gentle admonition' and not with hostility, hatred and indifference.

The issues which confront the world today are legion. Some are central, others peripheral. The Muslim *ummah* as a whole has to diagnose these at appropriate levels and present their Islamic solutions not only through sermons and literature but also and most especially through practice and example. It would not be an exaggeration to say that Western civilization is now passing through its most critical and perhaps its last phase of crisis and disintegration, and that the stage is set for the emergence of some new order based on values basically different from those of modern Western civilization. For various reasons, such as over-secularization, over-materialism and despiritualization of life resulting in a plethora of problems, the old order is beset by problems and difficulties point to its disintegration and collapse. How much time and how many more convulsions it will need before the new dawn no one knows. But there is little doubt that mankind is heading towards a major change. However, it would be naive and an oversimplification to claim that the stage is now set for the West's march towards Islam. Ideological and cultural movements take their own time and the historical course they assume to articulate themselves is neither linear, simple nor sudden. What can, however, be claimed with reasonable certainty is that there is an ideological vacuum in the West and, indeed, in many parts of the East under Western influence, and it is a law of nature that a vacuum must be filled. What ideology is going to fill it and over what period of time will depend on a variety of factors, most important of which is the nature of the *dawa* with which Muslims respond to the situation. Like other claimants, Islam also has a chance to fill this gap and the opportunity has to be seized appropriately and immediately. Any delay may prove fatal. A wide spectrum of groups and movements representing different participants in the search for spiritual meaning in life can be seen on the intellectual, literary and cultural scene. A variety of cults, hippy and yippy groups, as well as converts to Zen, Vedanta, Krishna and other more obscure religious manifestations, represent some aspects of this quest. Though these manifestations might be superficial, confused or even counterfeit, they do mirror the phenomena of simmering uneasiness of the soul and a quest for a genuine spiritual and ideological path. This presents Muslims with an exciting opportunity and a challenge of great magnitude.

This unique opportunity cannot be seized and the challenge cannot be met unless the Muslim *ummah* is well prepared and properly equipped for the task. Proper evaluation of the situation, leading to a thorough critique of Western civilization together with appropriate knowledge and education in Islam and the methodology of Islamic *dawa* are a prerequisite for planning and meeting this challenge. Moreover, the Islamic solutions to the problems and issues faced by the world at large and the West in particular have to be superior, comprehensive, practical and appealing. On all issues, whether it is the theory of knowledge, problems of race and colour, sexual politics or AIDS, disintegration of the family, economy or politics, war or peace, Muslims have to present appropriate solutions derived from the Quran and Sunnah and make known the merits of these solutions, using the appropriate language, medium and technology.

The theories of knowledge propounded by Islam and by the West are diametrically opposed. One depends on revelation and divine guidance and the other on speculation, observation, deduction and investigation. One is final and unchangeable and the other is in the process of evolution, embracing change whenever new theories emerge. Truth and absolute truth, according to Islam, cannot be discovered by deduction or scientific experiment. According to Islam, all means of knowledge, whether it is instinct, reason, intuition or experience, and all sources of deriving guidance on life, whether it is philosophy, history, law or science, are unable to lead to unimpeachable knowledge of reality and the ultimate values to which human behaviour should conform. Undoubtedly they have a part to play and a positive contribution to make, but they cannot make their true contributions unless they operate within a framework of Ultimate Truth as communicated by Divine Revelation. Human intellect, unaided by divine guidance is incapable of solving all the riddles of creation, of having a worldview of reality or of deriving principles that can produce peace and harmony in the human soul, create equilibrium and balance within human society and harmonize human behaviour with the movements of the cosmic forces and the overall dynamics of existence. It is the duty of Muslim scholars to show the world the superiority of the Islamic theory of knowledge and how it solves the riddles of creation and manifestations of the world which belong to the realm of *ghayb*, unseen, hence beyond human perception and experience.

Truth, by its nature and inherent logic, must be made known and manifest. Therefore, possessing the knowledge of truth must lead to *dawa*. The meaningful sequence of the first two revelations *Iqra, qalam* and learning, as the supreme manifestations of Allah's generosity coupled with the command in Surah at Muddaththir — 'Arise and warn, let the greatness of your Lord be the greatest' (Quran 74:2–3) — make it imperative to disseminate the knowledge of truth. In Islamic epistemology of knowledge, Allah is the source and possessor of all knowledge, *Alim* and *Khabir* and He alone can guide man to the right path. His greatness must demolish all false claims of greatness, arrogance and pride from all spheres of life, whether intellectual, or cultural or political. Therefore, one specific and enormously important and challenging task for the Muslim intellectual is the refutation and ultimate demolition of the man-made theories of knowledge, at the same time aiming at its complete Islamization, or shaping and directing all human knowledge to this truth. What Imam Ghazali accomplished towards the end of the eleventh century of the Christian era, first mastering all available theories of philosophical knowledge, then producing its complete and thorough refutation and presenting the true Islamic point-of-view, Muslim scholars and intellectuals, individually and collectively, have to do now. They have to demonstrate how the epistemology of Islam, with revelation at the centre of human knowledge and behaviour, can provide a far superior integrated system of knowledge. Unfortunately, during the past few centuries all human knowledge and philosophy of life has developed by ignoring Allah. The situation has to be rectified, but this is a daunting task, indeed. Muslim intellectuals must face it squarely and boldly. Although some laudable efforts have been initiated, such as the evolution and development of the disciplines of Islamic economics, Islamic science, etc., a lot more planning, co-ordination and concerted effort is needed to take up this gigantic task and to bring it to fruition. If this is achieved, it will be one of the best and most effective methods of *dawa*.

Dawa
A Practical Approach for the Future

Fadlullah Wilmot

The essential character of modern civilization is anti-religious. The modern world tends either to the active denial of the Divine Reality, seeing creation simply as a product of chance, or considers the Divine as marginal to the true and pressing concerns of man. Modern civilization is basically Western civilization which carries with it all the presuppositions and characteristics of the humanism of the Renaissance, the rationalism of the seventeenth and eighteenth centuries and the materialism and scientism of the nineteenth and twentieth centuries. For Muslims, therefore, modern civilization is not only alien in terms of its historical and geographical origins but also in respect of its metaphysical bases. However, it would be wrong to look at Islam simply as a passive respondent to modern civilization. Modern civilization itself is losing much of its cohesiveness and confidence as well as its naive faith in the pseudo-religion of progress, in the adequacy of rationalism as a means of cognition, and in the supremacy of Western civilization as the apex of all human history — these beliefs are fading as the realization grows that society and the individual in the modern world are confronted by apparently infinite and insoluble problems.

The historical and metaphysical baggage has apparently made religious questions irrelevant for modern civilization. Even self-proclaimed religious individuals have accepted the historical and metaphysical underpinnings of modern civilization as a sociological reality. Their religion remains as a spiritual and purely internal thing while their behaviour is affected by non-religious criteria, particularly by anti-religious propaganda. There has always been a gap between 'ideals' and 'action', but today this gap has become total, general and deliberate.

Perpetual, deliberate as well as unconscious anti-religious propaganda and its resultant psychological effects have made *dawa*, spreading the message of Islam, a difficult exercise in modern times. The psychological structures on which most modern societies are based are not favourable to religious beliefs. *Dawa* by its very nature must be slow and careful but modern propaganda quickly mobilizes the masses. The propaganda which bombards and manipulates modern man has made human beings increasingly impervious to spiritual realities and less and less suited to the individual moral responsibility every Muslim has towards the Creator. For modern man, truth is shaped by propaganda, and religion has been reduced to a level of ideology. Modern propaganda never considers the individual as an individual but always in terms of what one person has in common with others, such as motivations, feelings and myths. The individual is never considered as being alone but as a part of a large group. A true mob mentality is thus created, a mentality in terms of fashions, mindless group behaviour that can be manipulated this way or that. It is important to realize that modern propaganda does not seek to modify ideas, or present counter-arguments, but to provoke action. It is no longer aimed at changing adherence to a doctrine but to loosening reflexes. It consistently short-circuits all thought and decision, operating at the level of the unconscious. In modern society thought and action are being systematically separated. Modern man carries out actions which do not conform to his private beliefs. The two main means of pre-propaganda, preparing individuals for a particular action, are the conditioned reflex and the myth. The reflex is used by the communist and other totalitarian regimes and the myth is the dominant tool of manipulation in capitalist societies. Thus propaganda is one of the greatest threats hanging over mankind, more dangerous than any of the other commonly publicized threats.

One outcome of the domination of the propaganda culture, with myth and intuition at its base, is a tendency for oversimplification. Everything is seen in terms of black and white; and complicated and multifaceted issues are solved by monistic formulae: political freedom thus provides an answer for every ill of the so-called 'free world'; the economic factors play the same role in Marxist regimes. Muslims are not immune to this oversimplification. We have built up a narrow version of the Quranic injunction of commanding good and forbidding evil in the domain of morality. Thus *dawa* is mostly confined to the teaching of morals and the building up of a strong moral character. *Dawa* is considered synonymous with preaching by Christian missionaries. Islam, being a unique lifestyle, encompassing all facets of life, demands that there should be a wider vision of *dawa* work. *Dawa* should be the task of making fully operational the dynamic concepts of Islam in contemporary society. It should aim to develop personal commitment and orient our behaviour in the community according to the guidance of the Quran and the Sunnah.

Looking at the history and present needs of the Muslim ummah, *dawa* has to address many issues: spiritual, social, political, economic and educational. *Dawa* should solve the real needs of people in all the domains of their lives. It should aim at the abolition of exploitation in such a way that all human affairs are conducted in accordance with the norms of social justice and fraternal co-operation. *Dawa* should aim at the correct development of human and material resources to ensure prosperity for all. *Dawa* should eventually bring about an educational revolution in knowledge and training. Through *dawa* the individual and society should play a creative and constructive role in the reconstruction of mankind.

In Islam there is no priesthood, no theory of the separateness of the religious teacher from other Muslims; therefore, there is no necessity for special consecration or authorization for the performance of religious functions. This means that the convert to Islam does not have to be referred to some religious teacher to be formally received into the religion. Although it may be an exaggeration to say that in the past every Muslim was a missionary, it would be true that most Muslims expressed a keen awareness of Quranic the injunction 'summon to the way of your Lord with wisdom and kindly warning'. Therefore, side-by-side with religious teachers who devoted their whole time to *dawa*, the history of Islam shows that men and women of all ranks of society have laboured to spread the religion of Islam. There is a need to recapture the spirit of Islam which makes every Muslim a potential ambassador of Islam.

The Basic Problem

All discussion of *dawa* must start with a frank realization: most Muslim scholars and duat (those who practise *dawa*) today cannot serve as engines capable of propelling forward and steering the ship of Islam to the envisaged destination of revival and regeneration. However, they do serve as a heavy anchor which can stop this ship drifting in the wrong direction. The main emphasis of the ulama has been on the safeguarding and defence of religious dogmas rather than the revival of the true faith and a total Islamic way of life. The majority of religious scholars of every persuasion to whom Muslims look for advice are using their energy to propagate their special form of dogma and thus strengthen the roots of sectarian factionalism and mutual intolerance. Moreover, today's ulama have not studied modern science, social theories, and the philosophical thoughts and trends of the contemporary age as did, for example, Imam Ghazzali and Ibn Taimiyyah in their times. Hence, a sad truth must be recognized: most ulama are not competent to fulfill the real demands of furthering the cause of their religion on fruitful lines.

Another crucial dimension of our problematique is that Muslims, facing acute social, economic and political problems, have developed a false sense of security. They believe that reading the Quran is enough — it will bring them *thawab*, reward from Allah, even if they do not understand, let alone practise its injunctions; that going out to tabligh, on preaching missions, will secure a place in paradise; that writing pamphlets and propaganda sheets will gain support for Islam. Muslims all over the world have enslaved themselves into doctrinal chains and have lost the spirit of rationalism. Dogmaticism has become an end in itself, to the neglect of literature and the arts, learning and inquiry. Indeed, dogmaticism has suppressed the humanitarian instincts of Muslims and has led to oppression and torture, communal and sectarian strife in a number of Muslim countries. Dogmaticism has replaced social justice and creativity. Under such circumstances, inviting others to Islam does have its ironic side!

Further evidence of this problematique is to be found in the Muslim attitude towards culture and women. The plain truth is that much of contemporary *dawa* has a negative view of culture, and some *dawa* movements are actively opposed to the burning need of men and women for the aesthetic and the beautiful. For *dawa* movements, culture has come to be equated with ritual; and expression of art, music and literature are sacrificed at the altar of rituals of 'minimal Islam'. This negative attitude towards cultural expression and creativity, which is in total contradiction to the spirit of Islam, has given many creative people a negative impression of Islam. We can say the same about the Muslim attitude towards women. Most *dawa* movements have relegated half of the ummah to a marginal role in society. There needs to be a revaluation of traditional ideas about and attitudes towards women in Islam to bring them more into harmony with the true Quranic vision and the true Sunnah of the Prophet. Women in Islam are not meant to be mere bearers of children, kept at home playing no role in society. We need to learn from the role the women played in early Islamic societies, during the time of the Prophet and during the administration of Abu Bakr and Omar, the first two rightly-guided caliphs. Unless we change our obscurantic attitude towards women, there will be little development and even less *dawa* in Muslim societies.

In the final analysis, much of our talk about *dawa* is based on a dogmatic attitude to life, on assumptions which are contrary to the spirit of Islam. Like charity, *dawa* begins at home. We need to change ourselves before we can consider ourselves qualified to do practise *dawa*.

Dawa through Humanitarian Causes

Before he received his call, Prophet Muhammad was known as a man of compassion. *Dawa* does not mean imposition of the shahadah, the declaration of faith, on others or just inviting them to the truth. There must be credibility to this summons and the quality of the medium will determine the quality of the message. Without such credibility the whole effort of *dawa* will be rhetorical and devoid of meaning, no matter how great is the message. A profound saying of the Prophet is reported by Muslim:

> God would ask someone on the Day of Judgement, 'O son of Adam, I was ill but you did not pay a visit to me!' The man would reply, 'How could I have paid a visit to you? You are the Lord of the worlds!' Then God would ask, 'Do you not remember that one of My servants was sick, but you did not visit him? Don't you know that if you had gone to see him you would have found me by his side?' Then God would ask again, 'O son of Adam, I asked you to feed Me but you refused it to Me.' The man would reply, 'How could I have fed You? You are the Lord of the worlds!' But the reply of God would be, 'Do you not remember that one of My servants asked you for food? Don't you know that had you given him food you would have found Me by his side?' Then God would ask again, 'O son of Adam I asked for water to drink but you refused it to Me!' The man would reply, 'How could I have given water to You? You are the Lord of the worlds!' But God would reply, 'Do you not remember that one of My servants asked you for water, but you refused. Don't you know that if you had given him water, you would have found Me by his side.'

Notwithstanding the clear cut approach to *dawa* through humanitarian causes exemplified by this Hadith, it has been left to Christian missionaries to work on such lines. Their extensive network of services can be gauged from the following examples. Since 1948 the World Council of Churches Commission has been financing relief programmes among the Palestinians at the rate of some $1.7 million a year. The Lutheran Church while meeting in Caracas in 1979 approved forty-two developmental projects of which seventeen were to be implemented in Asia. This cost the church $1.4 million for the Asian projects alone. In Bangladesh many schools in towns are run by the Christian missionaries; they are also running fourteen hospitals, thirteen dispensaries, twenty-one charitable hospitals and orphanages and two leprosy centres. These services are in addition to other projects which aim at developing fishery and poultry. In many parts of Africa and Asia, Christian missionaries have developed co-operative projects with local money and manpower. It is this kind of evangelism with an unsurpassed zest, dedication and commitment of resources that has made Christianity acceptable to non-Christians. They are also using funds from the United Nations and other international agencies because Muslims are not organized well enough to obtain such funds.

While Christian missionaries are gaining fresh ground all over Asia and Africa, Muslims, despite their faith's emphasis on social services, have reduced *dawa* to abstract pronouncements. We are so convinced of the truth of Islam, its simplicity and its inherent appeal, that mere verbal or written pronouncements are thought to be enough. Muslims forget that there is something extrasensory in *dawa*, which is only achieved when souls establish contact with each other through the loving hand that places balm on the wound and feeds the hungry.

So pervasive is the dichotomy between *dawa* and humanitarian causes that it has afflicted even the Islamic movements. Their preoccupation with political change, in spite of their total outlook on life, has left them bereft of the benefit of adopting a multidimensional approach towards building their base in society. Both the Jamaat-i-Islami of Pakistan and the Ikhwan al-Muslimun of Egypt developed their initial methodology on humanitarian work, but over the years with continual dictatorship in both these countries and the governments' persecution, they have suffered heavy political defeat and have been left interlocked with the system. In both cases the workers had nothing to do during the political lull and many, feeling frustrated and dispirited with nothing to keep them in touch with the masses, left the movement. Some groups became obsessed with political change without a sufficient analysis of the power structure and without paying enough attention to the field of *dawa*, education and welfare. This, however, does not mean that political change does not deserve our attention. Indeed the root of all evils, as Maulana Mawdudi so succinctly said, lies in the government, but any passage to power doubtless lies through serving humanitarian causes. It is this link which has been ignored in the past.

A realistic programme of *dawa* must take into account the fact that the great majority of Muslims are poor, living below the poverty line either in rural areas or in urban ghettoes. It must also take into account the fact that 80 per cent of the Muslims in the world are illiterate. If *dawa* is to have any meaning for the poor masses of the world, it is necessary for *dawa* programmes to mobilize the people actively to participate in the improvement of their economic and educational situations. This requires a change in attitude towards what *dawa* involves so that appropriate attitudinal changes and value re-orientation can be developed. If *dawa* is to have any meaning for the poor and deprived Muslims who make up the majority of the ummah, plans must be worked out to deal with this problem of poverty which makes a dignified, fully human life impossible.

After eradication of poverty, the main focus of *dawa* must be on the development of systems and methodologies to improve literacy among Muslims. As the problem of illiteracy is related to home environment, socio-economic position, environmental stimulation, nutrition of both mother and child, as well as employment opportunities, it is necessary to tackle these problems as well. It is well known that a child has developed much of its intellect by the time it is five. As those in the lower socio-economic levels cannot provide a stimulating environment for the intellectual development of the child, *dawa* must provide ways to overcome this shortcoming. One method of helping would be to provide pre-school education for Muslim children where proper nutrition would be provided at least once a day. Such schools would teach Muslim children, through 'play and learn' methods to read, write and do simple arithmatic. The teaching of early reading is important because reading is essential to vocabulary development which is, in turn, necessary for the skills dealing with concepts. There is no reason why the mosques cannot be used for this purpose. An illiterate ummah is a disgrace to the Prophet whose first revelation from Allah was 'Iqra', read. A number of successful pre-school projects have been developed by the Muhammadiyyah movement in Indonesia, which operates over one-quarter of the country's kindergartens. In order to have healthy children, health care and nutrition in both rural areas and urban slums must be improved. The rate of infant mortality in Muslim countries is among the highest in the world, including those Muslim countries which have a fairly high per-capita income. The duat, or *dawa* workers, must have some knowledge of nutrition and be able to help Muslim women obtain good nutrition during pregnancy and while breast feeding, which may be encouraged as a religious obligation.

The workers for *dawa* must, therefore, re-evaluate their role from being the purveyors of abstract truths in a theological wrapping which has little relevance to the real and perceived needs of the Muslim ummah today. If a person is starving, does not have a proper house to live in, does not have more than one set of clothes, how can he or she be dedicated to living an Islamic life? The thrust of the *dawa* workers' efforts must be to train the Muslim masses, the poor and disadvantaged to participate in the development process. The *dawa* workers should, therefore, be motivators who enable the community to help itself and enable people to take up the responsibility to create structures and systems for co-operation.

Comprehension of the Worldview of Recipients

Effective *dawa* requires a change of approach and methodology. Planning is certainly essential but most *dawa* work, either to Muslims or non-Muslims, is unplanned and based on inadequate information. In improving our *dawa* it is necessary first of all to understand the underlying currents of a particular society and to make a study of its value system and the attitudes of different groups within that society. Many facts are available from statistics of average income, crime, social problems, poverty, what people spend money on and what is viewed as important in life. *Dawa* has to tap the interests of non-Muslims, but in order to do that the *dawa* workers must first understand them. *Dawa* cannot be a disorganized and haphazard affair. Random distribution of 'Islamic literature' and spasmodic talks and preaching must be substituted with careful strategic planning. An understanding of the history and culture of the target community is an asset in communicating the message of Islam. Ritual calls for this are made at most *dawa* courses, but it remains a vague desire without practical implications. People's attitudes are very much influenced by their historical and cultural experiences, fears and aspirations. Beliefs, worldview, faith and values are passed on from generation to generation. In order to perform *dawa* effectively, the worldview of others must be understood and there must be new approaches to building bridges between both the non-Muslims and Muslims who are the goals of *dawa*.

There is a formidable gap between the worldview of those involved in *dawa* and the worldview of the recipients of *dawa*. Perceptions of reality are patterned by societies into conceptualizations of what reality can or should be. The central assumptions, conceptions which are largely unconscious, regulate and govern their total behaviour. Behaviour, per se, is not a worldview but is the shadow of beliefs, assumptions and cognitive mapping. Another definition of worldview is ethos, personality, values and style. Though there is no uniform agreement as to the exact definition, the consensus is that the worldview governs the manner in which people order their living.

It should be understood that the mere fact of living in a community together does not mean understanding, let alone sharing a worldview. Human beings view things and evaluate them by past experience and present temper. Interpretation depends on the context and not the goodwill of the persons who intend to perform *dawa*. Past experience and present temper mould, translate and interpret events, symbols and gestures in different ways. The worldview is the soul of a people; it is the gate through which one can enter the mind, heart and life of an individual or people. Very few of our *dawa* workers understand the worldview of Muslims, let alone that of non-Muslims. It is necessary to use the receptor's categories for effective communication. The forms and thought patterns of the receptor's culture can be used to help the *dawa* worker communicate effectively. In other words, it is necessary to use a base for communication within the receptor's reference frame and worldview.

In spreading Islam, the early preachers did not try to destroy the indigenous culture and substitute it with Arab culture, because cultural diversity is the essence and the basic strength of Islam. *Dawa*, therefore, not only respects other cultures but seeks to strengthen them. In the classical period, Islam was spread by people who went to study other cultures, who adopted their languages and some of their customs, married them, and attracted people towards them by personal example. The spread of Islam in the Indian subcontinent, for example, was due to the ability of the duat to respect local cultural norms where they did not conflict with the fundamental teachings of Islam. The new ambassadors of Islam must learn from their own history.

Early Muslim workers in Java, for example, did not reject local culture but used it in spreading Islamic *dawa*. A person was not committing cultural suicide by becoming a Muslim. The spread of Islam in China among the ethnic Han Chinese, the Hui, is an example of Muslims who in their homes and culture remained essentially Chinese, with their houses and mosques looking, from the outside, just like any Chinese home or temple without, of course, the idols. However, inside the atmosphere is completely Islamic. Many of those active in *dawa* today seem to have lost the *hikmah*, wisdom, of the early Muslims. They do not seem to realize that entrance is gained into the world of others via the gate of the worldview. We can meet people better if we base our *dawa* on points of agreement rather than on confrontation. There are many values that Muslims hold in common with others which can be used as bases for discussion. The message of Islam needs to be tailored to each group of people. Tailoring is not devaluing the message but trying to understand the cognitive maps of the receptors and meeting them at convenient points in their worldview. It is not possible to build a Muslim community by extracting individuals from the setting of their own communities. People will accept *dawa* far more easily without crossing cultural and sociological barriers. It is necessary to use existing forms and thought patterns already held by individuals or their culture.

In looking at the worldview of others, the dichotomy between the bounded-set theory and the centred-set theory might be useful. It is possible to look at others from the point of view of the bounded-set theory, in which the boundary lines are firmly fixed. A person is in or out. Is this not the attitude of much *dawa*, not only towards non-Muslims but also to fellow Muslims? This is the Greek, linear pattern of thinking which is in sharp, clear-cut form. If we look at the history of Islamic *dawa* from the time of the Prophet through its spread through the Middle East, Africa, Europe and South and Southeast Asia, it is clear that this was not the method. There was a gradualness and a step-by-step approach. It took several generations for some groups to adopt the true Islamic lifestyle. The boundary between Islam and non-Islam is of course clear, but the Sunnah shows that Islam was spread in a gradual way and in a manner able to be understood and practised by those being reached. If we follow the bounded-set attitude, it also implies that once we are inside the set, the question of growth becomes unimportant.

The centred-set theory has boundaries, but they are not so rigid. They curl around the person who has turned towards accepting Allah and His Prophet Muhammad, even though there is still a long way to go. Once these two principles are accepted, however, he or she is our Muslim brother or sister and must be helped to grow and develop. It is important to note that people are heading in two directions vis-a-vis Allah: some may be heading closer towards Him; others, who were once close, may be heading away from Him. The attitude of the dai should be to find a way to bring mankind closer to Allah, but he or she will not be able to do this until appropriate bridges are built between people. If the centred-set concept is used to reach people, it will be realized that people may be arriving at the fundamental truths of Islam in different ways; there needs to be a wide range of tolerance for these different ways of arriving at the truth.

Figure 1.   Bounded and Centred Sets

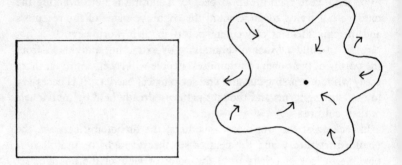

Bounded Set   *Centred Set*

As we know, Islam is the primordial religion, the natural religion of man; therefore, there are large areas of agreement between Muslims and all other people. Even 'non-practising', 'secular' or 'Westernized' Muslims will also accept many of the eternal values of Islam. There are many common beliefs between Islam, Christianity and Judaism. Islam shares the anti-materialistic stance of Hinduism and Buddhism's desire not to make this world the measure of all things. Confucianism's social morality agrees in essence with many of Islam's teachings. In *dawa* work, therefore, there is a need to seek what is held in common with the rest of humanity and not what divides. This is not an argument for watering down the unique message of Islam but an appeal for a more rational and realistic approach.

Planned Efforts towards *Dawa*

From the discussion so far, it should be obvious that the problems of Islamic *dawa* are not going to be solved by knocking on the doors of Muslims to remind them of their duty towards Islam, and the pleasures of heaven and the horrors of hell, while having nothing more to offer than an empty hand, hollow platitudes about brotherly love, and pious utterings devoid of all understanding of human psychology and the real problems existing here and now. *Dawa* needs preparation, and preparation begins with planning.

No scientific study of any problem facing Islamic *dawa* is of any use, if at all possible, when the gathering, interpretation, evaluation and application of data is haphazard and unscientific. No planning can take place where there is nothing but a search for supporting evidence based on unresearched generalizations together with a lack of analysis. Why are Muslims not interested in *dawa*? Are they apathetic? Is the message uninspiring or irrelevant? Do they understand its aim? Why don't Muslims listen to or read much Islamic material? Is it that they have heard hundreds of such sermons, taking a long time to say nothing and completely irrelevant to their immediate circumstances? What is the function of *dawa*? Does it fulfil this function?

These questions need to be answered by systematic research and study. We need to use a number of methodologies to study them, including system analysis and flow-charting as one method for overcoming the present mismatch between intentions and means. This planning should emphasize the proper place of *dawa* at the centre of the life of Muslims. No textbook on Islam for our youth anywhere in the world even devotes one chapter to *dawa* in the contemporary world, either to Muslims or non-Muslims. *Dawa* is not an optional extra nor should it be a response or reaction to the missionary activities of other religions. It is not a profession, an occupation that one may or may not engage in. No battery of paid workers, duat, literature, modern equipment or sermons can solve the problems unless we view *dawa* in its correct perspective.

In planning for *dawa* it is necessary to work out the resistance-receptivity axis. It is important to discover which groups of people are receptive to *dawa*. There are basically four areas which need to be investigated: locating the geographical area; the homogeneous group; the number of people being positively affected by *dawa*; and the location of people who are open to change.

People tend to be open to change where certain factors exist: for example, the breakdown of cohesive bonds due perhaps, to rural–urban migration, minority groups under pressure, politically disinherited groups, marginalized segments of the community needing empowerment. There are perhaps eight important indicators of societal change which precipitate people to make other changes: cultural change, political change, economic change, religious change, status of translation of religious texts, migration patterns, prototype image, and degree of influence of Islam. Taking these factors into account, proper research and the plotting of results on a resistance/receptivity axis would not only be a useful tool to evaluate the potential for success of *dawa* work but it would also help to sharpen the focus, determine the direction and the best means for such work.

Table 1. *Resistance/Receptivity Axis*

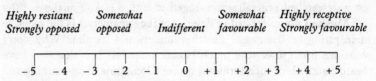

Highly resitant Strongly opposed	Somewhat opposed	Indifferent	Somewhat favourable	Highly receptive Strongly favourable

| -5 | -4 | -3 | -2 | -1 | 0 | $+1$ | $+2$ | $+3$ | $+4$ | $+5$ |

Thus, planning must be based on hard facts and from them we must work out the practical implications these facts have for *dawa*. We have to tap the interests and concerns of those we reach and we can only do that if we have sufficient information about them. The most common methods of *dawa* are still lectures and leaflets. However, modern people are crying out for personal contact, and two studies, one in Malaysia and one in America, have shown that 40 per cent of all conversions to Islam have been through personal contact.

In order for *dawa* to be effective, there must also be a revision of the attitude of Muslims towards knowledge. The late Professor Fazlur Rahman is so right when he reflects on the intellectual task of formulating an Islamic metaphysics on the basis of the Quran. Ziauddin Sardar goes further and argues for a contemporary epistemology of Islam. Faced with the lack of any contemporary scholarship activated by Islamic concepts and values, the absence of a modern operating model of Islamic theories of knowledge on the one hand and the coherent, powerful and inclusive, secular, materialistic disciplines of Western knowledge that compose their education, it is not surprising that young Muslims face so much doubt and disillusionment. The duat must help the ummah become capable of creative intellectual productivity in all fields of intellectual endeavour. The simple division of knowledge into 'secular' and 'religious', 'bad' and 'good', 'urgent' and 'less urgent', 'obligatory on the individual' or 'obligatory on the community' is not just dangerously obsolete, it can also sabotage *dawa* work. The modern world is a much more complex affair: the problems do not exist in black and white, but are found largely in the 'shade of grey'. Muslim duat, therefore, cannot give easy answers to modern problems. They have to be trained to differentiate between historical and normative Islam and should seek their solutions from Islam's normative teachings. The content of *dawa* must be normative Islam and not the complete historical legacy we have inherited.

The Psychology of *Dawa*

Psychologists have found that certain properties of the deliverer of a message, as well as the receiver of the message, help predict the probability of a change in the receiver's attitudes. Consistently it has been shown that a speaker who is perceived as highly prestigious is more influential in changing attitudes than one who is held in low esteem. Consequently, organized *dawa* efforts should focus on enlisting speakers who are not only competent, but have such qualities that others view as exemplifying competence as dignity, confidence, poise, precision in speech and intelligence.

Correlative to the qualities of the speaker are the hearer's qualities. For example, certain audiences are more open to debates and discussions, whereas others are influenced more by lectures. The lecture format is more successful with audiences composed largely of those who initially agree with the content of the lecture or of uneducated individuals, whereas the discussion format is more successful with more educated individuals or those who initially oppose the message. The implications of these facts for *dawa* are clear: try lecturing to blue-collar workers and secondary school students, but group discussions with professionals, college students and hostile audiences. A combination of a short lecture followed by group discussion unites both formats.

Consistency theories, including cognitive dissonace theory and balance theory, indicate that there are several actions one can take to aid others in changing their attitudes. Steve Johnson suggests that we should consider four factors. First, if we can get someone to act against his values or prejudices in accordance with the belief we want the person to accept, then the individual might change his attitude. For example, if you invite someone to dinner who is generally critical of your culture and he or she accepts the invitation, tries the food, plays with your children, and generally enjoys the occasion, then you increase the possibility that the person will develop a different attitude towards your culture. In other words, change in behaviour can cause change in attitude. This is the opposite of the typical *dawa* approach that assumes that we must change a person's attitude before their behaviour will change.

Second, both psychology and common sense tell us that presenting information that conflicts with a person's present beliefs might cause that person to change his or her attitude. This approach works best when the individuals are friends, but is much less effective with strangers.

Third, pointing out the inconsistencies in someone's beliefs can cause enough internal conflict that the person adopts a new belief. However, one must be aware that small attacks upon another's belief system might inoculate him or her to further approaches and cause him or her to hold onto the original beliefs more strongly.

Finally, it has been discovered that changes in law produce changes in behaviour and, consequently, changes in attitudes. With respect to *dawa*, this can be particularly important on college campuses. If students lobby to protest and change practices that discriminate against Muslims, marginalized minorities and other oppressed people, the abolition of discrimination can make Islam more acceptable to the masses of individuals and perhaps result in better attitudes toward Muslims and Islam. Similarly, Islamic communities should fight to change discriminatory laws. For example, if Muslims fight for the rights of the landless, disadvantaged segments of the society, the aged and the infirm, it might be a useful strategy for the Muslims' struggle to achieve the social conditions conducive to the spread of Islam.

Studies show that even if people change their attitudes they might revert to their old beliefs if a supportive environment is not provided. Therefore, Muslims committed to *dawa* must direct their attention to the new convert. Obviously the non-Muslim world is filled with temptations that are diametrically opposed to Islam. Since these converts are often eager to become involved in *dawa* work where their knowledge of the culture can be quite valuable, they should be welcomed and given appropriate guidance.

Practical Guidelines for Duat

Khuran Murrad has rightly brought to our attention some important points to be considered in regard to *dawa* to non-Muslims. First, we are not inviting people to a 'new' religion, but are inviting them to the oldest religion, indeed to their 'own' religion, the religion of living in total surrender to their Creator, in accordance with the guidance brought by all His Messengers. Indeed, we may be bold enough to say that we do not invite anyone to change his or her 'religion', to transfer allegiance to a rival religion. For Islam is not a new or rival religion among the many competing for human allegiance; it is the natural and primordial religion. All nature lives in submission to its Creator; all Messengers — from

Adam to Muhammad — brought the same religion. This does not mean a change in the basic position of Islam, for all religions, as they are, are not equally true. One will still be invited to follow the Prophet Muhammad, because he is the last Messenger, and to accept the Quran as the last revelation from God. But, proceeding from the position outlined here, implies a radical change in approach, tone, and style of *dawa*, and in the order in which the teachings of Islam are presented.

Second, the starting point and the basic core of *dawa* should be, as the Quran makes clear, total surrender to the One God, the Creator of all; accountability in life and after death; obeying His messengers; and building a new world on this basis where justice will prevail. This we may boldly affirm, without going into the question of empirical verification, is the core of every religion. To this the Muslim invites all:

> And We never sent a Messenger before you except that We revealed to him that: There is no God but I, so serve Me alone. *Al-Anbiya* 21:35
> The only [true] Way in the sight of God is total surrender to Him. *Al-Imran* 3:19

Therefore, we do not start by repudiating what is wrong with others but by inviting them to reflect on what is common between them and us. We ask non-Muslims to come to something they accept or which follows from what they accept: worshipping One God alone. The same approach was adopted with the idolators and mushrikin and the People of the Book:

> Say: People of the Book: Come now to the creed which is common between us and you, that we shall serve and worship none but Allah, and we shall not associate anything with Him (as God) and some of us shall not make others Lords apart from Allah. *Al Imran* 3:64

Telling people that we are not asking them to change to a rival religion, inviting them to the One God and His Messengers as their own religion, whose last revelation was to the Prophet Muhammad, should not be a semantic exercise. One important conclusion would be that we shall not be compelling anyone to accept all of 'historical Islam' as evidenced by Muslims over the last fourteen centuries. Therefore, we need not accept or try to justify everything done or said by Muslims in the past, or in our times.

Moreover, we should not start our *dawa* work by looking at the world as divided into two hostile camps: kafir (unbelievers) and Muslims, where every kafir is an enemy of Muslims, and therefore of Islam. Because of a long history of conflict, because of contemporary hostilities, because of our upbringing, because of our attitudes, we are prone to do so. Instead, we should ponder how Allah's Messengers handled their world. Their address was, in the beginning, always 'O my people' or 'O mankind'. In the beginning they never addressed them as 'kafirs' unless their kufr was demonstrated to be entrenched and deliberate. Similarly, the Quran treated People of the Book as a category separate from idolators, and addressed them as such, despite laying bare all their unbelief. Also, see how the Quran differentiates between those who are hostile to Islam and those who simply do not believe:

> It may be God will yet establish between you and those of them with whom you are at enmity, love . . . God forbids you not, as regards those who have not fought you in [the matter of] Din, nor expelled you from your homes, that you should be kindly to them, and act justly towards them, surely God loves the just. God only forbids you as to those one have fought you in [the matter of] Din, and expelled you from your homes, and have supported in your expulsion, that you should take them for friends.   *Al-Mumtahanah* 60:7–8

The history of the encounter between Islam and the West is a history of conflict at all levels — faith, morality, thought, politics, economics. For the last three hundred years the West has exploited and oppressed Muslims. Muslims, therefore, have genuine reasons to condemn the West for its hostility towards Muslims and Islam — in history as in the contemporary world — though the Western perceptions of Muslim domination in, for instance, Sicily or Eastern Europe are not very pleasant. We also have to expose the dangers of secular Western ideas, but does that permit us to engage in emotive diatribe and abusive polemic against the West, the white man? No. Someone is not evil because of being Western or white, but is evil because he or she is in rebellion against the Creator and His Messengers. Yet this sort of abuse permeates our attitudes and language. It is not that we should not provide an objective, powerful critique of kufr, of Western thought and society. That is our duty, although this duty receives little of our attention. Nor is it that we should not expose the Western powers' misdeeds in history or their present crimes. But these tasks should be performed with the compassion of the surgeon's scalpel, not with the brutality of a butcher's knife. We should reflect on the guidelines provided by the Quran in this respect. For example, the Quran forbids us to abuse even the idols; it condemns no one by name, except one person. It does not condemn people, it condemns their deeds.

Unless we have performed our duty of *dawa* and unless the message of Islam has been rejected by them, every non-Muslim should be seen as a potential Muslim, not as an enemy. Exceptions, of course, are those who are engaged in open aggression against Islam. This attitude is the logical conclusion of our position that man has been created in the best of moulds (*at-Tin* 95:4), that total submission to One God is the original and true nature of mankind (*ar-Rum* 30:30), that every Messenger brought the same religion. We must remember that language and themes are extremely important for *dawa*. The message remains the same, but it should be conveyed through a medium that is understood by its addressees. All the Messengers of God employed a language and took up the themes that were suited to their people. For example, the language of the 'Islamic state' may not be a suitable language for a Western society; instead, a just world order based on surrender to the One God and obedience to His Messengers is likely to evoke a more favourable response.

In all situations we should be kind and compassionate, just and fair to everyone, irrespective of their faith, race, colour or social status. These are the commands of God. We are ambassadors of the last Prophet, who has been described by the Quran as 'the merciful', 'the compassionate' and 'mercy for all the worlds', *Rahmatul lil-alamin*. Deep involvement in human welfare and service to mankind is basic to Islam and of central importance to *dawa*. The Quran places these values and conduct on a par with faith in God and His worship (68:27–37; 74:42–6; 107:1–7). Why should a Muslim be indifferent to the uncared for, the lonely, the old and the hungry who live in their societies?

We should make our basic *dawa* — the message of Tawhid, the Oneness of God, Risalah, Prophethood, and Akhirah, the Hereafter — relevant to the concerns and experiences of the average person in our societies. For example, why should Islamic *dawa* remain unconcerned with the questions of nuclear weapons, unemployment, underdevelopment? Indeed, Islam should be concerned with all matters of public policy and morality. The Prophet Noah's message dealt with caste and class differences; that of the Prophet Hud with imperialism, wastage of public resources and domination by tyrant rulers; that of the Prophet Lot with permissiveness; that of the Prophet Shuayb with injustice and economic maladies; that of the Prophet Moses with the tyranny and oppression perpetrated by the Pharaoh. In the same way our message must deal with the problems of our time.

Muslim communities need to develop a long-term strategy for *dawa* activities based on their material and human resources. There are several steps in this plan. First of all, we must study the situation scientifically with the benefit of news and trend analyses. Such an action plan would be implemented by training a small group of leaders who possess the intellectual capacity, skills and ability needed to lead others and to act as catalysts.

The action plan must include an attack on illiteracy, poverty, poor nutrition and poor health. If Islamic *dawa* fails to deal with these problems, it will be irrelevant for most people in the world. There is a need to train capable *dawa* workers who will not only have a clearer understanding of the needs of our community, but who will also have vision and the capacity to achieve this vision. In fact, many of the problems facing the ummah are due to the wrong sorts of persons obtaining leadership positions which they are neither intellectually nor spiritually competent to hold. No one has the right in Islam to take up a position for which he or she is not qualified — whether intellectually, morally or spiritually. It is only through *dawa* that the community can learn which sort of leadership they should choose.

The future of *dawa* depends on appreciating the contemporary needs of the human family. In the final analysis *dawa* is all about empowering the powerless, delivering the rights of the marginalized, securing justice for the oppressed, eradicating poverty and providing basic necessities to the vast majority of mankind. Only when these needs are made the focus of *dawa* will *dawa* become relevant to our time. Only then will *dawa* reach its true significance of 'inviting to all that is good'.

References

1. Ismael al-Faruqi, 'Islamic Renaissance in Contemporary Society', *Al-Ittihad*, October 1978.
2. Fazlur Rahman, *Islam and Modernity*, University of Chicago Press, Chicago, 1982.
3. Ziauddin Sardar, *Islamic Futures: The Shape of Ideas to Come*, Mansell, London, 1985.
4. Steve A Johnson, 'Dawa to Americans: Theory and Practice', Paper presented to WAMY Sixth International Conference, January 1986, Riyadh.
5. Khurram Murad, 'Dawa Amongst Non-Muslims in the West', Islamic Foundation, Leicester, 1986.

6. Raphael Israel, *Muslim in China: A Study in Cultural Confrontation*, Scandinavian Institute of Asian Studies, Curzon Press, London, 1980.
7. Abdul Wahid Hamid, *Islam: The Natural Way*, MELS Publications, London, 1989.

Dawa and Dialogue
Believers and Promotion of Mutual Trust

Syed Z. Abedin

Both Islam and Christianity are religions of outreach. In Islam, *dawa* (or call to Islam) is a duty incumbent on all believers:

> Call unto the path of your Lord through wise arguments and fair preaching, and argue with them [the non-believers] with arguments yet more fair, yet more becoming. *Quran* 16:125

Thus, in Islam the coming together of Muslims and non-Muslims is encouraged, even required. This even without the above textual reinforcement is inferable from the declared Islamic position that the Quran is God's last and final message to mankind; the Prophet Mohammad is a witness unto Muslims and Muslims are witness unto mankind. However, it is equally clear that this coming together is with a clearly defined purpose: 'Call unto the path of your Lord'.

The Christian believer, too, is required to carry the Gospel to the four corners of the earth. The purpose of the mission is to invite non-Christians to accept Jesus Christ as Lord and Saviour.

Given the mission orientation of both religions, is it possible for the followers of the two faiths to come together to promote trust and community? For example, can we have a Christian–Muslim dialogue aimed at promoting trust and community between the two sets of believers? Such a goal would require us to concede that although *dawa* and mission are legitimate exercises in their own right, under the exigencies of other factors (excluding the religious and spiritual) we are constrained to come together to promote trust and community. If such a premise is acceptable, then the next obvious question to ask is: do our respective religious beliefs allow for such a relationship? Obviously, this relationship in order to prosper has to be on a footing of equality. Are we ready to accept each other (religiously) in equal dignity and respect? Could we as Christians and Muslims, maintaining the primacy of our religious indentity, work in amity and accord in pursuit of a goal that requires the recognition by each other of our respective religious legitimacies? Or, could a Christian or Muslim 'believer' committed to witness or *dawa* suspend the witness and function outside the mission or *dawa* context? In order fully to understand the implications of these questions, there are a few facts that we need to examine first.

Lay Christians or lay Muslims do not ordinarily engage in organized missionary or *dawa* work. So when we talk of *dawa* or mission, we usually have in mind a particular group in each religion which consciously takes upon itself the responsibility of sharing its vision of truth with people outside its fold. In my view neither of these terms — lay Christians or lay Muslims or conscious Christians and conscious Muslims — quite fully describe this group. The most apt description of the role chosen for itself by this group is the one that is to be found in the Quran:

> Let there arise from among you a group that invites people to all that is good, enjoins [that which is generally regarded as] right, and proscribes [that which is generally regarded as] wrong. *Quran* 3:104

Such a group continues to belong to the 'lay' category in that it continues to be counted as a member in good standing of its ummah. Beyond this, it is also part of a self-conscious or committed group in that it takes its religious responsibilities, as compared to the lay group, more seriously. But added to these two roles, it has voluntarily taken upon itself a third role: it has stepped out of the confines of its own tradition and committed itself to promoting what is generally regarded as good. In the case of Christian–Muslim dialogue, it promotes trust and community across faith-boundaries. If we agree with this classification, then the questions I have raised gain greater urgency.

It is incontestable that by coming together in an enterprise of Christian–Muslim dialogue for promoting trust and community, we confer legitimacy on these aims. That is, from both our perspectives we see the dialogue as a genuine and worthwhile effort. But what about us: do we have legitimacy *vis-à-vis* each other? How do we see each other? Are we as human beings drawn together in expediency? Or, are we specialists of some kind who have agreed to take on a professional challenge?

To me it is clear that we are believers (in separate beliefs) who come together to find ways to circumvent this separateness and become one in a cause that transcends our 'separateness' and belongs to the realm of our common humanity. Now, what do our separate beliefs have to say about this? Am I as a *dai* (vehicle of Islamic *dawa*) permitted to function outside the *dawa* context? May I concede to my Christian friends, engaged in dialogue with me, a religious legitimacy, accept them on a level of co-equality in belief? These are questions that both Muslims and Christians should answer for themselves before any joint venture in the form of a dialogue can proceed and become genuinely productive.

The Muslim position with respect to these questions is well known. In the Muslim tradition human dignity and equality are basic rights of man *qua* man. Observe the words in the Quran 11:70 — 'Verily, we have honoured the Children of Adam' — or the following:

> O mankind! we created you from a single [pair] of a male and a female, and made you into nations and tribes, that you may know each other, not that you may despise each other.   *Quran* 49:13

This 'oneness' extends into the sphere of our spiritual and religious life as well: 'There is no people that God does not send a prophet or a warner' (*Quran* 16:36). All these prophets and messengers carried an identical message: serve God and eschew evil. The Quran in its own words, is not a denial, but 'a confirmation of revelations that went before it' (*Quran* 10:37). Hence, Muslims in order to be true Muslims are required to affirm:

> We believe in God, and what has been revealed to us, and what was revealed to Abraham, Ismail, Isaac, Jacob, and the Tribes, and in the Books given to Moses, Jesus and the Prophets from their Lord. We make no distinctions between one and another among them.   *Quran* 3:84

No declaration of the Islamic faith is complete without these verses. All men, then, came from the same source; they were all beneficiaries of God's favour, which was in all cases identical in content. There, therefore, exists a valid basis of continuing a relationship between Muslims and Christians, especially between those who practise what they believe (*Quran* 3:110).

> Those who believe [the Muslims], and those who are Jews, Christians and Sabeans — all those who believe in God and in the Day of Judgement and work righteousness, shall have their reward with God. They shall have no cause for fear, nor for grief.   *Quran* 2:62

The Quran, therefore, keeps the door open for interaction at all levels among the children of Adam. Beyond this, the Quran lays down another general principle to guide Muslims in their choice of conduct: 'Help one another in righteousness and piety, but help not one another in sin and rancour' (*Quran* 5:2). This principle allows Muslims as believers to co-operate in any effort toward the promotion of the good (in our particular case, the promotion of trust and community) with a view to creating a climate conducive to the survival of mankind and the attainment of peace and harmony and enrichment of the quality of life — goals which, I assume, we all share and are ultimately the end of our endeavour, more than simply strengthening Christian–Muslim relations.

In fact, in defining Muslims as an ideological group and in giving reasons for their status in the eyes of God, the Quran clearly states:

> You are the best of people, raised up for mankind [because] you enjoin right conduct and forbid indecency and you believe in God. *Quran* 3:110

Hence, participation in the promotion of the good is not merely an option open to Muslims; it is not a concession they condescend to make to the exigencies of a particular situation; it is a *sine qua non* of their faith–existence and their faith–status (*the best of people*). And this participation is in the context of humanity ('raised up for mankind') and not for themselves alone. And it is to be undertaken under the impetus of their religious belief, in fact derives from it (*you believe in God*).

These general principles I have briefly referred to seem to clear the way for Muslim participation in inter-religious and inter-group endeavours on a level of equality in origin and legitimacy in faith and moral status. But what about *dawa* and mission: the irrevocable obligation that rests with all believers? Isn't there a possibility, one may ask, that Muslims and Christians coming together on a precise platform (banning nuclear arms, for example; or promoting trust and community) may yet unwittingly or in simple good faith, make each other the object of *dawa* or mission and thus endanger the ends of trust and community? For, frankly speaking, we can promote trust only if we, each one of us, is assured that we do not have designs (however well-meaning) on each other.

Here, I think it is indicated that we look a little closely into these oft-repeated terms *dawa* and mission. Generally speaking, the meaning that the word *dawa* conjures up in the minds of many non-Muslims is that it is a device for conversion to Islam. It takes multiple shapes and forms: at times it is a theological argument, at other times (and such instances, in the perception of our non-Muslim friends, are or have been far more frequent) it involves coercion as well — economic, political, social, even corporeal (the sword theory, for example). Naturally, therefore, non-Muslims are wary of the word *dawa*.

As an aside, let me state that I hold no brief for all Muslims, past or present. Nobody's interests would be served, neither of Islam nor of Muslims or non-Muslims, if we made past or present Muslim conduct the basis of our inferences about Islamic doctrine. God did indeed guarantee the incorruptibility of the Quran, but I have yet to come across any textual reference that would even remotely suggest that Muslim conduct has also been thus guaranteed. Muslims, particularly those who exhaust their energies and fritter away goodwill in defending everything 'Muslim', should make a clear note of this. The Quran is the *al-furqan* (criterion). It, rather than history or any other measure, should be used to judge Muslim conduct itself. The Quran was not irrevocably or unconditionally given to any particular nation or tribe. It is a legacy, which like other spiritual bequests of man, belongs to all mankind. '[The message] is the grace of God, which He will bestow on whom He pleases' (*Quran* 62:4).

Now, going back to our discussion, even if *dawa* is accepted as an instrument for conversion in the hands of Muslims, a closer examination of the term would reveal that this could be only one of its aspects.

In the truest sense of the term, *dawa* is primarily inner-directed. It is essentially a means by which an individual Muslim ensures the vibrancy of her or his *iman* (faith), marshalling arguments 'ever more fair and ever more becoming'. This process in the widest sense has been termed as *tafakkur* (reflection), which is described by the Quran as a salient and ever-present attribute of the believer:

In the creation of the heavens and the earth, and in the alternation of night and day — there are indeed signs for men of under-

standing — those who celebrate the praises of God, standing, sitting
and lying down on their sides, and contemplate the wonders of creation in the heavens and the earth [and as a result they cry out]: Our
Lord not for naught have you created all this! Glory to you. Save us
from the punishment of the Fire.   *Quran* 3:190–1

Dawa in this sense is a witness that each individual Muslim presents in
the practice of daily life.

The second aspect of *dawa* is interactive in its connotations — it
relates to others; not *all* others, but Muslim others. After having become
a witness to the truths of Islam in his or her own life, a Muslim's next
concern is to see this witness in the lives of fellow-believers, peers,
friends, and the social environment. This process is akin to what the
Americans call a 'home mission' — setting your own house in order.

The third and final aspect of *dawa* is the one that relates to outsiders.
We have already touched upon this aspect. Its purpose is other-directed.
But certain connotations that have in time come to adhere to this process
in the perception of many non-Muslims (especially the notion that the
faithful *en masse* have been given free rein to target by any means
available those outside the pale of Islam) have, despite confirmed
or unconfirmed Muslim lapses in this regard, absolutely no basis in
doctrine.

Behind bearing witness to the truths of Islam through a life dedicated
to its precepts in all walks of life, the idea undoubtedly is that the picture
thus presented would be so attractive that those not in the fold of Islam
would be drawn toward it. And this is exactly the manner in which Islam
actually spread in *most* regions of the world. I concede that there are
parallel examples based on a different kind of testimony. But apart from
the fact that they are now recognized by impartial observers as not as
frequent as previously believed, they stand condemned as an aberration
by the clear testimony of the Quran.

According to one contemporary writer, the expansion of Islam
beyond the initial seventh century spurt was the work of traders and
itinerant sufis. This they achieved by learning 'to live lives of submission to God and to His Messenger in a pluralistic, sometimes even
unsympathetic environment. What eventually contributed to that environment changing to a "realm of Islam" (*dar al-Islam*) was not the
militancy of the Muslim minority but the religious interest of the non-
Muslim majority in what they came to recognize as a peaceful and attractive form of faith.'[1]

The Quran has been careful in laying down clear guidelines for this third aspect of *dawa*. All of us, I am sure, are familiar with the following Quranic statements:

> There is no compulsion in religion. The right direction is now distinct from error.   *Quran* 2:256

> He [man] has been shown the two paths.   *Quran* 90:10

> Whosoever will, let him believe, and whosoever will let him disbelieve.   *Quran* 18:29

> No bearer of burdens can bear the burden of others.   *Quran* 17:15

Our success or failure rests on how we exercise our freedom of choice. In the absence of this freedom there is nothing to judge; there is then no meaning in this entire enterprise. Muslims are thus persuaded against coercion, not so much for humanitarian or other considerations, but in order to retrieve and preserve meaning in life. Other examples of how Islam desires the process of *dawa* to remain within certain bounds are in the following verses.

> God forbids you not with regard to those who was not against you on account of your religion, nor drive you out of your homes, from dealing with them kindly and justly. For God loves those who are just. *Quran* 60:8

> And argue not with the People of the Scripture unless it be in a way that is better, save with such of them as do wrong; and say: We believe in that which has been revealed to us and revealed to you; our God and your God is one, and to Him we surrender.   *Quran* 29:46

> Call you unto the path of your Lord through wise argument and fair preaching and argue with them [the non-believers] with arguments yet more fair and yet more becoming.   *Quran* 16:125

> Turn not your face in scorn toward men, nor walk with insolence in the land for God does not love any arrogant boaster.   *Quran* 31:18

> And be modest in your bearing, and subdue your voice, for the harshest of all sounds is without doubt the sound of an ass.   *Quran* 31:18–19

However, there is one crucial aspect of the process of *dawa* that most people, even Muslims, overlook or fail to recognize: and this relates to the actual process of conversion. This would presumably reinforce our contention that *dawa* is primarily inner-directed.

The argument is rather lengthy, but the gist of it is that in Islam *dawa* has no relationship to actual conversion. The process of *dawa* and its results are not subject to body count or cost-effectiveness. Theoretically, the *dawa* process can proceed *ad infinitum* without 'saving a single soul', and still fulfil its purpose. The reason for this is that, according to the Quran, *dawa* belongs to the domain of man, whereas conversion or change of heart belongs to the domain of God. And if the Quran is testimony, God is quite anxious to protect His domain, so much so that He repeatedly intervened in the case of the first dai of Islam, the Prophet Muhammad, to underscore this truth. The tone of these interventions is sometimes that of a reminder, sometimes of caution and sometimes of even admonishment.

Had your Lord willed it, all the people of the earth would be believers [but He did not] would you then compel the people to believe? *Quran* 10:99

It is true you will not be able to guide every one whom you love; but God guides those whom He will, and He knows best those who receive guidance. *Quran* 28:56

Say: O men, the truth has now come to you from your Lord. Whoever will may be guided by it, whoever does not will, may not. And I am not sent over you to arrange your affairs [make decisions on your behalf]. *Quran* 10:108 See also *Quran* 6:104

We have revealed to you the Quran that you may convey it to the people. It is the truth. Whoever accepts it does so to his own credit. Whoever rejects it does so to his discredit. You are not responsible for their decisions. [In case people reject the revelation] say, I am only a warner to warn you. *Quran* 39:41

It is not required of you [O Muhammad] to set them [unbelievers] on the right path. But God sets on the right path whom He pleases. *Quran* 2:272

And say to the People of the Book and to those who are unlearned: 'Do you submit your whole self to God?' If they do they are on the right path, but if they do not, your duty is [only] to convey the message, and God watches over all His servants.   *Quran* 3:20

Thus we see that a Muslim's responsibility ends with the presentation of the message. Conversion cannot be the stated or measureable goal of *dawa*, because conversion, which implies a change of heart, is the prerogative of God. It goes against the very essence of freedom of choice which Islam wishes to protect and preserve even at the cost of war. Muslims are permitted the use of militant means in two situations: one, when they are the object of hostile aggression, and two, when a people's freedom of choice is being curtailed.

Of course, as I noted earlier, violations have occurred in the course of history; at times Muslims have *arrogated* to ourselves the power and authority that belongs to God alone. But it must also be considered that violations have occurred in all aspects of Islam, even in those which relate to Muslims ourselves and the dire consequences of which we alone have suffered. The point I am trying to make is that a clear doctrinal base, an unambiguous textual reference, exists so that Muslim conduct may at any time be adjudged with reference to our own sources. This should be somewhat reassuring to those who are disturbed by the historical evidence.

Hence, even if we equate dialogue with *dawa* (the reservations I have to this will come later), we find that these clear guidelines should rule out the possibility of any hidden Muslim agenda. Insofar as the present dialogue form is concerned, the credit for it goes entirely to our Christian friends. It is they who first recognized the urgent necessity of inter-faith trust and community, particularly the Catholic Church which through Ecumenical Council II courageously and imaginatively broke the ice of centuries and opened up the possibilities of dialogue between followers of different faiths. This step must undoubtedly reckon as one of the most significant landmarks in world religious history. Protestant churches soon followed suit. Even today, a quarter-century after Vatican II, it is mainly Christian bodies that are in the forefront of this effort and guiding it forward. The Muslim side, despite its hoary tradition of outreach, is still locked in reluctance, caution and a degree of timidity.

It is necessary at this point to examine briefly the factors behind this Muslim hesitance. If there is nothing in Muslim tradition, doctrinal or operational, as Muslims aver, to encourage them to turn inward and exist in a spiritual ghetto, why are we averse to grasping the hand of inter-faith exchange and discourse? To my mind, there are two reasons for it. One relates to the history of the past four hundred years or so, in which Christianity failed to perform its natural function of acting as a critique of culture. The internal consequences to the Church of this failure is not our business today and have now been valorously analysed by numerous serious Christian scholars themselves. But its external consequences touch directly upon our concerns here. I do not wish for a moment to suggest that in this respect only the Christians are to be placed in the dock of history, We Muslims, too, erred, but perhaps because of our own adverse tradition, or because of the lack of opportunity, our record of inter-faith hostility and aggression is not quite at par.

In the modern period, it was the Christians who were the dominant power; they had the means, the resources, the education, the will and the dreams. They are the ones who stepped out and made contact. They are the ones who rode roughshod over the enlightened elements of their own noble tradition and made inter-faith dialogue a dire prospect for followers of other, 'lesser' religions. Is this chapter now closed? Only our Christian friends can supply the correct answer. Insofar as the layman is concerned, one still hears of the phenomenon of 'Rice Christians' in parts of the world today, or so it is alleged.

If all this history is to be interpreted and understood in terms of a power syndrome, then the world of Islam is now catching up. In comparative terms it now has more power, more resources and a clearer will to exert itself. In parts of the world, religiously speaking, where there was no challenge, there is now a challenge. No one now is on the defensive, regardless of what each side would want to believe or want others to believe. In this emerging scenario, what guarantee is there that the Muslim side will not encounter the same pitfalls as the Christians experienced in their days of ascendence, or use the same rationalizations (civilizing the savages) and commit the same violations of our own enlightened traditions and the human ideals of tolerance, justice and equality? Perhaps soon a parallel new term may have to be coined and gain currency, if it has not been already: 'Rice Muslims'.

In consideration of such a frightening prospect, it is absolutely essential, and especially for Muslims, to seek ways of inter-faith communication, dialogue, mutual consultation and co-operation. If we Muslims find ourselves disinclined to take these steps for the sake of Christians or followers of other religions, we still need to do it for our own sakes, for the religious attitude described above is fatal not so much for the people at the receiving end (victims do survive) but for the perpetrators.

At this point let me clearly state that dialogue is not as I see it an invitation to suspend *dawa* or mission, Christianity as well as Islam would strongly resist this. The idea here is that proudly acknowledging our differences, we learn to work together. Let me repeat something that was noted elsewhere: there are certain salient characteristics that define our identity. These should not be in jeopardy in our coming together. But given these distinctions there are wide areas of belief and action wherein we can fruitfully co-operate and work for the betterment of mankind in service to our common Lord and Creator.

Identifying such areas and the rationale of such an approach needs to be briefly discussed, but before I do this there is one little point that I have skipped. In a way I ran ahead of my analysis of why Muslims even today experience a certain reluctance in participating in such inter-faith endeavours. In the earlier part of my presentation I have noted that Islam not only encourages inter-faith contact and dialogue, it provides it with a firm doctrinal base. It is my considered opinion that if this form is to proceed with meaning and gain genuine legitimacy, a similar statement of purpose, a definition, and clearly spelled-out guidelines need to be forthcoming from all participating parties. This would go a long way in creating mutual confidence and a more forthcoming attitude on the part of Muslims. This point cannot be over-emphasized.

I have already confessed at the outset that my experience in formal inter-faith encounter is very limited. My familiarity with Christian literature on the subject is even more so. But in the cursory attempts I have made to understand the accepted Christian concept of dialogue, its meaning and purpose, I have been struck by two salient features. One, despite the much longer Christian experience in inter-faith contact and their precedence in the recognition of such need, there is a striking absence of clear definitions and explicit expression of purpose. For one thing, there is an interchangeable and rather confusing use of such terms as dialogue, mission and evangelism. Each of these then comes out with varying connotations.

> To evangelize is so to present Christ Jesus in the power of the Holy Spirit that men shall come to put their trust in God through him, to accept him as their saviour, and serve him as their King in the fellowship of his Church.[2]

In similar vein, David Bosch in his very penetrating analysis on the subject entitled 'Evangelism: Theological Currents and Cross-Currents Today',[3] treats evangelism and mission in the same category, and then conceding that 'evangelism is understood differently by different people', sets about describing the various meanings of evangelism/mission.

In the several meanings discussed, one emphasis common to all is 'winning souls for eternity'. With regard to the ecumenical movement, it is averred that the use of mission, witness and evangelism is interchangeable, because ecumenism represents a total Christian ministry to the world, including conversion.

Later in the study, when a distinction between evangelism and mission is made, it turns out to be a territorial rather than a conceptual difference. Evangelism in this context is preaching the Gospel in Western society; *i.e.*, among those who are nominal Christians or are estranged from the church. And mission is communicating the Christian faith in the Third World; *i.e.*, among strangers. Now, since 'Evangelism that stops at calling people to accept Christ is incomplete and truncated',[4] one would expect a more distinct definition of dialogue to be forthcoming. But here, too, the issue is not quite clear. The following belongs more in the ambivalent category:

> Inter-religious dialogue would be unnecessary if all men believed in Jesus Christ and practised only the religion which He established.[5]

However, this is not the whole story. Tucked away in the background, but most assuredly there, is a parallel current of thought, a minority view, which has perhaps always been there and bears valid credentials. This current of thought has distinctly different emphases:

> . . . evangelism cannot be defined in terms of results; it is simply the preaching of the gospel whether any one gets converted or not.[6]

> Evangelism is invitation; it should never deteriorate into coaxing, much less threat.[7]

It cautions, however, that 'Both these — coaxing and threat — are often used in so-called evangelistic campaigns.'

The early Christian community, the founding fathers, so to speak, did not have to say, 'Join us'. Their 'conspicuously different life style became in itself a witness to Christ'. Evangelistic campaigns in our times are thus used to makeup for the lack of a 'conspicuously different life style' in present-day Christian communities.

In inter-religious dialogue the Church discovers the working of God in the other religions, elements of truth and grace, seeds of the Word,

. . . precious things both religious and human, and ways of the truth which illumines all mankind.

Fruitful inter-religious dialogue presumes that the partners participate in a spirit of openness, sincerity and involvement . . . It is built on respect and love for one another.[8]

To reconcile these parallel currents, whether in Christianity or Islam, we need sincerely to re-examine our religious ideals, a process that would in itself, by its own internal logic, lead to re-examination of our past performance in the realm of inter-faith contact and conduct. Such an exercise, I am convinced, will lead to a clearer doctrinal affirmation of religious pluralism and a recognition of the diversity of faith–beliefs and faith–practices. It would also, and this is a wish, come up with a definition of inter-faith dialogue that distinguishes it from evangelism and mission and represents a more forthright recognition of the equal identity and dignity of all participants in the process. Dialogue may then be defined as a

process wherein people with diverse faith–backgrounds come together and recognizing each other's confessional identity and integrity, join hands in equality and respect to resolve a common and mutually perceived threat to all.

In time, with the experience thus gained, understanding (even at the theological level) may very possibly result.

The mention of the theological component of dialogue raises in my mind another question. As I see it, the current form of dialogue has so far been rather overly burdened with theological content. Why do we have necessarily to start with ponderous issues such as Jesus in the Quran and Jesus in the Gospels, or the Christian estimation of the Prophet of Islam or their views on the divine origins of the Quran? What immediate purpose would be served? We come together, if my understanding is correct, under the constraints of not theological but mainly extra-theological factors: humanity is threatened with extinction, planet Earth has become or is likely to become the arena of perpetual strife. Those who subscribe to the belief in a higher life and have faith in the transcendent potential of human nature owe it to themselves to join hands and stem this drift toward extinction. Unless, of course, the purpose of dialogue is to convert all Christians to Islam or all Muslims to Christianity. Then, of course, the theological discourse becomes imperative and unavoidable. Even then I cannot altogether overlook the Quranic reprimand:

If God willed it, He could have brought them all together to the guidance. So do not be among the foolish ones.   *Quran* 6:35

There are numerous vital issues that in our present world constitute a cause of mutual provocation and tension between our two sides (or all sides). A better approach would be that we identify such issues — social, political, economic, attitudinal — one by one and make them the focus and the *raison d'être* of our coming together and see what working relationship we can develop in resolving them to our mutual satisfaction. Success in such a piecemeal enterprise would build confidence and encourage further interaction. Theological issues, on the other hand, by their nature strike at the roots of our self-identity; they challenge our very being as Muslims and Christians.

I regret that I find myself extremely reluctant to be carried away by the sentiments: since the Catholic Church has at last granted partial religious legitimacy to those outside the Church, or that there is revival in the Muslim world of the truly Islamic ethos, an era of spiritual cordiality or religious *bonhomie* is around the corner for the followers of different faiths as followers of different faiths. A lot more water has to flow under this bridge. But as I suggested above, there are ways of working toward that end.

References

1. Patrick Ryan, 'Islam and Politics in West Africa: Minority and Majority Models', *The Muslim World*, January 1987, p. 6.
2. John Scott, *Christian Mission in the Modern World*, quoted in the *International Bulletin of Missionary Research*, July 1987, p. 97.
3. *IBMR*, July 1987.
4. *IBMR*, July 1987, p. 102.
5. Vatican Secretariat for Non-Christians, *Bulletin*, 22: 2, 1985.
6. Scott, *IBMR*, July 1987, p. 97.
7. *Ibid.*, p. 101.
8. Francis Arinze, 'Prospects of Evangelization, with Reference to the Areas of the Non-Christian Religions, Twenty Years After Vatican II', *Bulletin* 20:2, pp. 114–15.

Part Two

The Future Role of Dawa

The Nature of Our Community
The Tasks Ahead

Kamal Hasan

Community development is one of the most neglected dimensions of *dawa*, but it must be a major concern if *dawa* is to have any real contemporary significance. The term 'community' usually describes a collection of people who occupy a geographical area, who together are pursuing economic and political activities and constitute a self-governing social unit, sharing common values and the feeling of belonging to one another. Communities may be a city, a town, a village, a kampong, a neighbourhood. However, modern life has become so fragmented, so isolated and involves so much mobility that the sense of community has all but disappeared. *Dawa*, therefore, should have community as a goal: the evolution of a community life, based on self-sufficiency and self-reliance, sharing and co-operation.

Dawa aimed at community development requires that we understand the nature of communities. In this chapter I will examine certain dominant global and local trends which will shape the future characteristics of Muslim communities everywhere.[1] For example, unemployment and underemployment among educated young people in most Muslim countries is on the rise. If this development continues, to use the words of Philip Coombs, 'the world of education and the world of work will become increasingly unbalanced and maladjusted' over the next twenty years.[2] It will lead to serious problems and challenges for Muslim communities everywhere. Another problem closely connected to the rise in unemployment is the rapid population growth in the Muslim World.

59

Today's world Muslim population of 1,000 million is expected to triple during the next thirty-eight years.[3] To keep pace with this demographic growth and to provide educational and employment opportunities, Muslim countries will require a continuing high annual rate of educational expansion. In addition, schools and colleges will need to improve the quality of their programmes and to adapt them to the changing environment. Muslim countries will also need to expand non-formal educational and training facilities.

Despite the large migration of rural Muslims to the cities, United Nations demographers estimate that between 1980 and 2000 the total rural population of the materially less developed regions will grow from 2,276 million to 2,774 million, an increase of 22 per cent. In Africa and South Asia the projected increase in the number of rural people due to high birth rates is from 349 million to 478 million and 1,069 million to 1,387 million respectively.[4]

This rapid increase means that the already deep and extensive rural poverty of Muslim countries in Asia, Africa, Southeast Asia and the Middle East is likely to spread, thus creating more pressures for arable land, educational facilities, water supplies, electricity, health and sanitation facilities, transportation and other essential household and community services. Under such conditions, the poorest families will be highly vulnerable to crop failures, devastating floods, prolonged draughts and epidemics. Already food production per capita has declined to dangerous levels in many of the poorest countries. That there will be an enormous need for effective health care services in the rural areas of Muslim countries, as essential requirements for raising the productivity of rural Muslim masses, is abundantly clear.[5]

It is also becoming increasingly clear that this Third Development Decade is witnessing the emergence of a crisis in development in many Muslim countries. At the root of this crisis are:

1. The continued dependence of the developing and under-developed economies [including many Muslim countries] on the industrial countries for investment, trade, finance and technology.
2. A lopsided internal socio-economic structure with great inequalities in wealth and income; and a neglect of certain sectors, especially food production.
3. The rapid depletion of natural resources, such as tropical forests, fisheries and minerals, which will have serious implications on income and the balance of payments.

4. A pattern of economic management and development planning based primarily on growth of output instead of emphasis on satisfying the basic needs of the people.[6]

Against this background of adverse conditions under which a substantial majority of rural people live in poor Muslim countries, the learning needs of lower-income groups are closely tied to their basic survival needs. To improve the Muslim family's health, for example, people must learn and apply new practices in nutrition, the use of uncontaminated water, sanitation, proper child and maternal care. To meet the occupational learning needs of the lower income groups, a great deal of pertinent education will be required by all those concerned, not through the schools alone but through a wide range of non-formal educational activities.[7]

The spectre of Muslim refugees, which today constitute the largest group of refugees in the world, suffering in their miserable dwellings in Pakistan, Iran, Jordan and parts of Africa presents yet another challenge to the Muslim community's capacity to meet the diverse educational and physical needs of those who have been forced to flee their own homes.

One of the most serious social problems in the world today is drugs — abuse, addiction and trafficking. Many Muslim countries and families are affected by this modern scourge. In Malaysia, it was estimated in 1984 that there were 101,038 drug addicts who were registered; the actual number, however, could exceed 500,000, most of them being Muslim–Malay youths.[8] It is gratifying to note that the international community has now recognized that drug abuse and illicit trafficking are global problems and has declared its commitment to combat both.[9]

Other major social problems in Muslim countries are corruption and its related misdemeanours of mismanagement, embezzlement and abuse of authority, which are not exclusive to Muslim societies. Although the forms of corruption may vary from place to place, corruption plays havoc in affluent as well as poverty-stricken societies. Whatever the form, corruption contributes significantly to human misery, and when it occurs at the lower levels of government bureaucracy it tends to affect the lives and behaviour of the less privileged sections of the community.

'It is partly responsible for the economic, intellectual and cultural dependence of the Third World, for continuing poverty in Third World societies, for the dominance of vested interests in agriculture, industry and commerce, for the destruction of the environment, for the rising cost of living, for the deterioration of goods and services, for political factionalism and political instability, for repression and communalism.[10]

It is unfortunate that in several Muslim countries, corruption in high places and petty bribery in government administration have become part of the Muslim way of life. Education alone does not seem able to eradicate this evil and, consequently, community development is severely affected. The separation of ethics from business and politics has also contributed to such scandals as breach of trust, conflict of interest, misappropriation of funds, kick-backs, financial manipulation and personal aggrandisements. In most Muslim communities, much of the material well-being depends upon the goodwill of political authorities, high government officials and the co-operation of the implementation agencies; the completion of any community project involving public funds and government agencies, may in some cases hinge upon securing such good will through adequate 'incentives' to all concerned.

Muslim Communities and Educational Development

A Muslim community may be large or small and may have democratic, autocratic, military, hereditary kingship or oligarchic rule. Any attempt to change the secularistic or dualistic educational system or improve the living and moral standards of the community needs the consent and support of the policy-makers and power holders. It was perhaps with these constraints in mind that the First World Conference on Muslim Education, organized by King Abdulaziz University and held in Makkah al-Mukarramah in 1977 offered, among other things, the following recommendations for Muslim countries:

Basic necessary knowledge must be imparted to all Muslims. To attain this aim, basic primary education must be provided for all children and illiteracy eliminated from the Muslim world.

The aim of this type of education should be to preserve the Islamic heritage and to resist the encroachment of alien cultures.

Ministers of Education in Muslim countries should take an active interest in student circles and unions all over the world, with a view to involving them in Islamic activities and providing them with material and moral support against hostile and subsersive currents.

Having reviewed educational systems prevailing in the world, namely the European, American and Marxist systems in addition to mixtures of such systems, and considered the traditional systems in some Muslim countries, the committee believes that it is time to formulate an alternative Muslim educational system to be adopted in Muslim countries, which will be designed to serve as a defence against ideological and behavioural deviation resulting from intellectual and ethical onslaughts.

Educational policy should seek to promote the formulation of Islamic theories in the field of economics, politics, sociology and philosophy in order to fill the vacuum in the minds of Muslim youth in these areas, so as to prevent intellectual invasion from outside.

Education could not be Islamic either in planning or execution unless the community and the state adopt the Islamic system. Therefore, all countries in which Muslims form a majority are urged to abide by the Shariah and make their economic, political and social legislation in accordance with Islam.[11]

The Conference, fully aware of the political and educational crisis in Muslim countries, advocated the removal of the existing dichotomy or dualism and the secular humanistic bases of modern education in Muslim countries.[12] Unfortunately, many recommendations of the five World Conferences have yet to be seriously considered by educational planners in Muslim-majority countries. The lukewarm reactions of many government authorities to the Islamicization of education are in part due to the intellectual gap between the Islamically-committed scholars and the secular, Western-oriented, nationalistic èlites who comprise the top official planners, bureaucratic bosses and highranking decision-makers in Muslim countries. These leaders are usually sceptical of ideas coming with the Islamic perspective. Thus, the resistance to Islamic views come from within the same Muslim communities. In non-Muslim countries, Muslim communities face different social and political problems, their principle obstacles coming from non-Muslim political, economic, intellectual and religious establishments.

Community Development and Muslim Minorities

In many parts of technologically under-equipped countries, community development particularly means improvements in agriculture and animal husbandry, provision for drinking and irrigation water, the building of roads connecting villages with highways, literacy and adult education, health and sanitation facilities, the stimulation of small family-based industries, land reforms, rural co-operatives and credit facilities.[13] It is the overall improvement of the way of life, embracing improvements in trade, commerce, industry, agriculture, education and health, and based on the objectives, principles, laws and values of Islam. Community development aims to integrate both material and spiritual needs of the individual and the society.[14]

The fulfilment of the objectives depends on the integrated functional relationship of the community development system, which is composed of clearly defined individual and group felt needs; people's voluntary, co-operative, active participation; the right kind of leadership; availability and effective use of funds, locally available human, material and spiritual resources; and functioning and participative organization. The following basic elements of community development should be borne in mind by Islamic leaders:

1. Activities and projects should meet the different needs of the community.
2. Changing attitudes and values in people are as important, if not more, than the material achievements of community projects during the initial stages of development.
3. The identification, encouragement and training of local leadership talents should be a basic objective of any programme.
4. Special projects aimed at the active involvement of women and youth should always be designed in view of the problems affecting both these vital sections of the community.
5. To be fully effective, communities' self-help projects require both intensive and extensive assistance from outside sources.
6. Organization of research, experimentation and evaluation.[15]

Insofar as community development aims at promoting the proper development in such areas as economics (business, trade, marketing, co-operatives, credits, banking, labour, industry, self-reliance), agriculture (land, irrigation, drainage, land settlement, water and water power, fishing, game and birds, conservation of natural resources, subsoil wealth, forestry, animal husbandry, poultry), social welfare (health standards, public safety, rehabilitation of drug users and ex-prisoners welfare services, social ethics), culture (arts and crafts, religious festivals, traditional songs, poetry, drama, dances), and religious education (Quran classes, Sunday schools, mosque activities, Islamic centres, lectures, training of duats, youth camps), Muslim communities will have to depend on the products of formal as well as non-formal education to supply the expertise and the trainers. This once again demonstrates the importance of pertinent education to produce the right knowledge, skills and attitudes in both the Muslim-majority and Muslim-minority countries.

The increasing self-awareness of the Muslim ummah has produced a keen interest in the conditions of the one-third of the world's Muslims who reside under non-Muslim jurisdictions. Three types of Muslim minority are defined by Dr M.A. Kettani:

1. Those which constituted majority states or communities before colonialism, and were reduced to minority status thereafter (examples are Muslim minorities in the U.S.S.R., Palestine and Ethiopia).
2. Minorities which used to control the states, but after losing political power became reduced to minority status (examples are India and the Balkan states).
3. Minorities which are formed through converts in non-Muslim lands, usually merging with a stream of Muslim immigrants.[16]

We can agree with Dr Kettani that it is imperative for Muslim minorities to organize themselves into community groups in order to survive. The community organizations should, in his view, express an inclusivist Islamic identity and not an exclusivist, racial, ethnic, sectarian or professional identity. Secondly, their constitutions should include a provision for mutual consultation. Politically, they should strive for the official recognition of their existence as religious communities on par with other religious communities.[17]

For the sake of brevity we may summarize the needs of Muslim minorities in terms of the following hierarchy of needs: survival, identity, employment, and development. These needs, in turn, entail different educational strategies and diverse learning skills. According to Dr H.H. Bilgrami, the Muslim minority communities, while utilizing the facilities of modern Western educational institutions, should establish facilities for Islamic education in order to preserve the ideological identity of their communities. His primary concern relates to the survival and identity needs; he stresses that the purpose of Islamic education (by which he probably means Islamic religious education) should be the following:

1. To maintain the means whereby Muslims in the West remain conscious of their identity.

2. To ensure a dynamic element which can face the onslaught of Western cultural influence on the minds of Muslim children.

3. To ensure that Muslim minorities remain conscious of their position as an ideological group with values different from those non-Muslims.

4. To function as a source of information about Islam to non-Muslims.

5. To serve as a means for the propagation of Islam, which is the sacred duty of every Muslim.

6. To ultimately raise a strong ideologically integrated community for the consolidation of the ummah on the basis of unity.[18]

In an overview of Muslim organizations in the West, Aslam Abdullah distinguishes two types of established organizations, 'mainly ideological' and 'purely cultural'. Many of them recreated the situation prevailing in their original countries. 'Most of the *dawa* organizations have now become ethnic groups with an emphasis on preserving their specific cultural and social identity.'[19] Muslim parents in the United Kingdom, according to one research finding,

> show concern only about the superficial problems of Islamic education. They do not perceive the real nature of the problems and hence fail to discover that their children should be provided with the meaning and message of the Quran, its essential elements, the characteristics of Islamic ideology and its culture, and that they should be given necessary lessons in Hadith, and should be taught Islam as the complete code of life for all humanity.

The Muslim religious teachers 'also have a limited knowledge of Islam, and their knowledge of Western ideology is much more limited. Hence, they are incompetent to solve the queries of Muslim children about British society.' As for the Muslim children, they 'are in a tug of war not between Islamic ideals at home and Christian concepts at schools, as it has been often incorrectly described, but are in a tug of war between incomplete and ambiguous Islamic ideas at home and Western concepts at schools.'[20]

It has been suggested that large and well-entrenched Muslim minorities such as those in India should ameliorate their educational backwardness not by demanding special reservations in national educational institutions, as this special reservation strategy seems to have benefited mainly the advantaged Muslim groups while the Muslim lower-middle class would hesitate to invest time, energy and resources in formal education, but by relying upon its own internal resources and private initiative for developing educational facilities. Muslims are urged to learn from the strategy adopted by the Jews in the United States and the Sikhs in India where 'both were able to overcome the chasm between secular education and religious instruction through a strategy which sought to emphasize the significance of secular education for the community and built an institutional framework where religious instruction could be pursued along with, rather than at the cost of, secular education'.[21]

Conclusion and Some General Suggestions

It is obvious that the priorities of Muslim-majority communities are different from those of Muslim-minority communities. It is imperative that Muslim-majority communities integrate religious and secular education in a single system, embracing both formal and non-formal education. In fulfilling the needs of the Muslim masses in the rural areas where poverty is acute and the communities backward, Muslim governments should direct more attention to the following matters:

1. The provision of non-formal skill-oriented training in agriculture, village co-operatives, animal husbandry, fishery, horticulture, blacksmithy, carpentry and cottage industries to local communities. These training programmes should not be divorced from courses in Islamic ethics, beliefs and fundamental religious duties for all age levels.

2. Skill training may be imparted on the principle of 'teaching by doing' and 'learning by doing'. In other words, the trainees, such as practising farmers, farm women, school drop-outs, illiterate youths, agricultural labourers and in-service field-level functionaries, are provided with opportunities to learn the skills by being involved in the actual process of various scientific operations.[22]

3. The establishment of more Islamic technical universities, such as the one sponsored by OIC in Dhaka, Bangladesh.

. The organization of international co-operation among Muslim countries in promoting vocational education using the Islamic integrated curriculum.

5. The establishment and preservation of the modern 'Pondok' or 'Pesantren' — traditional religious educational institution in Malaysia, Thailand and Indonesia which are privately owned and

whose curriculum is a mixture of religious knowledge and vocational training.[23]

6. The preservation of the harmonious combination of humanistic educational orientation and education for marketable skills in the scientific, technological age. The concern for 'employable skills' or 'manpower education' should not lead to the neglect of spiritual and moral values.

7. Educators must be encouraged to work in industry and agencies of government whose work has educational outcomes, such as those dealing with agriculture, fisheries, health and sanitation; vice versa, agencies and industries must be encouraged to maintain education and training units whose task is to provide training programs and/or educational materials pertaining to their development sector.[24]

8. Muslim youth leaders of Islamic voluntary organizations of the Muslim world should be trained in Islamic community services for long durations in several Muslim countries. The kind of training courses conducted by the Dawa Academy of the International Islamic University, Islamabad, should be emulated by the rich Muslim countries.

9. The infusion of informal learning — the spontaneous, unstructured learning that goes on daily in the home and neighbourhood, behind the school and the playing field, in the workplace, marketplace, library and museum, and through the mass media — with appropriate Islamic ethical values. In other words the channels of life-long education, such as radio, television and films, should not be allowed to be filled with materialistic and immoral values.

10. The encouragement of the Islamic movements to start projects in community development towards ameliorating the problems of capitalist exploitation, illiteracy, unemployment, drug abuse, prostitution, juvenile crime and cultural enslavement to the West.

11. The revitalization of the mosque as a multipurpose educational and community centre.

Muslim minority communities face the challenge of survival. They often become targets of assimilation by the governments of the dominant majorities. If they resist the social restructuring efforts of the government in order to preserve their identities, they will find it more and more difficult to survive economically and educationally. Their loyalty to Islam is sometimes used as an excuse to deprive them of employment opportunities in government services. For them the educational system remains dual; the secular-oriented national system which is the key to employment and social status and their own private religious education on an informal basis which is a source of religious identity and affinity with the larger Muslim ummah outside their frontiers. Undoubtedly, ideological unity, self-help programmes, and strong linkages with Muslim-majority countries are the key factors of survival for them.

Muslim religious organizations and voluntary associations should co-operate to select promising community leaders to be trained in the institutions of Muslim countries. Local Muslims are usually better equipped to function effectively in the long run, provided they obtain the necessary educational qualifications. However, recipient Muslim communities in Muslim countries should be vigilant against government agents or agents of vested interests disguising themselves as representatives of Muslim minority groups, so that funds meant for Muslim community development do not end up elsewhere.

Muslim religious movements in the minority and majority areas should be prevented from falling into the strait-jacket of ethnocentrism or regionalism. Aslam Abdullah says that

> many *dawa* organizations are run by people who are generally considered by the locals as immigrants. But their residential status should not make them behave as such. In order to act as the bearers of universal messages they have to go through certain painful experiences. They have to sacrifice their ethnicity, egoism, lethargy, and worldly interests. They have to make the natives feel that as followers of Islam they care for the problems of the society in which they live. If they fail to do that the information they are offering could just as well be obtained from museums.[25]

With the prospects of further decline in revenues of Muslim countries, the widening poverty gaps, increasing drug abuse, further persecution of Muslim minorities throughout the world, the oncoming tide of Islamic resurgence and hostile non-Muslim responses, Muslim governments should accommodate voluntary Islamic organizations in shaping the educational and development futures of Muslim communities. If such democratic self-reformation and internal correction are not undertaken, then the future world conditions may even make national states obsolete. After all, one of the ultimate aims of Islamic education and community development is liberation from human tyranny and dehumanization which sometimes accompany the national programmes of modernization.

Notes

1. For a general overview of global trends and the changes in store for us in the near future, see Edward Goldsmith and Nicholas Hildyard (eds.), *The Earth Report*. London: Mitchell Beazley, 1988.
2. Philip H. Coombs, *The World Crisis in Education: the View from the Eighties*. Oxford: Oxford University Press, 1985, p. 204.
3. 'Bilyun Muslim fil-alam al-yawm wa yutawaqqa ziyadatuhum ila thalathah balayin bada thamaniyah wa thalathin aman faat!' *Al-Rabitah* **267** (June), 1987, pp. 25–9.
4. Coombs, *World Crisis in Education*, p. 49.
5. See the statistics given by Ahmed S. Heiba in 'Agricultural Resources in the Muslim World: Capacity and Future Growth'. *The Muslim World and the Future Economic Order*. London: Islamic Council of Europe, 1979, pp. 296–315.
6. Khor Kok Peng and Evelyne Hong, 'The Third World Today: Crisis or Development?' Paper presented at the Conference on Third World: Development or Crisis?', 9–14 November 1984, held in Penang, Malaysia, pp. 5–6. For a detailed study of the structures and dependency of the Malaysian economy, see Khor Kok Peng, *The Malaysian Economy: Structures and Dependence*. Kuala Lumpur: Maricans & Sons, 1983.
7. As far as the future world economy is concerned, the Secretariat of UNCTAD predicts in its annual report, published on 16 July 1987, that economic growth will weaken in both industrial and developing countries. Commodity prices will suffer from slow economic growth and production growth rates in developing countries will decline due to falling commodity prices and a slowdown in growth of imports into industrial countries. In developed countries growth will decline to 2.3 per cent from 2.4 and 2.8 per cent in 1986 and 1985. *New Straits Times*, (K.L.), 17 July 1987.
8. *New Straits Times* (K.L.), 24 December 1984.
9. The International Conference on Drug Abuse and Illicit Trafficking held in Vienna in June 1987 and attended by 138 nations testifies to this new international awareness. See 'Global strategy to combat dadah abuse, trafficking'. *New Straits Times* (K.L.), 2 July 1987.
10. Chandra Muzaffar, 'The Scourge of Corruption', in *Corruption*. Penang: ALIRAN, 1981, p. 28.
11. S.N. al-Attas (ed.), *Aims and Objectives of Islamic Education*. London: Hodder and Stoughton, 1979, pp. 159–65.

12. S.S. Husain and S.A. Ashraf, *Crisis in Muslim Education*. London: Hodder and Stoughton, 1979.

13. Irwin T. Sanders, *The Community*. New York: Ronald Press, 1958, p. 404.

14. *Islam and Development*. Plainfield, Indiana: Association of Muslim Social Scientist, 1977.

15. For details, see Ernest B. Harper and Arthur Dunham (eds.) *Community Organization in Action*. New York: Association Press, 1959.

16. M.A. Kettani, *Muslim Minorities in the World Today*. London: Mansell, 1986.

17. See the book review by Reza K. Shah-Kazemi in *Muslim Education Quarterly* (U.K.), **4** (1), 1986, pp. 95–6.

18. H.H. Bilgrami, 'Educational Needs of Muslim Minorities', in *Muslim Communities in Non-Muslim States*. London: Islamic Council of Europe, 1980.

19. *Arabia Islamic World Review*, **6** (64), 1986 pp. 24–5.

20. M. Mumtaz Ali, 'Teaching of Islam to Muslim Children and Youth in Great Britain'. *Muslim Education Quarterly* (U.K.), **4** (2) 1987, p. 38.

21. Imtiaz Ahmad, 'The Problem of Muslim Educational Backwardness in Contemporary India: An Inferential Analysis.' Journal of the Institute of Muslim Minority Affairs, **3**, 1981, p. 66–7.

22. 'Enhancing the relevance and contribution of education to other developmental sectors'. A.P.E.I.D. Occasional Papers, **8**. Bangkok: Unesco Regional Office for Education in Asia and the Pacific, 1981.

23. *Profil Pesantren*, LP3ES, Jakarta, 1974.

24. *Ibid.*, p. 6.

25. *Arabia Islamic World Review*, **6** (64), 1986, p. 25.

Places, People and Poverty
The Challenge of Change

Ayyub Malik

In the creation of the 'modern' world, transformed so radically and made so complex during the last two centuries, the Muslim contribution, as people and countries, has been passive and negligible. For quite some time, a post-modern and post-industrial age has been in the making, and promises equally radical changes in the future. Instead of technical and productive efficiency, wasteful consumption and conflict-ridden human and material exploitation of the present industrial age, the new age will seek to redress not only the world-wide human and material inequalities created during the last two centuries, but will attempt also to balance the ever-depleting resources and the fast-polluting environment of the earth itself. It will aim not only to foster new attitudes and a sense of responsibility towards the life-sustaining structure of the whole environment, but seek a new moral and economic order capable of transcending the historic barriers existing between the dominant and dominating cities, people and nations to create a sustainable world based upon a new structure of relationships between peoples, progress, resources and the environment.[1]

If such a change does take place, and it may be less a question of if but of when, the followers of Islam — nearly a quarter of the world population — will have to contribute the social, moral and ideological concepts of their own system of values if they are to play an active part in the next cycle of world history. To participate in the evolving structure of such a post-modern world, their emerging consciousness will have to extend far beyond the present pious rhetoric. A genuine contribution to the construction of a post-industrial alternative future will demand neither merely reciting the moral and socio-economic superiority of their system of belief, nor recounting the cultural and intellectual achievements of the past, nor indeed just reacting to the impact of actions and ideas produced by others. First and foremost, it will require the active demonstration of their own system of values operating within their own communities and societies. To gain any credibility in the developing post-modern debate, Muslims will have first to begin to transform their own cities and societies to make them the proper reflections of their social and moral values and way of life. Not only will they have to set out a moral agenda and a coherent framework of action for such a world, but also, by making a proper beginning at home, they must demonstrate their concepts and ideals as workable in their own social, economic and living environment.

With the present system of information technology and rapid communications, of international capital, trade and industry, the economic system of the world has already become urbanized. By the end of this century nearly half the world population is expected to live in cities of fifteen million and more, and it is more than evident that a majority of this urbanization will take place in the countries least equipped to cope with such an expansion. Larger towns and cities of the future will in one form or another continue to remain the centres of power, material and human resources as well as consumers of most of the surplus. It is in these towns and cities, therefore, that a new agenda for change and a new order of priorities will have to be established. What actually does or does not begin to take place in the Muslim cities and urban settlements may decide the role that coming generations will or will not occupy in the next epoch of world history. With an emphasis upon the city, its people and their living environment, attempt is made here to identify some of the main concerns that demand concerted Muslim action if a new beginning is to be made at all.

Present Reality

Decades after the end of their political subjugation, and despite the moral and socio-economic system that can be derived from their own beliefs and the immense richness of their heritage, Muslim countries on the whole continue to accept a passive role as part of a larger 'underdeveloped' world, dependent on the intellectual and economic hegemony and system of values of those from whom they are now liberated. Much has been written about the decline of the Muslim world itself, and the political and economic rise of the industrial occident which has brought about the present structure of the 'developed' and 'underdeveloped' world where:

> The 'metropolitan' societies of Western Europe and North America are the 'advanced', 'developed' industrialized states; centres of economic, political and cultural power. In sharp contrast with them, though there are many intermediate stages, are other societies which are seen as 'underdeveloped': still mainly agricultural or 'unindustrialized'. The 'metropolitan' states, through a system of trade, but also through a complex of economic and political controls, draw food and, more critically, raw materials from these areas of supply, this effective hinterland, that is also the greater part of the earth's surface and that contains the great majority of its peoples. Thus a model of city and country, in economic and political relationships, has gone beyond the boundaries of the nation state, and is seen but also challenged as a model of the world.[2]

In this model, the twin images of the Muslim living reality — from one corner of the world to another — are all too familiar and recurring. In desolate urban and rural landscape, vast sections of Muslim populations are locked in degrading poverty, ignorance and deprivation; and in sharp contrast, meaningless and wasteful urban enclaves of an imported 'modernity' — with all its idols, images, and errors — still being acquired at great expense of scarce national resources to create symbols of progress mainly to display the preferences, wealth and power of their governments and new elites:

> Failing to communicate with the rest of the population, those elites carried on like regimes of internal colonialism running Head of State expenditure which, on a proportionate basis, outstrip the expenses of the Court of Louis XIV of France, wielding elaborate security organizations whose real purpose is to defend the regimes against their discontented populations, and which consume, in peacetime, more than a third of public expenditure. Those elites preside over top-heavy establishments which consume more than 50 per cent of revenues. They sustain a gap in payments and life styles between the highest paid and the lowest paid which could very well be described as salaried feudalism. . . . A middle-class is expected to lead development just as happened in the West. When no class is forthcoming to

play that role, because it is mostly engaged in distributive trade, exports and imports, real-estate speculation and money-lending, senior army officers are encouraged to step in and spearhead the middle-class role and proceed to build society in the image of the West.[3]

As a consequence, 'we are witnessing a change that is now forcing a complete rupture with the past; every concept and every value has been reversed. For house design in the Middle East, the introverted plan wherein family life looked into the courtyard was changed to a plan with family life looking out upon the street. The cool, clean air, the serenity and reverence of the courtyard were shed, and the street was embraced with its heat, dust, and noise'.[4] The modern Muslim architect, liberated by his modern education from the burden of his own history, art and culture, 'and unable to resist temptation, accepts every facility offered to him by modern technology, with no thought of its effect on the complex web of his culture. Unaware that civilization is measured by what one contributes to culture, not by what one takes from others, he continues to draw upon the works of Western architects in Europe and North America, without assessing the value of his own heritage.[5]

Most national and international experts still continue to commend such modernity as the necessary catalyst for economic and industrial growth benefits of which they promise will eventually reach the vast deprived populations of these societies. There are a few others, who see these cities as left over structures of an exploiting capitalism, decaying because of the inevitable decay of capitalism itself, and un-redeemable without fundamental changes in the structure of their societies.[6] But regardless, from one Muslim country to another, the pattern of development and change over the last few decades has been as repetitive as the compelling social and environmental consequences now evident in their cities.

Despite the 'modernizing' policies and efforts of the last few decades, the living conditions, experience and emotion of the fast-growing Muslim cities remain evident only in their social and cultural irrelevance, their environmental decay and despair, and their unremitting ugliness.[7] Any comparisons with the traditional environment and its quality of life and life styles, continues to bring home the conviction not only that the living environment of the past was somehow better, but also, that something unique and fundamental has been lost between then and now. Is this loss due to the progressive loss of the spirit of the community itself as the very foundation of the Muslim city and society? Can it be attributed to the loss of the moral, social and intellectual leadership and co-operative effort in that community? Is it due to the inaction and absence of those very institutions which were based on a certain sense of social and environment responsibility and socio-economic justice? Is this the loss which is now reflected in the plight of the contemporary living environment?

Community as the Basis of City and Society

The individual as a part of the family, the family as a part of the community, and the mosque as the centre of the community's religious, social and civic organization have been the bedrock of socio-spatial patterns of Muslim settlements whatever their size, place or time. Until the political and economic upheaval of recent centuries, the social structure of the Muslim society was founded upon the family as a unit of society, the community as its social and welfare institution, and the mosque as a place of congregation and social action. This organization of the community remained reflected in the social structure and the spatial arrangement of its living environment:

> The Medieval Muslim society was above all a religious society. . . . To religion it owed its social organization and its laws, for Islam had built up a new legal system obliterating, at least in all the civilized lands, the old social organizations and social inequalities. To religion it owed its corporate feeling, for Islam gave to every believer the sense of common fellowship in its universal brotherhood. Religion, in time, not only created the cultural background and psychological orientation of Muslim society, but supplied for its members a philosophy of living and ordained even the least activities of their daily life.[8]

The organization of such a society aimed to achieve unity by diffusing advantages, skills, knowledge and resources in such a manner that:

> All of the crucial political, economic, cultural, and religious roles of the society were entrusted to a broad and undivided class of professional, religious and commercial notables. The extension of the Shariah to virtually all communal concerns created one unspecialized stratum for the performance of adjudicative and administrative roles essential to the maintenance of society. Barriers of class stratification were reduced by relative ease of mobility and by the overlapping of the ulama with all the milieus and classes and communities of the

cities. The ulama were diffused throughout the society. Through
them all classes and groups found common social affiliations. . . .
Other solidarity ties cut across class lines, and knit together men of
diverse status and functions. Ties of patronage bound servants to
masters, workers and craftsmen to customers, professionals to clients, and ultimately all men to Mamluk state. Family, residence in
a common quarter, and ethnic or religious community united men of
high and low ranks. Affiliation to the law schools, circles of sheikhs,
scholars, and sufis bound men of different stations.[9]

As a dynamic for social change and collective action, Islam is as much a
religion of believing as of doing, as much a system of values as a form of
community, of stability as of continuous change. Its law aims to create
patterns for an ideal human existence as well as for an ideal society. The
fundamental principle of this law, as seen by one of the noted Muslim
scholars of this century, is that man has the right to fulfil his needs and
make all effort to promote his interest and achieve success, but:

> he should do all this in such a way that not only the interests of other
> people are not jeopardized and no harm is caused to their strivings
> towards the fulfilment of their rights and duties, but there should be
> all possible social cohesion and co-operation among human beings in
> the achievement of their objectives. In respect of those things in
> which good and evil, gain and loss are inextricably mixed up, the
> tenet of this law is to choose little harm for the sake of greater benefit
> and sacrifice a little benefit for avoiding a greater harm. This is the
> basic approach of the Shari'ah.[10]

The cornerstones of this law are the four rights and obligations imposed
upon man; the rights of God upon man: the rights of man upon himself;
the rights of other people upon him; and the rights of those powers and
resources which God has placed in his service and has empowered him
to use for his benefit.

The Shariah requires man to be just to himself and fulfil his personal
rights, but not to seek this fulfilment in such a manner that the rights of
others are violated. It prohibits economic activity of the kind where only
one side has to be the loser. Limits and restrictions 'have been imposed
by the law of Islam to prevent a man from encroaching upon the right of
others', in order to create a society in which 'people should not only not
violate the rights of others and injure their interests but should positively co-operate with each other and establish such mutual relations and

social institutions that contribute towards the welfare of all and the establishment of an ideal human society'.[11]

In such a society, the family is not only the first cradle but the cradle of civilization itself. The sphere of family binds together its members 'into one unity, . . . to make each one of them a source of support, strength and contentment to the other'. In a group of families, there co-exist the rich and the poor, the prosperous and the destitute, who have the greatest right upon each other directly as well as through charities and *zakat*. The law of Islam 'so regulates life that the welfare of one and all may be achieved'.[12]

After the family come 'man's relations with his friends, neighbours, dwellers of his own locality, village or city', where Islam bids its followers 'to help each other, to attend to the sick, to support the destitute, to assist the needy and the crippled, to sympathize with the trouble-stricken, to look after the orphans and the widows, to feed the hungry, to clothe the under-clad, and to help the unemployed in seeking employment'. It also forbids waste on useless ventures and extravagant luxuries. 'This injunction of the Shariah is based upon the principle that no man should be allowed to squander upon himself a wealth that can maintain thousands of human beings. It is cruel and unjust that money which can be used to feed the teeming starving humanity be frittered away in useless or extravagant decorations, exhibitions and fireworks.[13]

And beyond this immediate level is the wider community of Islam itself — the Ummah — at present made up of many a nation, whose proper strength will come less from their 'dress, etiquette, or fine arts', but from the 'right knowledge, science, discipline, organization, and the energy for action' where, when they learn from others, they will 'take lessons from their will to action and social discipline' and from 'knowledge and technical accomplishments' but not from 'those arts and crafts which breed cultural slavery and national inferiority'.[14]

Much more could, and perhaps needs to be said on the subject to illustrate the unique human and social dynamics of the Muslim community. Overlooking the minor variations in meaning and interpretation between different ulamas, the above ideals for the structure of Muslim community, its form and purpose remain central. These ideals are repeated to varying degrees in the observed and imagined cities of Muslim history and in the present malaise of their 'modern' cities. Together, these continue to delineate the fundamental oppositions inherent in a system based on Revelation on the one hand, and that of an economic and industrial 'modernity' derived from the historic evolution of occidental societies since the sixteenth century on the other.[15]

A Borrowed Modernity

In the last few decades the experiences and consequences of development in the Muslim countries have begun to elicit some fresh understanding and analyses from a new generation of Muslims who have
progressively articulated and underlined some of the oppositions
between their own system of values and tradition, and those inherent
and implicit in the form of 'modernism' imposed by others and adopted
by the few in power. They have criticized a 'modernism' not of their
own making — rooted neither in their own system of belief and ideals,
nor an outcome of their own needs and aspirations — but one shaped
and given meaning by cultures, systems and societies very different from
their own.

What has been accepted so far as modern and industrial progress in
the Muslim countries now appears to have been no more than the simple
transplant of certain industrial and manufacturing processes, buildings
and urban patterns without much attention to inherent oppositions.
Little thought has been given to their socio-economic relevance and
impact upon the existing productive systems in society; the ensuing
cultural and demographic changes and planned management of these
changes; the affordability of the 'modern' products by the producers
themselves; and more critically, the very visible and real needs of the
greater sections of their populations. The acquisition of this 'modernity' — or the lack of it — still remains assessed through the glamorized
symbols and visible imagery of this borrowed 'Modernism' and all its
inherent values, rather than through the provision of even the most
modest needs and public services for a much greater part of the Muslim
populations.

Modern industrial change by itself was a dramatic event in the occidental societies and radically transformed the nature of their human and
social existence. Among the many powerful forces of modernization
which radically changed the nature of the industrial individual and
society, the more acknowledged human and social consequences have
arisen from the direct effect of industrial change upon the production
and distribution of goods, services, and ideas; an emphasis upon the
individual's ability to control his natural and social environment; a belief
in an open social system and, a marked shift towards secularism. The
main individual-society-environment aspects of this transformation are:
it was based upon new sources of energy and modes of production and
upon new human skills and productive ability; radical changes in
the structure of education and skill specialization; loss of individual

autonomy; newer modes of mass transport and communications; concentration of manufacturing processes in fewer locations; new structures of money and finance; high levels of population mobility based on nuclear family; and, eventually, mass production, mass consumption and planned obsolescence.

More importantly, the modernization process transformed the modern individual's own view of himself and his society by making him alone responsible for his environment and his own destiny. Gone were the bonds of associations and loyalty to social groups and community and the belief in a divine scheme of creation. In an open social system of secular values, the 'modern' individuals' prime concern was with the condition of his own existence in this world alone, and with constant mobility from place to place and status to status, with the enhancement of personal advantages to acquire the goods and services produced by the new system. The socio-spatial arrangements of towns and cities were also radically transformed. Their development was based upon a new structure of the family and the society; a land use based on segregated functions of living, work and leisure; on mass mobility and rapid social and physical change to keep up with the changing demands of production, competition and profit maximization.[16]

In the analyses of one of its own concerned theologians, this 'modernism' meant 'the attempt to come to terms — in art, poetry, religion, or anything else — with the modern world supported by . . . the "five pillars" of modernity:

1. Sovereign national states as the legally defined units of the global political system.
2. Science based technology as the 'modern' world's principal source of its image of life and its possibilities.
3. Bureaucratic rationalism as its major mode of organizing and administering thought and activity.
4. The quest for profit maximization . . . as its means of motivating work and distributing goods and services.
5. The secularization and trivialization of religion and the harnessing of the spiritual for patently profane purposes, as its most characteristic attitude towards the holy.'

Together, these support 'an imposing edifice of art and music, literature and theology . . . which in turn refine, inform, and embellish the supporting pillars' and create 'the underlying institutional basis for the segregating of religion from political and economic power', to bring forth a human condition which forced Rousseau, the first to coin the term 'moderniste', to admit even that long ago that 'of all the things that strike me, there is none that holds my heart, yet all of them together disturb my feelings, so that I forget what I am and who I belong to'.[17]

New Search

Over the last century, the impact of such a borrowed and adopted industrial modernism and its science and technology has steadily pitted and eroded the social, moral and economic structure of Muslim societies. It has distorted the demographic and spatial patterns of their cities and stagnated the evolution of ideas and ideals for the creation of a living environment in resonance with its own belief and tradition and responsive to the changing pressures and needs of its Muslim societies. Laden with the values and structures of the dominant, inventing societies, its products have been packaged and promoted to dazzle and mesmerize the rulers, the decision makers and the urban elites alike into beliefs and attitudes of dependence upon occidental 'similar path' development in order to catch up with and become like them. Through heavy borrowing, aid and unfair trade, this path has been pursued by most Muslim countries at the expense of even the most modest human needs — of nutrition, health, shelter and education — for most of their populations.

The consequences of such developments are manifest in the urban and rural landscapes of Muslim countries. They are to be seen in the living conditions of most of their populations; in persistent poverty, deprivation, disease and pollution; in the structure of professions and the content of education, medicine and social welfare. Very little of what has so far been done or proposed about the Muslim environment promises much improvement and all future projections lead only to human and environmental catastrophe. Muslim hopes for the future now lie in the deliberate dismantling and replacement of the present course of development with a fresh perspective based upon proper analyses and understanding of the needs of their own societies and their longstanding social and environmental problems which have become very real and extremely serious:

In recent years, most intellectuals have come to believe that talking is no longer of any use, and that to speak of our sufferings is of no benefit. Until now, we have constantly talked and discussed our sufferings without doing anything or undertaking any action. We must therefore close the era of talking, and everyone must begin acting by reforming his family or his city.

In my opinion, this view is based on oversight, because in reality we have not talked up to now, we have not spoken of our sufferings, we have not closely and scientifically analysed our sufferings. All we have done is to moan in our misery, and it is obvious that such moaning is of no value.

Up to now, we have not discussed our psychological and social problems at all correctly. Sometimes the false impression may arise that we have diagnosed our ills and must now set about curing them, but unfortunately it must be said that we have not diagnosed our ills.[18]

If serious diagnoses and reforming is ever to take place, it will have to begin with the individual and the family, as well as with the city. It will have to involve the governments, decision makers, experts and ulamas — and there appears not much evidence of this so far — as much as the active participation of the community itself and its institutions equipped afresh to deal with the dominant human and social concerns. Proper identification of needs and priorities; allocation of appropriate human and material resource; planning, programmes and social action; the monitoring and modulating of these actions and their accountability can become purposive only when these are defined, identified and pursued by an informed and aware community.

Before examining some of the more dominant aspects which continue severely to affect vast areas of Muslim cities and their inhabitants, it may be of some help to set down a few observations emerging from the recent history of change and actual experiences in Muslim countries themselves as well as those in the advanced industrial countries:

1. Minds and societies do not gain independence through the simple change of one flag for another. The last few decades of developments, defined and initiated by others and continued since nominal independence have proved themselves simply an extension and reinforcement of the structures established by those whose real interests and values were not in unison with those of the Muslim societies.[19]

2. From the human and socio-economic consequences of these developments, it is clear they have only protracted and intensified the external and internal exploitation and dependencies created during recent history. They have led neither to desirable social change, nor to a

credible direction for the future. It is now overdue to learn lessons, draw conclusions, and change course.[20]

3. Having seen and experienced the consequences of 'modernization', there are ample signs of increasing disenchantment among the new generation of Muslims who have now begun to question and to search, interpret and articulate their own particular paradigms for the future of their own society and the appropriate shape of their own living environment.[21]

4. The value structures of 'modern' industrialism and its exploitive attitudes towards man and nature — indeed the entire concept of the universality of the occidental paradigms for a world modernized in its own image — stand jolted and indicted in occidental societies, and have no plausible and viable directions for their own foreseeable future.

5. As a result, the 'modern' societies themselves have become disenchanted with their own value structure of capital and industry and its social, urban and environmental consequences and are in search of alternatives for the future direction of their own societies.[22]

In this converging search for the value structure of a post-modern world, there emerge considerable common areas of problems, concerns and crises where a fresh Muslim perspective — at theoretical as well as at practical levels — becomes not only necessary, but vital. The moral force of Islamic beliefs and ideals of universal humanity; of economic and distributive justice; of social and environmental ethics — if made relevant and converted into public policy to create a social, economic and productive environment fundamentally different from that of the 'modern' industrial world — could become the basis for a new strategy of development in Muslim societies and could also be their contribution to the world at large. The way forward can lie no more in a borrowed 'modernity' which has already run its course. It can lie neither in the continued polarization and exploitation within their own societies, nor in the continued split between private piety and the long persisting structure of power, privileges and social inaction in their own countries.

The Challenge of Change

Every age must confront its own change and define its own modernity. Human and social ideals, visions, and worldviews need all to be spelt out in some detail by every society at each level of its reality and at each stage of its history. Change is constant and demands new needs to be met and new choices to be made at many interrelated levels of human existence. Changing individual and family needs demand new understanding, new institutions of change, and a new order for the allocation of scarce resources. Changing circumstances of the community — a collection of families in a small settlement or their complex collection in a large city — need to be identified, reconciled, planned, and adjusted. Choice of appropriate skills and technologies; their impact on individual lives and on society; demands of agriculture, transport, trade and commerce; nature and content of education and appropriate roles of the educators and the educated; aspects of evolving social practices and behaviour, and indeed, the observance of rituals themselves all need continuous adjustments and innovations in their separate and overlapping areas. Directly and indirectly, all change demands choices to be exercised and decisions to be made which — whether made or not, and irrespective of by whom and for whose benefit — continue to influence the living environment and the quality of human existence in it.

Leaving aside many of the complex areas relevant equally to the built and the natural environment,[23] it is proposed here to look briefly at those aspects — of poverty, the family and the community at large, and the distribution of advantages and resources within and among them — which, directly and indirectly, continue to remain central in the present plight of the Muslim living environment and the living conditions of most of its long suffering inhabitants.

Poverty

In all its many forms and expressions, poverty — individual and institutional, of quantity and quality — seems to have become so central to vast sections of Muslim society, that it makes most consideration of the proper shape and form of the contemporary living environment a most abstract and futile exercise. All aspects of poverty, needs and resources are related and relative, and without reference to the particular social and moral setting, the system of power and wealth distribution itself, continue to remain neutral and without meaning.

The living environment — urban, rural and natural — is a direct consequence of human life and not separate from its needs and concerns. It is a consequence of what people do, or do not do, or more critically, are unable to do around where they live and work and travel. Concern for the environment as a whole cannot be separated from concern for poverty and individual and collective need. It has to address not only the quantitative needs for human survival and for life chances, but has to go beyond the questions of 'basic needs', 'poverty lines', 'minimum shelter', and the comparative levels of incomes — important as all of these are. Fundamentally, it has to do with the creation of conditions conducive to the ways and ideals of family and community life and must be able also to lead to the fulfilment of life's possibilities with dignity, security, identity and intellect. None of these can become possible without the simultaneous creation of a corresponding social, economic and political environment.

Empirical studies in a number of Asian countries have revealed increased average incomes in all except one, in some cases quite rapid.[24] But despite this increase, the majority of the poor — rural as well urban — not only remained poor but actually became poorer.

> The initially high degree of inequality of income and wealth, the concentration of the economic surplus in a few enterprises and households, and the fragmented allocative mechanisms constitute a socio-economic context in which powerful forces tend to perpetuate and even accentuate low standards of living of a significant proportion of the rural population.[25]

This applied as much to those rural poor who fled to the cities, where 'the groups on which the government relies for support are the same groups which possess most of the wealth of the country, supply the majority of technicians and administrators, and provide the leadership of the army and the dominant political alignments. Economic and political influence are closely interwoven: those who possess purchasing power also possess political power.'[26]

One of the salient common characteristics of these countries is 'that many of the resources needed for development are at hand, unutilized or poorly utilized. Foremost among these is the intelligence, ingenuity, and effort of the labor force itself. . . . Labor is not the only resource that is poorly utilized; in many countries land and other natural resources are not efficiently exploited.'[27] This applied as much to large farms as to the smallest farmers who are 'forced to overexploit their land, with the result that useful land is destroyed through erosion and the exhaustion of soil fertility. Just as the economic system in the countries we have studied results in poor use (and even destruction) of parts of its human resources, so too it results in poor use (and even destruction) of parts of its natural resources.'[28]

Despite being caught in the web of such a system and being given the most minimum of resources and technical assistance, there is a well of untapped determination, innovation and effort among the disadvant-aged and the poor who somehow fulfil, as best as they can, their basic need for shelter, security and welfare. But the real cost remains — in physical hardship, ill health and family stress; in the lack of clean water, sewage, transport and education; and in the waste in productive and human resource. In the present context of the Muslim society — as individual nations and as an ummah — poverty, inequality and waste in all its human, material and institutional forms remain a direct conse-quence of the present structure of their society. The inequalities built up over a long period of time are reflected in the distribution of available skills and resources in a manner which perpetuates the very conditions of deprivation that corrupt not only the Muslim as an individual but the society at large, and as such, continue to pose some harsh and fundamen-tal questions both for the community as well as for its leaders.

The Family

With all its inherited values and attitudes, the family provides a funda-mental social institution not only for the survival of the individual but also for the survival of the social and cultural tradition itself. As a value and a set of values, it is one of the most important institutions for the development of a well balanced individual. Through stability, order, change and conflict, it provides the essential formative layers of human relationships and experience. As the basic unit of the Muslim commu-nity, the family has been the prime institution of individual and col-lective support and care, supplemented often by other institutions of social welfare whenever it was missing or found wanting.

If such a structure of the family is to remain the mainstay of the Muslim community, then it has to have reasonable means to support itself and fulfil its obligations towards other members of the family. The provision of suitable accommodation, health care, public services and education are not only essential needs but also the very preconditions for the creation of a civilized life and living environment. As collective social need and benefit, these can only be established and maintained by the co-operative effort of the community itself and its social and political institutions. An individual and family — bereft of economic resources, ill in the provision of life's necessities and ill in health, education and environment — will forever remain ill-equipped to become a part of the community and unable to participate in its productive and socio-spatial processes.

In the present structure of most of the Muslim societies, physical, economic and educational deprivation continues to frustrate whatever few efforts are made for improvements. Conditions continue to create barriers between people, knowledge and resources in such a manner that it is impossible for them to relate and interact to become the foundation of a community based upon a clear commitment to a certain public moral order, efficiency and quality of environment. Any commitment and effort towards improvements in the environmental condition will have to be matched with similar commitment to the improvement in the human condition itself, and this can be achieved only through a transformation of the existing social order to bring about a just and equitable distribution of the available human and material resources.

Resources

Degradation of the living and natural environment, first seen as a consequence of industrialization in the advanced countries, has increasingly become a matter of survival for most of the poor countries. On the one hand we have the increasing scarcity of raw materials and multinational industry's capacity to exploit, deplete and pollute the earth's resources; and on the other, increasing recognition of the structural inequalities existing among and within peoples and nations. Regardless of the level of national wealth and affluence, the questions of equitable balance between human needs and available resources now extend far beyond the mere physical to encompass wider concerns for socially and ecologically aware development and the protection of the whole environment.[29]

With all the advantages of being a world power, and after a century of welfare policies and a welfare state in Britain, the working of the 'modern' market and industry has created:

> a society in which it is structurally necessary for a certain proportion of the population to be at the bottom and in some degree of poverty; the individuals may change through the working of certain institutions like the schools, but the proportion of the population stays the same, and the relative differences do not alter. More than that . . ., we 'blame the victim' for being there. English society, and world society, patently does not contain equality in any sense, and show no signs of wanting to do so.[30]

Despite the state welfare policies and myriads of well organized voluntary institutions of social welfare, the combined effect of the present market and the welfare systems has created the conditions where:

the cycle of inequality is complete. Even in death the significant differences between rich and poor stubbornly remain . . . the wives of the professional groups have a far greater chance of giving birth successfully than the wives of semi-skilled and un-skilled workers. The children of the professional workers have a far greater chance of surviving the first year of life, and then living longer.

These children are unequal when they start school . . . The cycle of inequality is reflected in the income earned, the status at the workplace and in the housing the rich and poor occupy. These differences appear again in the differences in health and finally in death . . . differences in opportunities for life and health start at the cradle and continue through the life span.[31]

Without in any way arguing for absolute equality in the distribution of material goods and things, by all counts the living, health and environmental conditions among vast sections of the Muslim populations are not only worse but worsen everyday through the working of a 'modern' market system. What makes the Muslim condition even more helpless is both the lack of provision of new social and community welfare structures and the redundant nature of their inherited institutions ill-equipped to comprehend or cope with the present living reality of most of the people. In addition, there continues the social and intellectual irrelevance of their religious and professional leaders and the lack of policy and effort on the part of their governments to address either the basic issues of poverty and inequality or to begin to shift the balance of advantages between concentrated resources on the one hand and widespread deprivation on the other.

Resources exist in two main forms: material, as goods and money; and human, as knowledge and knowhow. Needs could be balanced only through equitable allocation of these resources which come from the two systems of society: the system of the market; and the system of community welfare. Being more direct and basic, the market system is always the more powerful. The strength of the social and community welfare system comes only from the better impulses of moral conscience and commitment in the society. Its effectiveness depends forever upon the material and human resources at the disposal of the community's voluntary institutions — be they through the social commitment and effort of the community leaders, or through voluntary efforts, philanthropy and welfare endowments.[32]

The relationship between what is needed by the Muslim individual and the family, and what is collectively available within the Muslim society as a whole continues to remain the central moral question in any meaningful consideration of Muslim cities and their populations and the desirable shape and form of their living environment. Considerable experience of welfare legislation and policies to achieve an equitable distribution of income and advantages in the affluent countries is ample evidence of the limitation of their approach. Simply, the increase in the quantity of national wealth and average incomes continue to conceal the plight of significant populations at the very bottom of the society. As is apparent from the material poverty and environmental deprivation of the Western inner cities much in the news at present, the accumulation of wealth first and the promises of redistribution later neither occurs nor alters the fact that primarily, poverty and deprivation is 'a product of a social system and reflects differences in access of various groups to sources of economic and political power'.[33]

An Equitable Future

Given the present direction of development and attitudes towards the living environment, the future of contemporary Muslim cities appears bleak and without much promise. The survival and prospects of the inherited environment — as places for living and as prototypes for study and investigation — is equally full of despair. Beyond the few selective areas of the capitals and the main cities, the official and public attitude towards the rapidly expanding urban environment and its organization and management continues to remain one of total indifference and apathy. It is this very indifference which now shapes the Muslim living environment everywhere and separates the modern city from the city of its history when many a poet, ulama and writer adopted the names of their cities with a sense of pride and distinction.

The pursuit of individual self-interest at the expense of co-operative effort for social development continues to find parallel expressions in the imbalance between resource allocation for the affluent private areas, state buildings and capitals on the one hand, and poverty, pollution and environmental despair everywhere else. Muslim cities of today express the social and environmental indifference of their urban and civic leaders, who understand neither the social history and dynamic of the city of the occident they wish to emulate nor the city of their own history which they sometime try to copy.

There exist neither any clear ideas, ideals and images for a contemporary Muslim city nor is there any relationship between the ideals of the Muslim community and the environment it continues to create. Those responsible for the environment — architects, planners, public authorities and social and religious leaders — show little interest in the distribution of space and the shape and form of their cities and the upkeep of their shared spaces, streets and services. Not many governments, local or central, take much interest in the problems of their urban, rural and natural environment and resources and continue still to rely upon international organizations for 'modern' solutions, often to gain some political advantage and recognition of their modernity.

Imams, Ulamas, Community and Environment

In the ever worsening problems and predicament of the Muslim living environment, any diagnosis, guidance and action from the religious and community leaders — imams and the ulamas — continue to remain remarkable only by their absence. A life time's study of history and theology enables them only to speak about private and public ritual, not about the poverty, ignorance, suffering and social polarization in their community. They talk about personal piety, prayer and ablutions but not about disease and the un-hygienic conditions and pollution in their living environment. They lead in prayers but not in education, health care and social reconstruction. They speak of the ummah but are unable to unite their own community into co-operative action and welfare. They memorize the Holy Book but remain unable to convey its message of equality, fraternity and socio-economic justice. They preside over thousands of mosques full and overflowing on Fridays but empty of social function and community action every other day of the week.

For too long, they have presented their faith and ritual as separate from action and knowledge, divorced from the actual problems of the community and the changed reality of their existence. Their emphasis remains upon private ritual and public display of piety and the mere rhetoric of the social and economic ethics rather than upon the real needs and problems of their community. Theirs is the presentation which refers more to the achievements, manners and institutions of an imperial past rather than to the complex realities of the present world and their own society as it is, and how it might be changed to face its own reality.

Even in the present awakening of a new consciousness and questioning they seek only to re-establish the ritual and structure of law, education and the socio-political order of their history, rather than relating the concepts and values of their Faith to the tragedy of their own community and the stark reality of their present world. Trapped in the web of their outdated knowledge and irrelevant institutions, they have become translators and transmitters of their history-bound knowledge to manipulate the ignorant and the simple-minded in their society, able neither to understand, lead and improve what is there, nor to foresee what can and needs to be done.

Who Builds Muslim Cities?

The true builders of vast areas of the Muslim cities are the deprived and disadvantaged people themselves who neither have much resources and rights nor much official help and technical assistance. Without any benefits from the trained professions, they build little by little over time on whatever land is available to them, or from wherever they are not evicted by force. These parts of their cities are built regardless of where they will find jobs, how they will get to them, how much it will cost to travel, and how their needs for public services, health and education will be met, if at all. They do not know who to ask for help or how to persuade those in power to help them improve their livelihood and living conditions. They need resources — material as well as professional and technical — but there are none who are sympathetic to their needs and problems and willing to work with them to help them do better what they can and have been doing themselves.

The making of shelter is not only one of the most essential needs but also one of the most ancient skills and activities. By far the largest area of any living environment consists of common place residential and every day buildings shaped by the common man and local craftsmen. Historically at least, the rhythms and juxapositions of the simple and unpretentious buildings — reflections of these inherent skills and social structures — have created as organic and appropriate environments as any created by the complex modern professions. In their apparent simplicity, they concealed not only the refined knowledge of materials, techniques and climates, but also represented vital human ability and productive capacity to shape a built environment which responded to their needs, and by creating a sense of place and belonging, continued to have meaning for those who lived there.

Yet, in the use and management of skills and resources, this very innate capacity is ignored, as is its possible enhancement to meet better at least some of the simpler needs for the creation of shelter, services and a responsive living environment. Little thought is given to the possibility of appropriately enhancing these inherent skills and capacities of the builders and the craftsmen who often evolved the many vernacular traditions and created the very environment so atuned to culture, climate, materials and resources.

Urban Professions

Trained and influenced by the imported urban models, images and culture of architecture, Muslim architects, planners and urban administrators continue to see their cities as collections of individual buildings on isolated pieces of land for those who already have means and resources. Confined within the boundaries of their separate professions, they remain unable to take account either of the culture, climate, geography and ecology; or of the needs, problems and deprivations of those from whom they have been socially, educationally and economically estranged. Like them, the shape and form of the new city and its architecture, with all its ugly, nonsensical applied forms and decorations, continue to remain estranged from the roots of their own history and the real needs of most of the people.

They seek their inspiration either from the urban imagery of Western countries, the history and evolution of which they rarely comprehend, or only from the royal cities, palaces and grand monuments of their own history — symbols of power long lost. In search of creative inspiration for the modern city and its architecture, some of them devote considerable effort to unravel the sacred and cosmic forms and patterns in the scattered details of their long-decaying towns and cities. Their inherited monuments, grand mosques and royal complexes do indeed represent the apex of Muslim urban and architectural achievements, but will the dead reveal their profound secrets to those unable to see the painful reality of their own living?

Muslim urban professionals do not need unquestioningly to accept or reject the urban and architectural experience of their own history or that of other countries. But they do need to seek a new kind of thinking which relies not on pastiche and repetition of the dead shapes of history but upon a critical exploration of fresh ideas and inspiration relevant to the ideals and reality of their own society. Mere use of history as decoration and stage sets can mask neither the present vacuum of intention and intellect nor, estranged from most of its society and its needs, can it become a serious possibility for a future relevant environment. They can make a new beginning only by first seeking a critical validity of their own ideas and ideals of change, movement and destiny to discover an architecture of relevance, need and meaning, able not only to draw upon the essence of its own values and history but capable also of responding to the decay, despair and deprivation in their present environment.

At the highest level of its achievement, the city and its architecture celebrates life and 'immortalizes and glorifies something', yet there can be no meaningful city and 'no architecture where there is nothing to glorify'.[34] Human suffering, poverty, inequality, visual and environmental indifference are not the ingredients for the creation of cities which celebrate life with beauty and meaning. Cities can acquire purpose from their own history and the sense and understanding of the past, the present and the future of their creators and the participation and culture of their inhabitants. Environment is what everyone needs to sustain life, and development is what everyone does to enhance the quality of human existence. A balanced and sustainable environment cannot be created by those without skills, knowledge, resources and self confidence. Neither can it be created by the socially indifferent disciplines and professions isolated in their own separate subjects; it can hardly be entrusted to the passing political whims of the civic and municipal leaders.

Community, Leaders, and the Living Environment

The need of the Muslim community is not for a bureaucracy which delays, exploits and terrifies, but for socially sensitive public administration which understands the needs of those it is meant to serve. Its need is not for doctors and medicine ill-affordable by those most in need but for a structure of medical and health care which prevents malnutrition and disease in the first place. The need is not for architects trained to work only for those who can afford, but for those able to understand the needs of their communities for shelter, transport, services and hygiene; not just for teachers of script and literacy but for a system of education which can lead to knowledge, understanding and liberty; not for imams and ulamas who preach private ritual and literal interpretations, but for those who can understand the social and economic dynamics of their system of belief and are able to work for social and environmental justice and collective action in their communities.

Somehow they will all have to become socially sensitive and environmentally conscious of the wider issues in their societies so far excluded from their education and public debate. New ways of thinking about wider interpretations of climate, ecology, resources and the living environment will be necessary to mobilize an active rather than a passive community. A deeper understanding will be needed of the structures, attitudes and forces which now shape the social and spatial order in

Muslim cities — understanding that could lead to fundamental changes
in education, professional attitudes and social responsibility. A range of
new skills, subjects and disciplines will be needed to enable the educated
to articulate, communicate and understand the needs of their own
societies.

The creation, care and management of the living environment is an
ongoing process which can be sustained only by the continuous effort
and participation of the whole society. It demands time, effort, skills and
resources from individuals, institutions and governments as well as from
the community and its civic and professional leaders. A well informed
and participative community based on shared aims, collective effort, and
a sense of environmental responsibility is essential to balance ever
changing needs, problems and opportunities. A commitment to those
values which first recreate communities based upon mutual obligation,
caring, compassion and social justice is vital to heal social and economic
divisions which now exist. It will be necessary first to sponsor the very
conditions which enable everyone to belong, participate and share in the
creation of their living environment. A deeper understanding of the
links between poverty, inequality, and environmental degradation is
crucial and will require fundamental changes in attitudes and in the way
Muslim societies are structured. Re-creation of an aware and informed
community itself is the essential first step towards the creation of cities
and environment.

Muslim cities will change and renew themselves only if those who live
in them will identify with their own communities. Any new strategy for
social, economic and community reconstruction will have to take full
account of the entrenched divide in the Muslim society and the decay in
its living environment. Creation of such an environment cannot simply
be the creation of physical patterns and structures alone; it must also take
into account their relationship to the nature and location of productive
work and needs for transport, health and education. Fundamental questions — the relevance of industrial and technical development, the
imbalance between the modern city and the rest of the environment, the
inequalities between urban centres of power and rural areas — are all
linked as much to the questions of poverty and inequality as they are to
the present process of decision-making and resource allocation. A strategy for improvement in the living environment cannot be based just on
a few better-designed buildings and parks in the modern quarters of
cities. Its objectives must come from development and environment as
participative and political issues and from the many areas of decision-
making and resource-allocation which influence social and economic

progress for those without knowhow and resources.

To build cities and shape urban forms is not to ignore social reality and economic problems or to believe that architecture and the city by itself can create a living environment. Commitment to art, architecture and city making has to go far beyond just art and decorated buildings for their own sake. It has to do with making connections with the urban and visual tradition, historic continuity and with the stimulation of ideas and debate conducive to the creation of a balanced and equitable living environment which is humane and socially, visually and ecologically purposive.

If the Muslim city and its architecture is to fulfil its ideals and become a significant expression of its own society, then society will have to initiate the kind of changes which will enable it to become a society of its own ideals. If its city and its architecture are to regain the social, spiritual and environmental relevance which seem to have been lost, then it has to find ways to connect with the whole of its society and its inherited and present problems. This can be the only way to put back into architecture and environment not only that which has been misunderstood and lost during the last century but somehow to achieve this in the full understanding and awareness of today's problems and opportunities; not just in the forms of building, decorations and details, but also, by balancing human and material needs and available resources in a manner that achieves maximum benefit with minimum harm and waste.

References

1. The possibility of a post-modern age, and how it might influence the existing social and human condition (not the current post-modern style of architecture) first came to be discussed through the writings of Schumacher and Illich. For a recent study of the global issues and concerns, see, for instance, the Report and Recommendations of the World Commission on Environment and Development in *Our Common Future*, Oxford University Press, 1987.
2. Williams, Raymond, 'The New Metropolis'. In H. Alavi and T. Shanin (eds.), *Introduction to the Sociology of Developing Societies*. London: Macmillan, 1985, p. 363.
3. Al-Mahdi, Sadiq, 'The Economic System of Islam'. In Salem Azzam (ed.), *Islam and Contemporary Society*. London: Longman, 1982, p. 111-2.
4. Hassan Fathy, *Natural Energy and Vernacular Architecture*. Chicago: University of Chicago Press, 1986, pp. xx–xxi.

5. *Ibis*, p. xxi.
6. For a brief evaluation of some of the many theories of development, see T.G. McGee, *The Urbanization Process in the Third World*. London: G. Bell and Sons, 1975, pp. 13–34. For a detailed exploration, see Ian Roxborough, *Theories of Underdevelopment*. London: Macmillan, 1985.
7. '. . . architecture cannot exist except in a living tradition. . . . As a direct result of this lack of tradition our cities and villages are becoming more and more ugly. Every single new building manages to increase this ugliness, and every attempt to remedy the situation only underlines the ugliness more heavily.' See Hassan Fathy, *Architecture for the Poor*; Chicago: The University of Chicago Press, 1976, p. 20.
8. Ibn Battuta, *Travels in Asia and Africa*. London: Routledge and Kegan Paul, 1929, pp. 26–7.
9. Lapidus, Ira M., *Muslim Cities in the Later Middle Ages*. Cambridge: Cambridge University Press, 1984, pp. 185–6.
10. Mawdudi, S. Abul Ala, *Towards Understanding Islam*. London: The U.K. Islamic Mission, 1980, p. 108.
11. *Ibid*, p. 115–6.
12. *Ibid*, p. 118.
13. *Ibid*, p. 119.
14. *Ibid*, p. 122.
15. For a wide ranging analysis, see Ziauddin Sardar (ed.), *The Touch of Midas: Science, Values and Environment in Islam and the West*. Manchester: Manchester University Press, 1984.
16. See 'The Consequences of the Industrial Revolution'. In E. Eames and G.G. Goode, *Anthropology of the City*. Prentice-Hall, 1977, pp. 46–9.
17. Cox, Harvey, *Religion in the Secular City*. New York: Simon and Schuster, 1984, pp. 182–4.
18. Ali Shariati, *On the Sociology of Islam*. Berkeley, Mizan Press, 1979, p. 39.
19. 'The conclusion to which both theoretical analysis and historical experience lead is, thus, that for the vast majority of the peoples of the periphery, dependent development yields not a better life and a brighter future but intensified exploitation and a greater misery'. See Paul M. Sweezy, 'Centre, Periphery, and the Crisis of the System'. In A. Hamza and T. Shanin (eds.), *Introduction to the Sociology of Developing Societies*. London: Macmillan, 1985, p. 217.
20. 'It is an illusion, perhaps widespread but reflecting ignorance of

economic history, that industrialization somehow lies at the heart of the process of economic development. On the contrary, it is the final act and crowning achievement of economic development; and there is no direct route to its successful realization, though countries like Germany and Japan, which were relatively late in embarking on the development process, could learn (as well as borrow) from their predecessors and in this way avoid mistakes and shorten the time required. But those countries that, to use Samir Amin's phrase, "imported" the industrial revolution without laying the necessary agricultural foundation have succeeded only in creating new forms of dependence.' *Ibid*, pp. 213–14.

Reference to Samir Amin relates to the foot note in 'The New International Economic Order', *Monthly Review* (July–August 1979):16, which clarifies that: 'a failure to lay the necessary agricultural foundation for industrialization is not to deny that they have experienced certain kinds of agricultural development. The trouble is that these have centred on the cultivation of at most a few specialized crops for export, and in the process have tended to withdraw the best lands and other rural resources from vitally needed domestic production. The consequence is the paradox, almost universally observable in the periphery, of countries with predominantly agricultural economies unable to feed themselves and forced to import a large and increasing proportion of their requirements for grains and other staples from countries of the centre. This is why the first rule of a strategy for independent development in the periphery must be a determined move towards agricultural self-sufficiency, including food production. And this means that industrialization must first and foremost be geared to the needs of agriculture'.

21. See, for instance, Sardar, *The Touch of Midas*.
22. See, for instance, Fritjof Capra, *The Turning Point: Science, Society and the Rising Culture*. London: Flamingo Fontana, 1987; and Edward Goldsmith, *The Great U Turn: Deindustrializing Society*. Green Books, 1988.

RIBA Conference, 'Building Communities', 1986; the appointment of a ministerial team to deal with Britain's decaying inner cities and the founding of Urban Corporations for various cities; 'Remaking Cities' Conference this year in Pittsburgh, PA., addressed by Prince Charles who is personally conducting similar campaign at home, are some of the recent attempts to bring into focus the social and environmental problems and deprivation in the Western cities.

Regional/Urban Design Assistance Team (R/UDAT) is a

programme developed in the United States in which a multidisciplinary team of experts is invited into an area by community leaders to spend a weekend's brainstorming session with all sections of the community, examining environmental problems and devising programmes of action. The British equivalent of the programme is Community Urban Design Assistance Team (CUDAT). For a wider debate and examples, see Nick Wates and Charles Knevitt, *Community Architecture: How people are creating their own environment*. Harmondsworth: Penguin, 1987.

23. For a discussion of many such areas, see Ziauddin Sardar, *Science, Technology and Development in the Muslim world* (London: Croom Helm, 1977), and *The Future of Muslim Civilization* (London: Mansell, 1982).

24. Studies were carried out to determine the trends in the absolute and relative incomes of the rural poor in seven Asian countries — Bangladesh, India, Indonesia, Malaysia, Pakistan, the Philippines, and Sri Lanka — and could generally apply to most of the Muslim countries. For percentages of the rural populations below the 'poverty line', see K. Griffin and A.R. Khan, 'Poverty in the Third World: Ugly Facts and Fancy Models', in H. Alavi and T. Shanin (eds.), *Introduction to the Sociology of Developing Societies*. London: Macmillan, 1985.

25. *Ibid.*, p. 244-5.

26. *Ibid.*, p. 245.

27. *Ibid.*, p. 241.

28. *Ibid.*, pp. 241-2.

29. For a survey of ecological and environmental consequences of development, see Avgit Gupta, *Ecology and Development Third World* (London: Routledge, 1988), in particular, 'Urban in the Development and Environmental Modification', pp. 57-68.

30. Hardy, Jean, *Values in Social Policy*. London: Routledge & Kegan Paul, 1981, pp. 91-2.

31. Field, Frank, *Unequal Britain*. London: Arrow Books, 1974, p. 62.

32. For a general survey of Muslim Welfare institutions, see Gregory C. Kozlowski, *Muslim Endowments and Society in British India* (Cambridge: Cambridge University Press, 1985), particularly 'Endowments in Muslim History, an overview', pp. 10-40.

33. Alavi and Shanin, *Introduction . . . Sociology . . . Developing Societies*, p. 250.

34. Wittgenstein, Ludwig, MS 167: 1947-8; Von Wright and Nyman (eds.), *Culture and Value* (Oxford: Blackwell, 1980), as quoted in *The Architectural Review*, July 1985.

Meeting Basic Needs
The Example of Bangladesh

Mir Qasim Ali

The message of Islam was revealed to the Prophet Muhammad who took up his mission in a community that was no stranger to poverty. The tribulations of the first Muslims in Makkah prompted the *Hijra*, the emigration to Medina, where again the first Muslim state knew much hardship. It is therefore not strange that the Prophet spoke several times about the effect of poverty and deprivation on the human character, that poverty saps peoples' sense of worth and leaves them prey to a whole range of moral ills.

The Prophet did not just give cautionary words on the poverty trap, but took practical action to help release people from the stranglehold of poverty. When one young man asked for aid because he was poor, the Prophet bought him an axe and rope so that he could set up in business for himself, cutting and selling firewood. Islam makes the eradication of poverty a responsibility of the entire community. The institution of *zakat* is a basic religious obligation in which the community itself must be active. Once the Caliph Umar was criticised by members of the community when he allocated three camels as *zakat* to one recipient. His response was that the intention was to ensure that the following year the man paid *zakat* and did not seek *zakat*. The resources of the community were to be mobilized to generate self-sufficiency.

Dawa is the obligation of all Muslim men and women to invite others to Islam, to witness to their faith and communicate its meaning. All the Prophet's words, deeds and actions are a unified model, the enduring standard against which all Muslims at all times and in all circumstances must match themselves. Hence, *dawa* can never be understood merely as preaching the words of Islam. The example of the Prophet is indeed his *practice* of Islam, from which we cannot escape the lesson that *dawa* must be an all embracing undertaking which includes direct, determined and constant endeavour to tackle the scourge of poverty and enable all members of a community to meet their basic needs.

The Prophet lived out his mission by establishing a state, a government and administration for an entire community. However, the need for a public administration did not deter the Prophet from taking individual action in the face of need. The Quran is full of instances where individual *sadaqa*, charitable contribution, usually taking the form of feeding the needy, is commended. Islam does not lead us to see the creation of a state administration as lessening the obligation of the individual or group to put into operation the principles of Islam. In the modern world the nation-state has grown into a concept which is all-pervasive and all-powerful. The institutions of government appropriate to themselves more and more tasks for the organization of society. Yet it is clear that the governments of Muslim nations are often unable to marshall the resources necessary to meet the needs of the people. They lack financial, material and human resources to meet basic needs. Foreign aid, which has for many governments become an all-consuming way of life, also falls far short of meeting the evident needs. Major aid donors have in the last decade made more and more mention of attuning their assistance to meeting basic needs, yet the whole system of delivering project aid militates against achieving this objective. Even worse, foreign aid still seems resource-poor in terms of the growing poverty of the aid-receiving countries. The truth of four decades of so called 'development' is that there is now more poverty, and the poor are getting poorer. Yet the ideology of the nation-state maintains that tackling basic needs is the job of government.

The effect of this ideology of omniauthority of government and administration is a growing inertia among the populace. It is not only states that have fallen into the 'dependency trap'. Individual recipients have lost their self-reliance and have become part of a constant cycle of unremitting need. Where the state has assumed all responsibility, the citizen and the community are often hamstrung to a bureaucratic process that patently cannot meet the needs of all. This is in stark contrast to the traditional, historic workings of Muslim society, where we find *waqf*, the charitable trust endowed with economic resources for the alleviation of poverty. *Waqf*, an institution of the community mobilized resources not called upon by the state and therefore supplemented the total resources available to tackle the problems of deprivation. As an institution of society that was distinct from government, it provided the practical example that the community could act for itself.

If *dawa* is to find its proper role in the life of the Muslim community today, we urgently need strategies of action to meet our needs without waiting for some invisible hand to marshall all the resources necessary. We need a genuinely integrated approach which cares for and nurtures the whole human being.

In the light of these clear guidelines, a specific programme to tackle poverty at the grass-roots level has been initiated by Rabita in Bangladesh. In keeping with the source of inspiration for the project and the requirements made clear by that source it has been called 'Comprehensive Integrated Development Programme' (CIDP). CIDP is a long-range plan that aims to promote self-sufficiency among the rural population by providing economic and social service packages to tackle poverty, ill health, illitracy and social malaise. It is a departure from the *dawa* of preaching Islam that has been all too common in Bangladesh and a move to enacting Islamic *dawa* in its full and proper dimensions.

Bangladesh is the second largest and the poorest Muslim nation. Since its birth in poverty, low productivity, dense population and frequent natural disasters have been the common lot of its people. The statistics make grim reading. Per capita income was just $130 in 1984–5 and the distribution of income in the country has changed little in the last 20 years — the top 20 per cent of the population earned 45 per cent of the national income while the bottom 20 per cent eke out their lives on just 6–7 per cent of the national income.

Agriculture is the mainstay of Bangladesh, amounting to just over half of all economic production and providing a living for 67 per cent of the labour force. But Bangladesh produces only 85 per cent of the food grains it consumes. In seeking to close the food gap there is little new land to bring into cultivation. Agricultural development will depend on increasing crop intensity and yields.

Industry has only a minor share in the economy, 9.05 per cent in 1986–7. Performance of major industries has been uneven since 1972, with the biggest growth sector in the service industry. The expansion of small enterprises outside the major cities holds the greatest potential for increasing employment.

Over half the population of Bangladesh earn less than the cost of a minimum viable diet. For the year 1976–7, the United Nations Food and Agriculture Organization (FAO) estimated that 83 per cent of the people lived below the poverty line. Since then nutritional surveys show a drop in per capita consumption of cereals, protein, vegetables, pulses and vitamins. Rapid population growth and relatively slow growth in incomes and productivity has led to an increase in landlessness over the last two decades. With the labour force increasing at 3.8 per cent per year, the country needs to create employment for an extra 1.5 million people every year. As agriculture can absorb only about one-fifth of these, a great deal needs to be done in non-farm sectors of the economy.

The consequences of poverty bring human misery. There are crushing rates of infant, child and maternal mortality, with the highest rates among the poorest. The problems of poor health, hygiene, nutrition, lack of safe water and sanitation create a syndrome of disease. Lack of ability to earn means people cannot buy the food they need to maintain their health and causes widespread malnutrition, making people easy prey to illness. Government programmes to provide health care in this desperately poor country have proved inadequate.

The general climate of poverty engenders an erosion of moral values, promotes pervasive fatalism about the possibility of a better life and supports superstition. This is compounded by the limited access to educational opportunities and leads to an illiteracy rate of 77 per cent. Primary education is inadequate both in terms of content and coverage; the irrelevance of the curriculum leads to the high drop-out rate and inadequate enrolment. While the state education system does not provide moral and religious education, the traditional *maktab*, religious school, suffers from resource constraints and poor management.

If the general situation in Bangladesh is horrifying, then the plight of the most vulnerable group, the women, is appalling. Women occupy the bottom place on all the usual indices of quality of life and economic development. Large numbers of women live a life of destitution as a result of being abandoned, divorced or widowed, and desperately need jobs outside the home for simple survival. Poverty and natural disaster have also left a large body of abandoned and orphaned children, many growing up as 'street children', a prey to all the whole range of moral and social evils as they scratch for a meagre survival. The human costs of poverty are a long-term threat to the social and moral fabric of the nation.

Faced with these realities, Rabita Bangladesh devised the pioneering CIDP project to help Muslims to live a life of human dignity. Income generation is the key component of the programme, which also covers health, nutrition, education and vocational training. The cornerstone of the strategy is community participation in planning, implementation, monitoring and evaluation of the programme. The plan of action is to be implemented through local Bangladeshi voluntary organizations.

The principal objective of the CIDP project is to improve the socio-economic, moral and physical quality of life of the most disadvantaged Muslims through a package of economic and social services aimed at the eradication of poverty, disease, illiteracy and social ills. It seeks to achieve moral, spiritual and material development of the individual and society by providing religious and development education to enhance the peoples' consciousness, maximize the community involvement and participation, and the mobilization of local resources within the context of Islamic concepts. The practical effect will be a drive to raise the level of income by creating employment in farm and non-farm activities and to improve health, nutrition, education, and other related conditions through a package of basic services.

The implementation of the project is through local voluntary organizations, selected for their past experience, viability and Islamic commitment. These organizations will select sites throughout Bangladesh to establish village-level groups involving local imams, primary school teachers and the participants in the project who will be responsible for its implementation within the village.

Participants in the scheme are entitled to a starter capital in the form of loans. Before receiving their loans their project proposals will be discussed and various orientation and training activities will be made available, including project staff to assist in better management and implementation of the projects. All participants will be required to attend the regular weekly *Dawa* service meetings. It is at these meeting that the on-going village monitoring and evaluation programme is conducted, providing the integration of the religious and development functions of the scheme. The operating costs of the loan scheme is realized through such mechanisms of Islamic economics as equity participation and partnership. Repayment of loans is used to further extend participation in the programme.

A crucial part of the income-generation programme is vocational training, made available to participants in the starter capital loan scheme to increase their skills as a stepping-stone to self-employment. Rabita Bangladesh's existing vocational training centre has trained more than 800 young Muslims over the last five years, most of whom have gone on to become self-employed workers in a variety of trades from airconditioning, refrigeration, electrical work and welding, to plumbing and driving. The CIDP will make use of the existing Vocational Training Centre and will engage other recognised vocational training centres in the country.

The income-generation programme will run alongside a primary health-care programme. This will be developed by training cadres of village youths as rural health workers, who will undergo an intensive one-year training directed by doctors at Rabita's Hospital in Cox's Bazaar. The Rural Health Workers will be agents for the delivery of both health care and *dawa* services to their communities. Once in place the rural health workers will receive a token fee from participants in the programme to enable them to be self-reliant. This programme is based on an evaluation of an existing Rabita Bangladesh project which has shown that the 150 rural health workers already in place have become effective in their mission and have the respect and confidence of their local community. Health care services will be complemented by initiatives to provide safe water, sanitation and health education. The entire programme will complement such government initiatives as universal immunization and diarrhoea diseases control.

The rural health workers will also be involved in the nutritional programme, providing nutrition education and monitoring the nutritional status of women and children. Part of the income-generation project will be a drive to increase production of more nutritious foods.

Each village participating in the CIDP will also be the focus of an education programme based upon the village *maktab*, the religious school attached to the mosque. The *maktabs* will be strengthened in terms of their supplies and teaching staff, and their curriculum will be broadened to embrace religious education, functional literacy and numeracy programmes, and development education. Special emphasis will be given to reach out from the *maktab* to serve the educational needs of women and school dropouts. The overriding priority for the *maktab* education programme is to be relevant to both the development, religious and moral needs of the people; it will cover more children than are currently engaged in formal primary education. The initial cost will be borne by the CIDP; however, when the conditions have been created, the continuity of the education programme will be undertaken by the participants themselves.

Rabita Bangladesh's pioneering plan will tackle the whole spectrum of the ravages of poverty. It seeks practical remedies to the spiritual and moral erosion of the complex ills of poverty as well as the economic, social and material ones. In devising their scheme, Rabita Bangladesh is expressing the full meaning of the Islamic concept of *dawa* to bring both Muslim consciousness and the practical realization of the Islamic ideal of human dignity and self-reliance to one of the world's poorest and most disadvantaged nations.

Educating the Other Half
No Half Measures

Aisha Lemu

The search for knowledge is a duty for every Muslim, male and female.

Fourteen hundred years ago the Prophet spelled out the need and obligation for female enlightenment and education, which should not make Muslims complacent. World statistics indicate that most Muslim countries are at the bottom of the literacy league table, and at the bottom of the bottom are Muslim women.

More painful still is the fact that this position of women is not due to poverty or inability to teach women, but to indifference or even to deliberate witholding of education from females on the grounds that it would be unnecessary or in one way or another bad for them — in direct contradiction of the Hadith. This resistance to the education of women was prevalent in many parts of the world, including Europe, in earlier centuries, and reflected the common view that women were intellectually negligible. Religion in these parts of the world taught nothing to the contrary, and it required the secular women's movement to challenge the status quo and prove there was nothing defective in women's intellects. Women could not only learn the theory and pass their examinations as well as men, but given experience and responsible tasks, could make practical use of their knowledge and even pioneer new fields of discovery and ways of doing things. Whatever may be the future course of human social development, one cannot foresee any major regression to the view that women should not be properly educated.

If Muslims have belatedly awakened to the implications of the Prophet's sayings on knowledge for all, it is surely time for a focusing of minds on the elimination of illiteracy within the shortest possible time as an essential step towards an Islamically enlightened and well educated society. It would be natural to expect the lead to be taken by our national and international Islamic organizations — a setting of target dates for universal literacy, a development of strategies and methodologies, a mobilization of energies. Yet this appears to be the exception rather than the rule, perhaps due to a too-narrow conception of *dawa* on the part of some of our Islamic organizations.

Classical Muslim scholars developed the view that the prerequisite of an Islamic duty was itself a duty. If every Muslim, male and female, is charged with the duty to search for knowledge, then the provision of collective means for universal education, especially in the basics of literacy, numeracy and religious instruction, is a fundamental responsibility of the community whether by voluntary organizations or governmental provision. What is inescapable is the universality of the responsibility set out in the Hadith.

In the early days of Islam, the spread of education was one of the dynamic factors in its success. It is the principal task of *dawa* today to retake this initative by following the example of the priorities set by the Prophet and the first Muslim community. It is central to the Islamic outlook that its guidance to a total way of life is a constructive programme that gives practical effect to success in both this world and the world hereafter.

Illiteracy and the generally low level of education among Muslim women acts as a drag upon the whole *ummah*. Their level of knowledge, even of Islam, is limited to what they are told or taught by local ulama. The level of Islamic knowledge of such ulama is often very low, and dangerously mixed with local customs and beliefs. The little that illiterate women know about Islam is thus passed through the filter of tradition, and tradition is identified with Islam. Given such a background their belief and practice of Islam is bound to be defective.

It follows from this that illiterate women cannot be fully effective as wives and mothers. If an uneducated woman is married to an educated man, there is bound to be a gap of understanding between them. They are more like master and servant than man and wife. An educated man would not normally choose an uneducated servant as his close companion and confidante, because their ways of thinking would be far apart. The consequence may be tensions within the home and the loss of that mutuality in their relationship that is the Islamic ideal. Similarly, the uneducated or illiterate woman can do little to promote her children's education. She cannot teach what she does not know. She cannot supervise her children's homework, or give them useful guidance or counselling in their school affairs or choice of training and career. She may even have a negative effect on the education of daughters, discouraging them because she feels inferior or left behind, or because she sees them departing from what is traditionally expected of females; she cannot see the need for their having more than the bare minimum of education. By virtue of the lack of education women are prevented from achieving their potential and realizing the full potential of the home as the microcosm of Muslim society.

If an illiterate woman is a problem within the home she is unlikely to be able to contribute anything, other than manual labour, to the family or society in general outside the home. She can carry water, collect firewood, do farm labour and crafts. But even in these fields her potential for improvement in the quality of her work or in devising value-enhancing methods that generate economic and social benefits is limited by her illiteracy.

Every programme for social development, education or health introduced by governments runs into problems with the illiterate. Conveying the most basic messages for any form of uplift has to rely on visual techniques, speeches or demonstrations. This is a labour-intensive means of spreading information and, thus, expensive and slow. Many programmes never reach the people in greatest need in remoter towns and villages because there are not enough trained personnel, without whom such methods cannot succeed.

The pernicious consequences of the lack of female education are seen at their most stark in the case of illiterate women, especially those in poor rural communities. But undereducation or attitudes prejudicial to the education of females are by no means confined to the poor and rural areas they have spread and become pervasive throughout the *ummah*. The task of *dawa* then is to recapture the proper sense of priorities that must centre upon education for all Muslims, male and female, and be reflected in strategies for educational provision that are rooted in Islamic principles. These strategies must be capable of being adapted as practical programmes according to local circumstances to fit the actual needs of a particular community.

It is necessary for any educational programme that sets out to be practical to have clear and achievable aims. 'Clear aims' implies a coherent philosophy of education. 'Achievable aims' implies taking into account the background of the people to be educated, the existing educational programmes and the potential resources of finance and staff. In the case of education for Muslim girls, it is necessary to consider not only the theoretical role of women in Muslim society but also the needs of the Muslim community as a whole and its interaction with non-Muslims.

In most parts of the world the education of both boys and girls is undertaken by the state through established government schools, supplemented by private or voluntary agency schools, such as those run by churches or Islamic organizations. In some countries government control over education is total. The aims of all education accord with state policy; the curricula, syllabi, textbooks, examinations and teacher training programmes are fully centralized. Any change or development required by Muslims in such educational systems has to be through the Ministry of Education with the approval of the government in power. In other countries some powers over education are devolved to regional or local authority levels or to school heads. At the other extreme are countries where the government permits private and religious schools to operate with complete independence, the only constraint may be the need for students to prepare for and compete in the entrance examinations of higher education.

When we consider 'practical' programmes for girls' education, we should be aware that some programmes may be relevant, but the government may not permit them, either due to its opposition to or ignorance of Islam, or due to fear of the reaction of non-Muslim sections of the population. In this sense what is practical in one country or region of a country may be impractical in another.

If the government exercises control over education, whether at national, provincial or local level, Muslims should make every endeavour, collectively and individually, to influence those in authority to make the system as a whole acceptable to Muslims, or if that is not possible, to make provision for the special needs of Muslims within the system. This lobbying of officials is the task of those Muslims who are qualified to make their case in a proper manner. In some areas where Muslims are not satisfied with the way government schools operate, they only complain privately to each other and no collective effort is made to convey their views to those who control policy. In other areas Muslims lack well-qualified, articulate leaders who can put their case in a way that commands respect, or they spoil their case by putting it forward in an unreasonable manner. However, it may happen that the views of Muslims are expressed by competent people, but the government is simply unwilling to listen or to concede any point.

Whatever the reasons for a government's failure to meet Muslims' needs, it becomes the duty of the *ummah* under such circumstances to supply what remedies it can outside of the formal education system, making use of evenings, weekends or school holidays, and if possible opening their own Islamic-based schools wherever this is permitted. Having mentioned these points which apply to the education of both boys and girls, we turn to discuss girl's education programmes.

It has been common in the past, and in some areas is still common, to regard Western education as a preparation for employment. Since most women did not take jobs there was no need for them to be given such education, a view seen as increasingly out-of-date. First, education is not just job training. It is, or should be, a part of the process of civilization and human development which cannot be limited to one sex without creating an imbalance in society. Girls and women have shown themselves to be mentally and academically as able as men, and have great potential to contribute to human welfare. To deny them education is to treat them as subservient, in the same spirit in which earlier generations of Europeans refused to educate Africans because they were born to be 'hewers of wood and drawers of water' — suited only for routine menial tasks and not for thinking. Second, we have also reviewed the way in which the gap in understanding, knowledge and culture between educated husband and uneducated wife is a source of friction within marriage. Such unequal marriages lead to dissatisfaction and often to divorce. Third, we have also considered that the uneducated Muslim wife is not generally able to give sufficient support and guidance to her children in their education; in competitive multireligious societies, the children of educated mothers tend to do better in school. Fourth, a community with a residual pool of illiterate and uneducated women will have difficulty in tackling the root causes of ill health and poverty and of employing the opportunities of technology. Many of the areas of life that directly relate to health and the family are either traditionally the sole responsibility of women or are areas over which women have considerable influence.

Among those who have conceded that Muslim girls should go to school, however, there are some who would like their curriculum to be restricted to a sort of higher level version of what they previously got at home; that is a more modern, 'scientific' approach to home economics, plenty of religious and moral education, basic literacy, numeracy, a few arts subjects, and possibly some technical training in skills or crafts. While such programmes may appear to meet the needs of a large number of girls of average or below-average ability, they are obviously not adequate for the above-average girl or woman either as a Muslim or as a contributing member of the *ummah*. She needs exposure to the full range of subjects at higher levels, and the appropriate preparation for such education. Both male and female Muslims are required to seek knowledge as a religious duty. There is no restriction on the level or the subject of study, provided it is not something in itself *haram*, harmful or prohibited, for both male and female. The only restriction on areas of inquiry is established by reasoned criteria derived from the operation of the total value framework of Islam; this value framework applies equally to male and female and must be applied equally by them if these standards are to be agents for creating a thriving Islamic civilization. The Quran tells us that 'only the learned among His servants truly have *taqwa* (God consciousness)'. We are urged to look for the signs of God in the universe and in ourselves, and to use our reason to understand the significance of these signs as a means of attaining *taqwa*. It is this *taqwa* that lies at the root of our moral and spiritual development. Therefore, it is quite unwarranted to deny girls and women access to scientific and technical knowledge where these insights into God's creation are often obtained.

It is essential for large numbers of female Muslim students to qualify in all fields of study in order to become the teachers of the next generations. In multi-religious societies this is particularly important, because if Muslim women are not qualified for these jobs the next generation of girls will be taught instead by non-Muslim women or men, both of which can have dangerous side effects. The same applies to the fields of medicine, nursing and social work where there is a specific need for qualified Muslim female workers to cater for the fellowwomen and girls.

In mixed religious societies if Muslim women do not qualify in all fields of human endeavour, the whole initiative of female leadership becomes dominated by non-Muslim women. This has already happened in many countries where non-Muslim women, due to their higher qualifications and work experience, occupy by right high posts in professions, administration, politics, journalism and the general leadership of women's national organizations. In this way they become spokeswomen on women's affairs and are able to exert a strong influence on other women's way of thinking, while Muslim women are often silent or apologetic.

For all these reasons, whatever the type of schools or colleges concerned, whether they be government, private or religious, they must make provision for Muslim girls to have access to the full modern curriculum at the appropriate level. Leaving aside the question of single-sex schooling, the general principle that must run throughout educational provision is education of equal quality and content for both boys and girls. Having established this point, we can now consider the common deficiencies in girls' education in the modern school system, and discuss how these deficiencies could be remedied. It should be clear that some of these deficiencies apply equally to boys as well.

From the Muslim point-of-view, the major defect of modern schools is their secular basis and marginalization of religion. From an Islamic standpoint, knowledge of religion should be at the core of the curriculum and other subjects should be seen in its light. Instead, in most modern schools the secular perception of the arts and sciences forms the core of the curriculum, while religious knowledge is squeezed in with only two or three periods a week and is often not regarded as a serious subject. This, of course, reflects the common Western view of religion as something personal and restricted to private belief and spiritual life.

It is not easy to persuade government schools to make any substantial increase in the time devoted to religious education. The authorities concerned can point to the existing pressure on the time-table in a broad-based curriculum, and in the higher classes few people want to divert the students from concentration on their examination subjects. Muslims can, however, appeal to the government to make religious studies (Muslim, Christian, or other, as applicable) a compulsory examination subject at all levels so that even if its time allocation is not much increased it is at least taught to every young person throughout adolescence and is considered a serious examination subject. A cogent case for making it compulsory can be made by stressing its importance in upholding and transmitting the moral values essential for the survival and success of the nation as a whole. It may even be possible for Muslims and Christians to make a joint appeal on this issue, which the government would find hard to refuse.

A second area where a great deal of effort is required is in campaigning for and facilitating the teaching of the Arabic language to non-Arab Muslim students. In most ex-colonial territories, the only foreign languages taught are English or French. It is necessary to campaign for the viability of Arabic. However, even where this is attained, the problems are by no means over. Arabic is not an easy language. It requires the mastery of a new alphabet and an unfamiliar grammatical structure. There is the problem of modern local dialects. Unfortunately, there are very few good textbooks available designed for young foreign learners, and the teachers are usually unfamiliar with language learning theory and modern methods of foreign-language teaching. Consequently, even where Arabic is taught in secondary schools the standard achieved is low and the pupils often avoid it for fear of failure. The ideal of making Arabic once more the *lingua franca* of the Muslim world is being frustrated by our own incompetence and lack of will to turn aspirations into realities. An international Islamic body should be established to achieve a breakthrough in availability of standard syllabi, textbooks, tapes and international teacher training. Facilities and liaison should be maintained in such countries to monitor progress and provide programmes and assistance as required. The British Council has done solid work of this type for the English language, and the Alliance Française for French. We should take a leaf from their books. Those concerned should not neglect to find means of including women and girls in their programmes.

Obviously, private and religious schools in countries which allow free experimentation in the curriculum, such as the United States, have much wider scope for adopting the policies of expansion of religious education and proper teaching of the Arabic language. They are also free to experiment with full Islamization of knowledge in all the other subjects, both arts and sciences. The results of their experiments, new curricula, syllabi and teaching materials should be advertised and made available to schools in any part of the world where their use is feasible. The Islamic Academy in Cambridge, England, is working along these lines.

However, where it is not possible to persuade the government to meet Muslims' needs and aspirations in the schools, it is important that Muslim organizations step into the breach. They can employ and loan Islamic studies teachers to institutions free of charge and organize vacation courses, evening classes and weekend classes. In traditional societies girls were groomed for marriage and home care. Feminist ideas over the past twenty years have opposed this idea, in the belief that the running of the household and the bringing up of children should be shared equally by husband and wife. However, it is now apparent that even in the most developed countries, this sharing has not worked out as planned.

Weekend and vacation courses, operated by Islamic organizations for secondary-level girls where mature Muslim women, not necessarily professional teachers, instruct the girls, are an opportunity to introduce them to a whole range of life skills in the Islamic way. The course content might include:

The Islamic concept of marriage.
Moral conduct with the opposite sex before marriage.
The right choice of partner.
Husband and wife relationship — mutual obligations.
Good qualities to be cultivated in a Muslim wife and mother.
Management and care of the home — creating an Islamic
  environment.
Pregnancy, childbirth and infant care.
Family diet and healthy living.
Treatment of common illnesses and first aid.
Child management and teaching; socialization of children.
Common causes of marital breakdown and how to avoid them.
Moral conduct at home: importance of example to children.
Moral conduct in women who go out to work.

Such courses should preferably not be taught by the girls' regular teachers. They need to see new faces. The classes should be small and so that the girls will feel free to discuss any matters which give them concern about their future role as wives and mothers. Other resource persons should be brought in if possible, so that the girls are exposed to a number of responsible women with whom they can identify and who can guide them in their moral and social development, and encourage them to take pride in the development of their skills in homemaking in balance with their academic development.

The second area where the weekend or vacation programmes are needed for girls is in general Islamic knowledge, the ability to read the Quran correctly and a knowledge of Arabic. It is difficult to obtain enough teaching time in government schools for Islamic studies, because of pressure of other subjects. Islamic organizations, particularly women's Islamic organizations or women's wings of Islamic organizations can organize extramural courses for girls to supplement what is taught in the schools. In countries where Islamic studies is not taught at all, this may be the only organized Islamic teaching available.

A philosophy of education is crucial. However, it can do nothing to reach the most serious and enduring problem of women's education in the Muslim world — illiteracy. We need a strategy for educational provision, but first we need to ensure that all females get some form of education. This need is just as pressing for women who are past school age and therefore cannot be catered for by the formal system. Is is incumbent upon all Islamic organizations to be active in promoting the provision of basic literacy. It is even more essential that Islamic

organizations become directly involved in mobilizing their own energies
and resources in providing such courses as a major priority.

Governments in many countries have introduced literacy programmes with varying degrees of success. Many involve women, and are
sometimes a part of adult-education programmes aimed at social and
economic development. This utilitarian approach sometimes fails to
arouse much enthusiasm, particularly in traditional Muslim societies
which tend to regard all secular-based education with suspicion. The old
Quranic schools were respected because of their religious ethos. Whatever their defects in course content and methodology, at their root lay
the concept of a pious person teaching the young how to live and worship in ways acceptable and pleasing to God. There was blessing in the
teaching and in the learning.

It is in traditional Islamic areas that there is often the greatest resistance to modern government literacy programmes. Yet, experience in
some areas has shown that if literacy courses are incorporated in Islamic
education programmes, they become not only acceptable but keenly
desired.

In Nigeria over the past ten years there has been a widespread upsurge
of Islamic classes for married women, many of which include literacy in
the vernacular in their subjects of study. Some of these are run by
Islamic organizations, some by individuals who may either teach or play
a supervisory role. An increasing number are being taught or run by
women. Some of the large cities have as many as twenty or thirty such
schools, and even some small towns have three or four. In Lapai in Niger
State some large rooms in the Emir's palace are loaned as classrooms,
and some of the local Quranic teachers come there to teach hundreds
of women. However many classes are opened, demand for places still
outstrips the supply. This is in contrast with government secular
schools where the authorities sometimes have to resort to threats or even
arrests of parents who refuse to send their girls to school.

Women who attend these classes are of any age between sixteen and
fifty. A very few have some secondary education, others a few years of
primary schooling, but the majority never went to any school except for
perhaps a few years of Quranic school where counter-productive methods usually result in minimal learning. The majority are therefore illiterate when they begin. There is enormous variation in what is taught in
these women's classes, and to what depth it is taught. Subjects may
include Quran and its meaning, Hadith, Arabic, literacy in the vernacular, *tawhid*, *fiqh*, moral education, *sirah*, comparative religion (Islam,
Christianity and traditional religion), the rights and duties of Muslim

women in marriage and divorce, the teaching and Islamic upbringing of children and so on. Some schools restrict themselves to Quran, Hadith and Fiqh, and in the absence of literacy depend on memorization.

For many women their experience in these schools brings changes in their lives and greater Islamization of their behaviour. For those who attain literacy, they can for the first time read newspapers and write letters. They have access to books in the vernacular and thus to knowledge in any field that interests them. Some of the women are extremely intelligent and on completion of their course are gaining admission to Government Arabic Teachers' Colleges and even to Islamic Studies Diploma courses in the universities. Many of them are keen to teach other women. This movement offers much hope for Muslim women and multiple long-term benefits to the Muslim community and the nation as a whole.

A variation on these Islamic schools is a 'Women's Home Islamic Literacy Programme' which is being tested in several places by the Federation of Muslim Women's Associations in Nigeria (FOMWAN). It could be adapted to suit almost any environment, provided there is an effective Islamic organization to administer it, and some educated women with basic Islamic knowledge who are ready to give some of their free time to teaching. This programme is useful particularly where there are no classrooms available, or where women live too far away from the nearest Islamic school.

It makes use of the desire of many educated Muslim women to help their uneducated neighbours. The method of organization begins with the recruitment of women volunteers who are ready to teach in their own time in their own homes. A standard course syllabus is prepared to be distributed to all the teachers, covering:

Literacy in the vernacular.
Memorization of ten short surahs of the Quran and their meaning for use in prayer.
Fifteen selected Hadith from an-Nawawi's collection of Forty Hadith.
Basic moral teachings of Islam.
Practical performance of prayers and other Islamic duties.

Then the women teachers are given weekend orientation courses to familiarize them with the selected textbooks and methods of teaching. They are given a small blackboard and copies of the books. The sponsoring organization must then make available application forms and give wide publicity to the existence of the scheme to encourage women to apply. Applicants are sorted according to the area where they live and attached to the nearest teacher.

Normally there should not be more than ten people to a group. This number has been selected since the scheme draws its inspiration from the Prophet's literacy scheme after the Battle of Badr when he promised freedom to any prisoner of war who would teach ten Muslims to read. Ten was thus the number chosen for its historical associations with the Prophet's own emergency literacy programme. Also, most women's homes do not have the space for larger numbers, while many women who enrol need individual attention since they may not even know how to hold a pencil, let alone know the letters of the alphabet.

Once the groups have been allocated, the students are conducted to the house of their local teacher and together with her they agree on the days and times that are mutually convenient. Once the lessons begin an attendance register and markbook are kept. The programme supervisor visits the classes regularly to monitor their progress and resolve any problems. The standard course is to be completed in ten months, followed by central examinations which contain written, oral and practical sections. Those who pass are awarded a certificate. Those who fail go back to their teacher for further lessons and re-sit the examination when they are ready. It has been found convenient to start the course immediately after Ramadan, so that the examinations can take place before the next Ramadan. This enables the organizers to use the occasion of women's gatherings for vernacular *tafsir* during Ramadan to recruit new students and also to present certificates to the last batch of successful candidates. At the same time special awards can be presented to the most successful volunteer teachers as a recognition of their achievement in getting their students through the examinations.

This women's home literacy programme has a number of advantages. It requires little finance. The expenses of the organizing body are only blackboards, teachers books, examination papers, certificates and awards. Students should provide their own textbooks and writing materials unless they are too poor, in which case they can be helped to obtain them. As a whole, the programme fosters good neighbourliness and closer relations between women of different classes and backgrounds who would otherwise not get to know each other. In this way it promotes mutual care and social solidarity of the *ummah*. Because the classes take place in other women's houses in the locality, there is little objection from husbands who are concerned about *purdah* and would not like their wives to be taking taxis to distant parts of the town, or to be taught by men. Women who have benefited from the programme may be able to become volunteer teachers themselves and to help spread the literacy and knowledge they have gained.

Experience has shown that supervision is important to this scheme. Without a supervisor who has time to pay regular visits, the teacher may feel isolated and lose the sense of being part of a corporate effort. The supervisor can correct mistakes in methods, and help to resolve any administrative problems which could otherwise result in drop-outs or the collapse of her class.

Obviously the structure of these classes could be adapted to include the teaching of other knowledge and skills to local women. Units could be included on health education, nutrition, child care, first aid, home farming, food processing and cooking, needlework and various crafts. It could also form the basis for developing co-operative production and sales of local produce. In this way the educated woman would be carrying out a form of 'national service' to the uneducated which is wholly in accordance with the Islamic ideals of passing on knowledge and not treating it as a monopoly to be used for personal enrichment. The network of groups becomes a mechanism for harnessing and sharing skills of the uneducated in an environment where they can be upgraded and mutual benefits can be brought to a whole neighbourhood. The religious motivation for teaching and learning is retained and is felt as a source of blessing and ultimate reward from God.

The literacy and other programmes we have mentioned imply the existence of women's Islamic organizations and women's wings of Islamic organizations. Where these do not exist, it should become a priority to foster their development under the leadership of women who are sincere, patient and hard-working. To flourish, they need the leadership of women with organizational ability; their operation offers an ideal place for women to acquire confidence in a range of organizational skills that make women's Islamic organizations themselves a practical learning environment of great potential benefit to the *ummah*. But women's organizations also need the support and encouragement of the men, especially in promoting a general understanding among husbands that some sacrifice of their own comfort may be required if their wives and daughters are to give this service to the *ummah* as a whole.

Too often, plans are made for educational programmes that are useful but are designed entirely for boys and young men. The planners often fail to consider the special needs of girls and young women, who thus lose out on the opportunities of their brothers and as a result feel demoralized. We not only must look forward to giving equal thought, time and attention to the sisters, we must positively and actively work to ensure this is provided. If they have special problems or requirements, these must be resolved and met — not avoided. The full participation of women in the Islamic movement will be a criteria for its earnestness and a harbinger of its success. The mobilization of the *ummah* for self help and self sufficiency can have no better starting point than the eradication of the greatest scourge of Muslim civilization, illiteracy.

Across the Muslim world, Islam remains the most potent rallying cry to popular participation. We need to harness this fact, to mobilize it. Too often we have seen Islam used as mere sloganeering, as rhetorical flourishes that have been devoid of the solid substance, the Islamic content of true *dawa*. Too often *dawa* itself has been a matter of lecturing and exhortation on either purely spiritual topics or discussion of an Islamic ideal that is quite disassociated from the realities of the lives of the vast majority of Muslims. We all take pride in that fact that 1,400 years ago the Revelation of the Quran established the best possible status for Muslim women and gave them rights women in other societies are still struggling to achieve. *Dawa* that does not engage itself with reality, however, perpetuates the gross deformity of the Islamic ideal in the lives of the majority of Muslim women today. Quite simply, today the majority of Muslim women, thanks to traditionalism and a range of other misguided notions, enjoy neither the status nor the full possession of the rights Islam gives them. *Dawa* must mean a practical engagement to bring the lives of women in line with the teachings of the Quran and the example of inclusion, care and active encouragement to participate in the life of society set by the Prophet himself. In today's world, achieving literacy and securing adequate educational provision is the first essential in fulfilling the Islamic vision of the status and rights of women. Attaining this goal within the context of *dawa* is the best way to recapture the original meaning of invitation to Islam.

A Nation in Exile
Tackling the Problems of Refugees

Ayman Ahwal

Over the past four hundred years, the lands of the Muslim world have come under increasingly destructive pressures. In the sixteenth century the glories of Islam still shone throughout the world and a Muslim could travel from present day Morocco to Indonesia without the possession of a passport, protected and provided for with local valid currency. Nowadays, what is left of the Muslim world can hardly be called such, so much has it been fragmented. Following the Crusades, the European powers continued the assault on and fragmentation of Muslim lands. Colonizing the greater part of the Muslim world, they left in their wake the deadly legacy of their own boundaries, which reflected their inter-European rivalries rather than any homogeneity or even diversity in the lands they colonized.

The break-up of the Ottoman Empire and Caliphat was the final blow to any international Islamic political entity. Since the Russian Revolution and the birth of Communism, the onslaught on Muslim lands has continued, although the nature of the war has changed. The antagonists are the same Christian nations which formerly conquered by force of arms, although nowadays few of them would admit to being 'Christian nations' per se. Whereas the Eastern or communist block of nations has continued to overwhelm Muslim lands with its armies, the Western and capitalist block of nations has continued the war in a more covert but equally insidious way — through economic exploitation, which is just as destructive. The cultural and social onslaught has never failed to follow in either case. The result of both war and economic exploitation are destruction, oppression and famine, when it is time for the inhabitants to flee for their very lives, becoming refugees.

According to the United Nations High Commission for Refugees (UNHCR), there are officially some twelve million refugees in the world. The true figure is more likely to be nearer fifteen to eighteen million, if those who have not actually left their countries are taken into account. According to UNHCR criteria, a person cannot be considered as a refugee while still in his or her own country, however uprooted the condition. This of course means that those actually considered by the UNHCR are at the end of the line, having through fear, disaster and despair left everything — land, possessions and livelihood — to cast themselves into the arms of fate and uncertainty.

The overwhelming majority of the world's refugees are Muslims. Collectively, they are a sad testimony to the state of the Muslim world today. Huge numbers of refugees from Afghanistan, Ethiopia, Palestine, Kurdistan, Iran, Iraq, Chad, Uganda, Mozambique and Somalia live in the squalor of refugee camps in lands other than their own. Together they constitute a nation in exile strung around the world. Having fled their country to escape war, famine, oppression and natural disasters, they are to be found living in sprawling communities near to the border of the first country of sanctuary they come to.

A further category of migrants, also mostly Muslims, are economic refugees who have left their countries in search of better lives. Europe is full of them. They have left their countries before the more decisive cataclysms of war and famine strike, when the economic degradation has already made deep inroads into their lands. There are some three million Turks in Germany and Switzerland, three million North African Arabs and West Africans in France and the Benelux countries, Indonesians in Holland, more than a million Pakistanis, Bangladeshis and Yemenis in the U.K. Although they are a category of refugees not classified by the UNHCR as refugees, nevertheless they deserve mention. These migrants who come mostly from less educated milieux, peasants and townfolk, now constitute the majority of the Muslim presence in Europe; it is thanks to them that nowadays we can reckon the Muslim populations of European countries in millions rather than a few thousand, as was the case before the prosperous years of the 1950s and 1960s, when they first migrated.

The third category of Muslims are those who have left their countries, usually individually or with their families, because of oppression and war to seek sanctuary elsewhere. These asylum-seekers, as they are known, come largely from the professional and educated classes. Specific clauses in the Geneva Convention are designed to protect them. Numerous human rights organizations worldwide are geared to monitoring them, drawing public attention to their plight and defending their international rights. These asylum-seekers form the most mobile section of the refugee community. A number of them, notably Palestinians and, more recently, Kurds, encounter many obstacles in finding permanent asylum for themselves and their families in any one country; they often find themselves in the situation of being shuttled from country to country in search of a haven. However, many of those who succeed in finding asylum settle to commence new lives in exile. As many asylum-seekers were politicians or held public positions in their countries of origin, they form a kind of international elite of refugees. Many continue their political activities in their countries of adoption, newly geared to their status of exile.

Muslims should always be mindful that the Prophet himself was a refugee, a migrant, that the Muslim calendar is dated from his *hijra* (immigration) to a place of refuge, and that those who migrated with him, the *Muhijirin*, became the core and inspiration of the Medina state. This prototype Muslim nation of refugees is to this day the example for all Muslim life, secular and spiritual. Thus the very condition of being a refugee can be seen as being sanctified, the evolution of such a society as having the best possible exemplary model, and its aspirations and outcome as having the most momentous possibilities.

The situation of refugees and the esteem in which they are held is a very different matter now. Their very existence is a cause for collective shame on the part of the world community. Few would dream of imitating their life styles; indeed, the most laudable attention meted out to them is one of pity and a somewhat paternalist desire to improve their miserable condition. The fact that there are pious Muslims among them and that there are often countless men of religious learning is rarely included in information about them. A refugee settlement may well be a devout praying community, but it is of little consequence to most of those that rush to help them. Few imagine that they have anything to learn from those they are helping.

Refugees of Today

The twentieth century metropolises of misery, which refugee communities have become, are improvised cities of tents, shacks and makeshift shelters in Pakistan, Somalia, Sudan, Palestine and Lebanon. Unlike other cities of similar populations, they do not have inspired city architects and planners to beautify and improve their amenities, avenues, public buildings and services. These cities are at the end of the line of human despair. These people are the main beneficiaries (or victims) of the aid agencies' attentions. The dedication with which many of those that work for the agencies is of a very different brand to that which inspired those first Muslim refugees who arrived in Medina.

Nowadays refugees' status and rights are enshrined in international conventions. As is to be expected in these days of nation-states, the bases and substance of these international instruments are purely secular. The integral language of Islam which framed the first constitution of the Medina state and which was loathe to separate the spiritual from the secular, is absent. There is no reference nor special respect afforded to believers and people of faith. All is framed in the cold secular jargon of bureaucratic equality and laudable legality. As in modern legal practice, there is no original example by way of final reference but only legal precedent, which necessarily supersedes a legalist absolute by way of fine adjustment. However there is much of worth in these international instruments and even sometimes a familiar ring to the fine language of many clauses.

The UNHCR is the international body with special overall concern for refugees. Formed at the same time as the United Nations Organization itself, the UNHCR is charged with direct responsibility for the welfare of refugees on behalf of the world community of nations. From the moment that persons or communities become eligible by clearly phrased criteria, defined as refugees and subsequently registered as such, they become an incumbency on the UNHCR. The most important of these international instruments for refugees and stateless persons is the UN Geneva Convention of 1951. Many references are made in the Convention to the Universal Declaration on Human Rights proclaimed by the UN General Assembly in 1948. Other international declarations which affect the status and welfare of refugees are the International Covenant on Civil and Political Rights agreed by UN General Assembly in 1966; the International Conference on Human Rights agreed in Tehran in 1968 and the simultaneous co-operation with the UNHCR in 1968; the Convention on the Prevention and Punishment of the Crime of Genocide, approved and agreed in the UN General Assembly in 1948. Indeed, the declarations make impressive reading.

Other regional agreements concerning the status and protection of refugees and asylum-seekers have been ratified by the Organization of African Unity (Addis Ababa, 1969), the European Convention on Human Rights (1950), the International Conference of American States, and the Asian–African Legal Legislative Committee (Bangkok, 1966), to name but a few. It is by the problems as assessed by these international conventions that refugee issues are judged and provided for. In the effort to be egalitarian and on account of the multi-religious composition of signatory states, the terms of reference adroitly avoid questions of religion. This being so and as the majority of the world's refugees are Muslims, it becomes clear that many problems of most refugees are ignored and uncatered for in the international instruments concerning refugees.

Afghan refugees make up the largest refugee community in the world. Pakistan government figures register 2.9 million as of 30 June 1987, although this figure is widely challenged. A more accurate figure is probably in the region of 3.4 million in Pakistan and a further 2 million in Iran. It is estimated that nearly one-third of the entire population of Afghanistan is living in refugee settlements outside Afghanistan. They live just over the borders in some 320 refugee villages, 75 per cent in Pakistan's North West Frontier Province, 20 per cent in Baluchistan and a further 3 per cent in the Punjab. Another estimated 1.8 million live in camps in Iran. Mostly from rural areas in Afghanistan with its largely land-based population, women and children make up nearly three-quarters of the total Afghan refugee population. The men have either stayed behind or returned to fight the Russian invaders. The land has been emptied of life. Truly a nation in exile fighting and waiting to return.

As the Palestinians were sent into exile with the tacit approval of the UN itself by the formation of the State of Israel and the subsequent balkanization of the native population, the UN saw to it that a compensating UN body was formed with the special assignment of administering to the needs of Palestinians. In such a way the question of Palestinian refugees was effectively channeled and isolated in a separate agency, the UNRWA, which has an annual budget of around $200 million, provided almost entirely from voluntary contributions by governments and non-governmental organizations. At first UNRWA's role was principally as a relief Agency, bringing food aid and material assistance to the disaster-struck Palestinians when they lost their country in 1948 and regrouped in refugee camps throughout the middle East, in Gaza, Jordan and Lebanon. The agency now instead, provides, education, health care and welfare services. A 1984 UNRWA report declares apocalyptically:

If the Agency is compelled to cut down some of its programmes due to lack of funds (a real possibility), this would inevitably lead to the closure of many UNRWA schools. This would create a serious security problem for the host country's inhabitants, as thousands of UNRWA's children would be turned 'out into the streets', and would contribute to the overall instability of the Middle East.

UNRWA's budget *has* been drastically cut over the past years.

In many respects the second largest community of refugees, those who have fled from Ethiopia, has much in common with those from Afghanistan. Refugees from Ethiopia are largely Muslims from various ethnic rural communities and have fled a Communist regime, which by nature sees Islam as a threat to its policies. They live in camps in Sudan, Somalia and Djibouti. However, the Ethiopian situation is, if anything, yet more insidious. The ruling Coptic Amharic (Christian) minority is in fact exactly the same minority as that which made crusades and war against Muslims under the emperors. Only the name and the vocabulary of oppression have changed. The fact that the Amharic regime is basically a Christian-Communist one is important in mitigating the attitude of Western governments towards it and goes a long way in explaining their ambivalence towards it. The Copts are past masters at exploiting this ambivalence and turning it to their advantage. The fact remains that not only the majority of refugees from Ethiopia are Muslims but also that many have actually fled from concerted religious persecution. Massacre, pillage and rape by Ethiopian armies are equal causes of the huge Ethiopian refugee communities. The much publicized famine is no more than a by-product of this persecution of genocidal proportions against Muslims.

The infamous Ethiopian Resettlement and Villagization plans can only be seen as attempts to uproot and destabilize the entire Muslim community in Ethiopia, where they are a majority. These plans, which are a priority in Ethiopian national policies, are directly responsible for causing the massive refugee situation in that country. Until the revolution, land was owned by absentee Amharic Copt landlords, whereas land ownership by Muslims was prohibited. However, Muslims still retained possession of much of the land, after as before the Revolution, imbuing it with their own way of life, even if they could not own it. Hence the Resettlement and Villagization Plans were devised to get Muslims off the land they have farmed for centuries. There is no doubt that these plans are equally responsible with war and famine for the refugees. The matter should be discussed at the highest possible level and steps taken in the international arena to discourage their implementation, which constitutes an abuse of human rights on a vast scale. This must be a matter of urgency in order to avoid further tragedy, genocide and refugees. As it stands, Ethiopia has hardly figured in agendas of the annual Geneva Convention sessions on human rights since 1979, although Ethiopia is arguably the worst offender on record in modern history.

Special attention should also be given to Eritrea, and other individual territories within the Ethiopian Empire, which are effectively liberated from central government control by successful resistance groups, but whose populations have nevertheless fled the war zones to find safety elsewhere in their country. As the liberation movements hold effective military control of the land from the Ethiopian government's point of view, famine must be seen as the most effective and perhaps the only way of exerting pressure on Eritrea. However, following the political considerations of Western nations, food aid from outside directed at relieving suffering in Eritrea is nevertheless mainly sent through Ethiopia. This is because in sending it through purely Eritrean (i.e. liberated) channels, they would be offending Ethiopia's sovereignty over Eritrea since Eritrea is not an internationally recognized country. Since its annexation by the Ethiopians, Eritrea is the only country whose borders were defined by Western colonialism but is not today an independent country. This is in spite of the fact that Eritrea is effectively controlled by liberation movements and that alternative liberated channels of communications are possible and viable. In their insistence that only liberated channels be used, convoys travelling through Ethiopian routes are attacked and destroyed, causing much hurt to self-righteous Western humanitarian organizations whose declared intention is 'merely to relieve hunger in Eritrea'.

A similar situation is also prevalent for the Afars, whose Mujahidin are also in a controlling position to harrass and destroy convoys passing through Ethiopian channels. To a lesser extent, but progressively as the liberation movements gain momentum, the same applies to Oromia. Some Western aid agencies, notably the Christian ones, have covertly channeled food aid through purely Eritrean (i.e. liberated) channels. Quite naturally, perhaps, they choose to support the liberation movements which are Christian-dominated or which have a large proportion of Christians in them.

Significant communities of refugees are to be found in Iran and Iraq. These are mostly Kurds who fled from involvement in the Iraq-Iran war, since their territory straddles the two countries. Other sizeable communities of Muslim refugees are to be found in Uganda, Chad,

Mozambique, Burkino Fasso, Niger, Mali and other countries of the African Sahelian regions. These refugee communities include persons displaced for reason of war, famine and acute agricultural deterioration but who have not actually left their lands of origin.

The Aid Game

Countless aid agencies, many of which raise vast sums of money from ordinary individuals, vie with each other in what has become known as the 'Aid game'. Many of the agencies are run by religious organizations. Some agencies, such as World Vision, directly reflect the policies of their countries of origin. But whether they are *de jure* government agencies or not, there is no doubt that most governments view the aid agencies based in their countries as the humanitarian face of their countries. Accordingly, many aid agencies, while nominally and constitutionally independent and free to operate, raise and spend money as they think fit, receive large allocations of funds from the governments of the countries in which they are founded.

In a similar vein the UNHCR, the largest of all the aid agencies, also reflects the policies of its 'government'. UNHCR's aid programmes tend to express the policies of the major donor countries to the UNHCR budget (i.e., the Western block of powers). The UNHCR invites governments to contribute to its various funds for individual refugee-producing situations. It is then up to the individual governments to allocate funds for each project in turn. The UNHCR also receives funds from international corporations, trusts and individuals, which may be designated to a given area or to a general fund. For instance the Jihad in Afghanistan is overtly supported by official U.S. State Department policy. The war produces the largest refugee situation in the world. Accordingly, the largest U.S. contribution is to the UNHCR Afghan fund. On the other hand, in the case of Ethiopia, the U.S. does not support any one of the national liberation movements against the central, albeit Communist, government. Accordingly, the U.S. contribution to UNHCR funds for refugees from Ethiopia is more circumspect and emphasis is put on development programmes within Ethiopia and repatriation. The former is usually of more benefit to the Ethiopian government than it is to stricken farmers and the latter is often cause of further hardship. The attempt to repatriate Afar refugees in Djibouti to Ethiopia is a recent example of hastily formulated refugee policy, into which the UNHCR had been manoeuvered by various interested governments. Fortunately the programme was aborted and the main body of

Afar refugees in Djibouti are still there. The repatriation operation was halted by the protests of human rights organizations around the world.

As can be imagined, the major effort of the aid agencies is directed towards the purely material support of refugees and the related logistics of distribution. When refugees arrive in new settlements, they are exhausted in body and spirit. They have to start their lives from nothing, on often quite barren territory which is not their own. They arrive and wait, helpless. Apart from their most intimate (and religious) personal activities, newly arrived refugees have neither livelihood nor familiar neighbourhood around which to base their lives. Many have lost even their most immediate families and cannot even count on this essential stabilizing factor. The psychological deprivation of refugees is just as much a calamitous factor as is the need for material sustenance.

At first life is centred around the organization of the refugee camps and the distribution of food and aid. This, of course, puts the aid agencies in a powerful position for influencing the lifestyles of these supremely vulnerable people. As the majority of aid agencies are Western based, the priorities, sense of social responsibility and morals of aid workers are correspondingly guided by Western mores, which may be subtly expressed and with few overtly ulterior intentions. But sometimes methods are blatant and uncompromising. For instance, a rule was made in one refugee camp that only young girls were to be given rations of a certain commodity. In order to defy this rule, young boys were encouraged by their parents to dress up as girls in order to qualify for the handout. This subsequently led the distributors to check the recipients more carefully! However shocking this particular instance may be, it illustrates both the desperation of the communities in their need and to what extent the distributing agencies can influence the actions of refugees and their families. Similarly, many distribution policies insist on giving aid to individuals according to the individual's need rather than to the head of the family as would be the normal practice in most Muslim communities. Frequently women may be given priority to receive aid, causing tensions in family hierarchies and loyalties. Rather than reconstituting or patching up the homogeneity and cohesion of refugee societies, aid distribution, especially when it comes through Western agencies, often serves only to continue the disintegration of well-worn life styles and traditional family structures.

As refugee communities grow in size, so does the scope of the aid programmes. Aid is no longer a question of providing basic assistance and food to beleaguered communities. Improving their condition now involves countless researchers, sociologists, anthropologists, experts in nutrition, psychology and childcare, doctors and teachers. Many aid workers readily admit that refugee communities are no more than raw material out of which to remould society.

The power of the aid agencies in some cases can be tyrannical and their influence is often wielded in far from diplomatic ways. In places where there may be little or no local government infrastructure or control, an agency or a group of agencies become a law unto themselves and virtually control everything that happens in their areas of operation. Clearly this is a danger for the untypical situation of an agency, which may have the resources of a multinational corporation and may be spending sums of money equivalent to a significant proportion of the GNP of the country where it is operating. Sudan recently expelled seventeen foreign aid agencies for allegedly meddling in the internal affairs of that country.

Most difficult to contend with is the almost unassailable moral self-righteousness which agencies adopt to justify their methods and operations,: 'because they are in the country' they say 'to help refugees and bring relief and humanitarian aid, therefore, anybody that criticizes them must be immoral'. This attitude, which is indeed a tricky one to contend with, gives them enormous and sometimes uncontrollable freedom to act as they please. Usually the countries in which they operate have no choice in the matter by the sheer economic reality and need. Neither do the governments in which the agencies are based say much; they hardly hide the fact that in the absence of direct colonialism, the presence of the aid agencies is better than no presence at all.

In the last decade a number of Muslim aid agencies have come into operation, increasingly catering for the welfare of Muslim refugees. As yet these agencies are still relatively inexperienced and certainly they are not yet in any measure geared to supply the needs of all the Muslim refugees in the world. Furthermore, the fact remains that the UNHCR is primarily dominated by non-Muslims and it is this body which governs overall world refugee policies. However, the presence of the Muslim agencies does to an increasing extent assure that now many Muslim refugees can receive food and aid from Muslim hands. This is more important than it may at first appear. Most refugees in camps are from uneducated rural communities, who even in better times would be reluctant to receive food or anything else from the hand of a non-Muslim. An important psychological threshold is crossed when a rural Muslim is obliged, albeit through necessity, to accept food from a non-Muslim. He who gives the food can to a large extent call the tune.

However experienced and effective the effort of the Muslim aid agencies become in the foreseeable future, with resources at their present level it is unlikely that they can cope with the massive dimensions of Muslim refugees in the world. This does not mean, of course, that the Muslim agencies should just resign themselves to their inadequacies, but that they should tailor Muslim aid programmes to have maximum effect in the preservation and reconstitution of the Islamic identity of Muslim refugees. The right balance must be sought in planning aid programmes to inspire and reassure Muslim refugees with the Islamic approach and to counteract the one-sided secular effect of Western aid. This would suggest that the emphasis in the Muslim aid effort should be on education rather than on food aid. Food and shelter nevertheless are extremely important and must not be underestimated.

To illustrate the secularizing effect of the Western aid agencies, the following scenario is a typical one. In most camps, soon after the need is perceived, schools are established for primary education of refugee children. These schools are often formed by religious teachers who naturally enough begin instruction with the basics of religious teaching. Subsequently, the UNHCR agrees to pay for the cost of the schools, including teachers' salaries. Then, when the schools have been going for some time, the UNHCR refuses to pay for the salaries of imams and teachers of religion in the schools on the pretext that it (the UNHCR) is a secular organization and cannot be responsible for religious education, which is considered by it to be the responsibility of each individual. That many of these schools have originally been founded by the only available teachers among the community (i.e. religious teachers) no longer seems relevant to the UNHCR once the schools became ongoing concerns. Doubtless, the UNHCR is a secular organization, but the children in the schools are not, but are from Muslim families. Clearly there is here a role for the Muslim aid agencies to make good the deficiency in education.

It is of prime importance that refugee children are not deprived of the most basic Islamic education from the initial level. Fortunately, the more established Muslim aid agencies, such as the International Islamic Relief Organization, the Islamic Relief Agency and others, have begun to devote much effort and attention to the question of education. It is essential that this trend continues in the most concerted manner possible. Educational projects should necessarily include basic training in skills and trades for young refugees. As many scholarships and grants as possible for further education should be made available to refugee students, so that when eventually the refugee community returns home there will be quailfied people for every function in the future development of the country.

The composition of the executive body of the UNHCR is of prime importance in the formulation of UNHCR policies. With perhaps the notable exception of Sadredin Ali Khan, a former UN High Commissioner for Refugees, both the High Commissioner and the composition of the Consultative Committee reflect the policies of the major donor nations and are easily manoeuverable by means of careful lobbying and in-committee strategies to express policies that are actually detrimental to Muslim refugees. Few notice the political in-fighting and manoeuvering which goes on, since most of it is done behind the scenes.

Some Positive Steps

The fact that there are now a number of Muslim aid agencies should give Muslim voices at least a say in refugee affairs at the international level. This is not only on account of relief work in the field, but principally because the aid agencies themselves constitute an important lobby within the UNHCR, for the aid agencies are represented in the Consultative Committee of the UNHCR and are thus able to bring issues to its notice.

By UN Charter refugees are an incumbency on the world community. The UNHCR is, so to speak, a managing agent on behalf of the world community. It is one of the functions of the UNHCR to authorize other agencies or projects in any given area or refugee-producing situation. In this respect the discretion of the UNHCR is final. Alternatively the UNHCR may select an aid agency to act on its behalf as overseer which will fulfil these functions, even in quite far-reaching policies. This is often the case in particularly sensitive situations. Thus we see situations in which the UNHCR is both managing agent and on-the-field agency directly involved in the administration and distribution of aid. In other cases, where the UNHCR has delegated its administrative role to another agency, it will be this agency which has the power to appoint and approve other agencies and their operations in a given refugee-producing situation. UNHCR Funds are channelled through the sub-contracted aid agency delegated with overall responsibility. Such is the situation with the sensitive refugee area of Nicaragua–Honduras. In this case most of the administrative and field work is carried out by Christian agencies.

The better established Muslim aid agencies should equip themselves with personnel experienced in a quasi-political situations, such as within the UNHCR. They will then be ready for the in-committee wranglings when it comes to appointing agencies to overall positions of responsibility, which affect profoundly how a refugee situation is managed. Then, especially in cases where a refugee situation is exclusively a Muslim one, the Muslim aid agencies can be in the position not only to influence the direction and tone of programmes and their overall policies, but also to receive ample funds for doing it.

The Muslim World League is an independently constituted international agency in much the same mode as the UN itself, and would thus be eminently suited to administer both the immediate needs and the formulation of long-term policies for a number of refugee situations in the world. The financial onus nevertheless, remains, on the world community through the UNHCR. The League would in turn appoint agencies which it considers suitable for the distribution of aid in a given situation. It may even appoint non-Muslim agencies where circumstances require it and may also act on its own behalf as an aid (distribution) agency. Such an arrangement can offer great benefits, both practical and intangible, integrating all dimensions of refugee needs, including the material, social, cultural and religious. But the proposal also requires the amassing of expertise and an active commitment to practical humanitarian work that the *ummah* has so far been slow to marshall on such an organized, international scale.

Complementary to this proposal, it is clear that adequate research and information should be made available. There are already sizeable research departments in Europe and America, which specialize in refugee studies. The most significant one is the Queen Elizabeth House Refugee Studies Programme in Oxford University. As with most other similar departments, the QEHRSP is part of the department of anthropology. Some excellent work has been done and much valuable research exists which is of vital use to an aid agency in almost any given refugee situation.

Research already done should be made use of and a refugee studies programme set up to which all interested agencies can both contribute and have access. There now exists a standard format for compiling data on human rights and refugee issues. First developed in Holland, HURIDOCS is now used by many organizations involved in refugee studies and human rights. In this and other ways, efficient networking of information can be achieved. Already the Oxford Refugee Studies Programme is linked with a similar studies programme in Juba, Sudan, and is soon to be extended to another centre in Peshawar, Pakistan.

A separate centre for Muslim refugee studies could be founded for networking with existing sources of information and data. This would be with an aim both to adding a specifically Muslim angle to input on

Muslim refugee situations, agencies and programmes and to be provided with up-to-date information on the activities of other agencies, programmes and situations. Such a centre would most appropriately be founded in the form of a separately constituted department in a university of international status. Accurate information is essential not only in the treatment of refugee situations but can also be useful in their prevention, quite apart from material needed for the training of those who work in aid agencies. It is obvious that when a refugee-producing situation occurs, action can only be a palliative. Part of the role of such a Muslim refugees studies centre would be to research into the root causes of these situations in order to alert the world community to take steps to deal with the source of the problem before it is too late. Extensive research should also be made into Muslim minorities and more positive action to protect them urged at the highest possible level.

With the increasing pressure now felt throughout the Muslim world from war, famine and economic degradation, many Muslim lands are experiencing a breakdown of national security — or an excess of it. Both situations cause individuals to flee their countries to seek refuge elsewhere. This, together with the huge numbers of Muslim migrants workers in Europe, has contributed to a situation in which Europe and the so-called free world see themselves beseiged with foreigners (again mostly Muslims) seeking a livelihood, refuge and asylum. One might say that the empires are coming home to claim those very same rights with which they were formerly wooed. Accordingly, the gates of Europe are becoming increasingly difficult to prise open, and often remain firmly closed even to the most deserving asylum seekers. All kinds of pretext and letters of international law are mooted in order to justify this situation, which is contrary to the high ideals enshrined in the same international conventions which the European powers have themselves instituted.

The UN Geneva Convention of 1951 insists that everyone, who has justified reasons to fear for life in his or her own country through reasons of race, politics or religion, has the right to claim political asylum in any signatory country of the Convention and that a signatory country is obliged to provide asylum. Nevertheless, it has become very difficult to obtain asylum. For instance, if a refugee leaving a country travels first to a neighbouring country and then to a European country where he or she claims asylum, the European country will probably refuse that person on the grounds that a refugee can only claim asylum in the so-called 'country of first asylum', even if the first country was only transited by plane. There are also tragedies when a person stays first in a country which is not a signatory to the Geneva Convention. If an Eritrean, Afghan or Palestinian works in one of the Gulf States (non-signatory to the Convention) and leaves when the work contract expires, rather than return to the country of origin where there might be untold difficulties, this person may go to Europe and claim asylum. However, the European country will not grant asylum on account of the 'country of first asylum' clause. The refugee will then be sent back to the Gulf State in the knowledge that he or she will not be allowed to re-enter the Gulf State in question because the contract and visa have expired. Alternatively the person will be sent directly back to Ethiopia, Afghanistan or Palestine to a singularly uncertain future. Endless bureaucratic ruses have become common practice in the avoidance of extending political asylum in Europe, thus putting an ever increasing number of Muslims on a circuitous globe trot in search of refuge.

The situation of the Kurds is a tragic example of how international politics can affect refugees. Kurdistan, spreadeagled over the frontiers of Iran and Iraq was wholly caught up in the imbroglio of the Iran-Iraq war. Iraqi Kurds fled to Iran for refuge and vice versa. As both sides were hungry for manpower to send to the war, refugees found themselves in the dilemma of having to fight for their newfound protectors against the country they had just left. Increasingly, they are fleeing to European countries to find asylum there, having already fled both countries. One of the protagonists is thus considered to be the country of first asylum. As the European nations try ever harder to stem the flow into their own countries by bureaucratic pettiness, Kurds are sent back to a very uncertain fate in a warring land.

One well publicized individual case of an asylum seeker can be extremely effective in changing public opinion about the policies of a country, which may be persecuting large numbers of anonymous people within its borders. On the other hand in the international political arena it is often a more difficult task to alert the world to persecution of a minority by a government, however outrageous or flagrant the oppression might be. Not only is most persecution covert, to begin with at least and most countries are eager to keep it that way, but also most countries have skeletons in their cupboards, and are anxious to retain their good reputations in human rights. Thus there is often a tacit understanding between countries not to expose another's misdeeds in matters of human rights for fear of having its own abuses exposed. It is nearly always refugees who are among the first to suffer from these conspiracies of silence. Nearly always adequate information concerning the plight of an individual or a group is sufficient to prevent a human tragedy or an injustice.

There is a case to be considered for the creation of a 'holding country' for Muslim asylum-seekers. Such a project would involve a country willing and able to receive Muslim asylum-seekers, whatever their country of origin, according to well defined, internationally recognized criteria. Such criteria as well as the election of such a holding country would have to be discussed at Islamic Conference level. The numbers of asylum-seekers from Muslim lands, especially in recent years from countries of the Middle East, are beginning to attain disaster proportions. As so many asylum seekers are qualified people and could normally fulfil useful roles, the waste of valuable human resources is obvious. The stay of asylum-seekers would be considered as temporary until a further, more permanent resettlement solution could be found for them. A precedent for such an arrangement is Austria which is a holding country for East European refugees. Such a project could be financed by the UNHCR in a similar way as is Austria.

Muslim refugees are a charge on the entire *ummah*. It is clear that the UNHCR, as the overall and overtly monopolist agency in questions of refugees, cannot be relied upon to act in the interests of Muslim refugees. Its increasing co-operation — identification — with the World Bank cannot be regarded with anything but suspicion. Administrative structures within the UNHCR as well as the 'democratic' composition of the committees and election of policy-making officials are further reasons for anxiety.

There is no doubt that development can go a long way in preempting a refugee situation when the causes are purely famine and agricultural deterioration. But these causes in themselves have their origins in more far-reaching and deep-rooted political causes, which are to blame for war and devastation in Muslim lands. In any case refugees constitute a hideous wastage of human resources. Unless Muslims are able to recuperate and regenerate living societies out of this exiled nation, the situation can only worsen as more and more Muslim peoples are cast into exile. It is most important that Muslim refugees remain ever conscious that they form a unified part of the worldwide *ummah* and that the *ummah* knows how to heal the open sores on its wounded limbs before the sores spread and the pain engulfs the whole body.

Part Three

Contemporary Communications of Islam

Muslim Print Media
Present Status and Future Directions

Aslam Abdullah

In all periods and in all Muslim societies print media form part of the literary output. But interrelated publications with a variety of content overlap so that it becomes difficult to separate Muslim media from the mass. This difficulty is heightened while the media are being formed in Muslim societies. In addition, although no firm definition of Muslim media exists, the determining elements of content, media ethics and commitment to Islam are often used as rough guides.

A publication may be oriented to Muslims and their societies without commitment to their interests or religion. For example, the *Muslim World Review*, published by a Christian trust in the United States, is about Muslim societies but can never be classified a Muslim publication. Nor can the daily *Hurriyat* of Istanbul, produced mainly by Muslims with a secular worldview for a Muslim readership. Although *Soviet Muslims*, published in Arabic, Persian and four other languages by the official Muslim religious board from Tashqand, claims to be an Islamic publication, most Muslim media analysts disagree.

No systematic study has identified or classified Muslim media, and hardly any record exists of the history, role and function of Muslim media. At the first Asian Islamic conference in 1978, it was decided that co-ordination should be developed between Muslim journalists and media people to counter the Zionist-controlled monopoly of mass media which were deemed antagonistic towards the Muslim world. The scope defined at this Karachi conference was vast: publications produced by

137

Muslims to counter zionist-controlled media could be classified as Muslim media. However, this scope was narrowed at the first international conference of Muslim journalists and media people in Jakarta in September 1981, when a covenant for Muslim media people was endorsed. The two main points of the covenant are that all Muslim media people should follow Islamic rules of conduct in their journalistic endeavours, and that the Muslim media should work towards achieving integration of the Muslim individuals' Islamic personalities.

From this definition, we may distinguish between Muslim world media and Muslim media. Muslim world media portray Muslims, but are produced from secular, socialist or communist viewpoints, whereas Muslim media portray Muslims in particular and the world in general from an Islamic perspective. This distinction is not found in existing literature, which can be classified in four main categories.

1. Books, articles, research theses and reports published by Muslim or non-Muslims in Muslim countries.
2. Books and articles published by Muslims in non-Muslim countries.
3. Reports and articles on the Muslim world media appearing in Muslim periodicals.
4. Documents and papers on the Muslim media presented at media conferences organized by leading Muslim organizations.

Print Media in Muslim Countries

The substantial literature on the status of print media in Muslim countries includes government-produced books, independent research studies and unpublished theses submitted to various universities. Most of this literature is in indigenous languages, although some books on the subject are also available in English and French.

These books discuss the Muslim media in the national context with occasional references to Islamic and Muslim issues. Those written by independent researchers concentrate primarily on media functions, media systems, media behaviour, media politics, and ownership and readership patterns, whereas those sponsored or published by governments deal mainly with the facilities available to media people, the role of the media in struggles for independence or on media laws.

However, there is no systematic study of the print media in the Muslim world in any language. Even single-country studies on the subject are rare. Single-country works that do exist are mostly in Arabic on the Arabic press, in Persian on the Iranian press and in Urdu or English on the Pakistani press. No up-to-date book analyzes the role of the print media in Muslim countries, the motivations of and constraints on Muslim journalists and governmental pressures. A few regional works are available, but the two best known are in English: *The Arab Press* by William A Rugh and *Daily Journalism in the Arab States* by Tom McFadden.

Muslim-owned Press in Non-Muslim Countries

Some single-country studies are available in Urdu, French and English on media in non-Muslim countries. The bulk is in Urdu, published in India. Imdad Sabri has published a five-volume work on Urdu journalism, analyzing the Muslim-owned Urdu press in the Indian subcontinent. Journal articles and newspapers contain information on the Muslim-owned press in Burma, the Philippines, the U.K., the U.S.A., France and other Western European countries. These studies provide an historical perspective on the development of Muslim-owned periodicals in non-Muslim countries; a few are analytical, but most discuss the births and deaths of Muslim-owned print media in non-Muslim countries.

The Muslim Print Media in Muslim Magazines

Many articles and special reports on the Muslim world print media have been published in newspapers and magazines in both non-Muslim and Muslim-majority countries. These articles are mainly on three issues: the dependence of Muslim media on Western news agencies, the distortion of Islam and the Muslim world in Western media and the media status in the Muslim world. The monthly *Inquiry*, published in London, included a twenty-eight-page special report on Muslim media in its January 1986 issue. *Arabia: Islamic World Review*, which has now ceased publication, published a five-page report on the status of media in the Muslim World in 1987. The Delhi-based *Radiance* in 1984 published a long article on Muslim media in Britain. *Crescent International, Impact International, The Islamic Order, Islamic Message, Concept* (Pakistan), *Islamic Herald* (Malaysia), *Islamic Horizon, Minaret* (U.S.A.), the *Saudi Gazette, Milli Gazette and Islam* (Turkey), *Jordan Times, Kayhan and Teheran Times* and many other publications have published articles on Western coverage of Islam and the Muslim world.

Only a few of these articles contain hard data. Most are mainly pole-mical, emphasizing the level of dependence of the Muslim world media on Western sources of information or the distortion of Islam and the Muslim world in the Western media.

Conference Papers on Muslim Media

During the past fifteen years there have been three major international conferences on the subject of Muslim media. The World Assembly of Muslim Youth (WAMY) organized an information conference in 1976 in Riyadh to discuss the future strategies for the Muslim media. In 1981 the World Muslim League organized the first International Islamic Media Conference in Jakarta. Earlier the U.S.-based Association of Muslim Social Scientists held an information and communication con-ference in Chicago. These conferences presented various proposals to bring about a positive change in the Muslim media. Some papers were reflective, and a few dealt with the status of Muslim media in Muslim majority countries.

In addition, the issue of Muslim media has been discussed in several papers presented by media analysts to national and international confer-ences on Islam. In 1971 at the first All India Urdu conference held at Lucknow, issues related to the development of the Muslim media were debated. Similarly, in 1987 in a conference of world religions held in Istanbul, the future of the media was discussed at length by participants drawn from leading Muslim institutions.

At several conferences organized by Unesco and the Non-Aligned Movement on the new information order, the status of media in Muslim countries figured prominently. But the emphasis was on the dependence of the Third World media on Western news agencies rather than media status in the Third World itself.

Is it feasible to identify Muslim media on the basis of existing litera-ture? If we analyze Muslim owned and produced media in Muslim majority and minority countries in the light of the covenant adopted by Muslim journalists at the 1981 Jakarta conference, we may draw a broad outline of Muslim media.

Historical Background

From historical accounts it is possible to conclude that the early media development in the Muslim world was greatly influenced by Islam. Muslim media passed through three stages before it achieved regularity.

The first stage was the publication of single-story sheets or papers. In Abbasid Baghdad, Umayid Spain and Muslim India such accounts of events were written after the occurrence. For example, travellers' accounts were reproduced in handwritten form by Muslims in different lands to be read in public. Accounts of religious debates were also frequently reproduced in this form, not for mass circulation, but for an interested readership. There was no regularity in this type of publication. They were produced in Arabic in the Abbasid period and Persian in Muslim India. For comparison, this stage in Europe began in the seventeenth century.

The second stage was the periodical account of occurrences on successive days. In Muslim India, for instance, during Alauddin Khilji's period, weekly, fortnightly or monthly accounts of military expeditions were available to interested readers. At one time the information was compiled by people close to the department concerned with defence matters of state. This type of weekly or monthly account began appearing in Western Europe in 1640, after the Thirty Years War which provided the main content for most of the news publications of Europe.

The third stage was when information about different events began to appear in a formal form, though not very regularly. Thus, Muhammed Bin Qasim's military expeditions in Sindh, or Aurangzeb's military campaign in the south of India, or even Shah Waliullah's sermons during the 1150s after Hijra were produced along with other events in sheet form. Some of these publications appeared under the title of 'Ahwal Nama'. Shah Waliullah's address to the *ummah* in which he called upon people to give up un-Islamic traditions was, in particular, circulated in large numbers throughout India. It was distributed in mosques by Shah Waliullah's disciples. When Shah Waliullah returned from Hejaz where he went in 1143 AH, his ideas about the unity of *ummah* were circulated in a series at frequent intervals throughout North India. It was not only Shah Waliullah's sermons that were in circulation in a written form, but there were many other events made public through this dissemination system.

The information produced in early stages was confined either to religious issues or military expeditions with the exception of a few items about the social life of the Muslim community. These early efforts, however, did not result in the development of an indigenous media, as was the case in Western Europe. These three stages presented most of the prerequisites for such a development in the Muslim world. But it was only in Europe and to a certain extent in North America that the establishment of the technical and administrative framework helped develop a definite media tradition in the eighteenth century. In 1708, one Dutch publisher called it 'the century of newspapers'. For the Muslim world it was the century of the end of newspapers.

In the Muslim world the political and intellectual crises were so deep that the third stage did not immediately result in the publication of periodicals using available technology. But these were not the only reasons. The tradition of oral communication in the Muslim world was so strong that it often discouraged printing. Families were close, friendship circles were wide, public gatherings were frequent and the mosque system was strong. Face-to-face communication was considered more important than impersonal media information. The traditional reliance on information from friends and other personally-known individuals was strong. But whenever these forums and channels were put under pressures, the people evolved their own means of communication. In India, for instance, during the Reshmi Romal Movement (silk handkerchief tahreek) political groups produced regular accounts of events which were pasted on city walls or distributed secretly.

Print technology was introduced in India and other Muslim centres as early as the eighteenth century, but periodicals were not immediately published. It was not until the mid-nineteenth century that the first periodical was published in Turkey.

Sadly, the history of the press in the Muslim world is written from the date when Western European colonial governments took control of Muslim lands. Early developments are ignored. Thus, the first publications started in Indonesia in 1744; in Turkey in 1768; in Sierra Leone, 1806; in Iraq, 1816; Egypt, 1820; Algeria, 1847; Lebanon, 1858; Tunis, 1861; Syria, 1865; Libya, 1866; Yemen, 1879; Morocco, 1889; Malaysia, 1896; Sudan, 1899; Saudi Arabic, 1908; India, 1822; and Afghanistan, 1925.

Although modern media developments in the Muslim world are attributed to colonialism, the media in Muslim countries have played an active role in the struggle for national independence. With the growth of nationalism in Muslim countries in the twentieth century, periodicals were attracted to the cause of liberation from colonial rule. They were drawn into political issues, nationalistic, anti-imperialistic themes that are very strong even today. The fact that the British, French, Dutch and Portuguese had the tradition of a free press at home did not help the development of a free press in countries under colonial rule.

Governments and colonial administrations in the Muslim world used every means to control early publications. Several newspapers and magazines were banned because they were critical of the colonial administration. It was expected that when the media came out of the colonial stage it would diversify and play a dynamic role in the reconstruction of Muslim societies. However, the media in Muslim countries by and large ignored the role played by their pioneers from the thirteenth century. They did not encourage good and discourage evil by providing news that honoured truth and called for participation in public affairs. In the colonial and post-colonial Muslim world, the media slowly incorporated into an international secular culture. Eventually the media succumbed to the information order that considers conflict, contention and disorder as hard news. But much more than that under the political pressures of the age, it neglected its role as an instrument of change.

The Present Status

More than 5,000 Muslim periodicals are published in the world today, with about 3,000 produced in the forty-five countries of the Organization of the Islamic Conference. These include 587 dailies, 1,087 weeklies, 1,167 monthlies and 128 quarterlies. The remaining 2,000 are published in countries where Muslims are in a minority. In India alone the number of Muslim-owned media is over 700. In addition, there are some one hundred news and feature agencies including forty-two national news agencies in the Muslim world.

Periodicals are produced in almost every significant language, the two most widely used being Arabic and English, followed by French and Urdu.

In the eighteen African countries with Muslim majorities, except for Nigeria, there is no significant print media. Other Muslim countries, such as Turkey, Malaysia and Egypt, have long print media traditions. Some countries are making use of new technologies, whereas such countries as Indonesia and Bangladesh still depend on sixty-year old technology.

In the nineteenth century the few newspapers and magazines published by private individuals appeared in Egypt, Syria, Lebanon, Morocco and India. Muhammad Baqir started publishing his Urdu periodical from Calcutta in the mid-nineteenth century. Khalil Khuri printed *Hadiqat al Akhbar* in Beirut in 1858. *Wadi al Nil* and *Al-Ahram* appeared in Egypt in 1867 and 1876, respectively, and *Al-Maghrib* started in Morocco in 1889. Today, however, private ownership has increased to 62 per cent of the periodicals in the Muslim world.

Periodicals in Muslim countries have concentrated in the more densely populated urban areas. In most Muslim countries one or two cities serve as the political, economic and commercial centres and that is where most daily newspapers are published. It is only in India that popular provincial news media have started appearing in different regional languages. But by and large the provincial press is negligible.

Media Density in the Muslim World

The print media in the Muslim world can hardly be called mass media. It is subject to many constraints: high rates of illiteracy, multiplicity of languages, low GNP, lack of adequate printing resources, high cost of news print, inferior telecommunication facilities for transmission of news and inadequate or non-existent transportation. The number of regular newspaper and magazine readers is probably under 10 per cent of the Muslim world's population.

The literacy rate is not the only factor which limits the circulation of newspapers and other periodicals. Others are the level of urbanization and purchasing power of the people. In such small wealthy states as Kuwait and the United Arab Emirates, where populations are largely urbanized, periodicals have substantial circulations. In addition, a long tradition of reading and periodical publishing influence the circulation of publications. In Egypt, Syria, Turkey, Malaysia, Lebanon and Jordan, where the literacy rate is above 50 per cent, the circulation of newspapers is above fifty per 1,000 persons. Kuwait and Malaysia have remarkably high circulations: Kuwait's is 208 per thousand and Malaysia's is 133 per thousand. In African countries periodical circulation is weak, even in countries with high literacy rates. Benin and Sierra Leone, for example, have above 20 per cent literacy rate but the number of readers per thousand is only three. The political instability and lack of proper transportation facilities are two main reasons for this low circulation. Moreover, in many African countries the oral communication channels are regarded as more reliable than newspapers.

Table 1. *Newspaper Circulation in Muslim Countries*

Countries	Literacy rate	Daily Papers per 1000	Radio (one per person)	TV
Somalia	5.2	x	42	x
North Yemen	8.3	x	68	x
Bourkina Fasso	9.1	x	56	438
Niger	9.8	1	38	553
Mali	10.1	6	72	30
Djibouti	11.9	x	19	x

Mauritania	17.0	x	19	x
Chad	17.8	x	63	x
Guinea	18.7	4	36	769
Afghanistan	20.0	4	124	1340
Comoro	20.0	x	9	x
Gambia	20.1	x	6	172
Sudan	21.6	7	15	188
Senegal	22.5	7	19	122
Sierra Leone	23.6	3	37	171
Saudi Arabia	24.6	23	3	3
Benin	27.9	3	53	287
Guinea Bissau	28.0	7	31	x
Bangladesh	29.2	5	117	357
Jordan	31.2	58	4	12
Pakistan	31.8	18	14	77
Nigeria	34.0	15	2	180
South Yemen	38.9	x	19	733
Algeria	41.8	28	6	16
Egypt	41.9	54	6	12
Iran	42.8	127	6	21
Iraq	43.8	21	6	19
Tunisia	47.4	46	6	24
Libya	52.4	12	21	20
Oman	55.0	x	5	75
Turkey	60.0	89	11	13
UAE	68.0	32	4	10
Bahrain	69.8	71	3	3
Cameroon	70.2	6	11	x
Morocco	70.7	14	9	26
Indonesia	72.0	18	23	51
Lebanon	73.4	90	2	7
Gabon	75.0	14	13	65
Malaysia	75.0	133	8	12
Brunei	77.8	x	4	7
Syria	78.4	79	5	24
Qatar	78.7	x	4	1
Maldives	81.1	6	72	x
Kuwait	86.7	208	12	3

Note: The figures are compiled from country year books and the World Bank annual report published in 1985–6.

Literacy in the Muslim world is on the rise in the 1980s. At present the literacy rate is highest in the under-thirty age group among both males and females. Paradoxically the number of newspaper and magazine buyers is the lowest among this group.

The GNP, communication development, literacy rate and political structure affect most aspects of media, including the careers of those involved in it. Salaries of journalists are low and professional standards are generally uncertain, but the overriding problem is the media's inability to remain independent. Financial support is sought, usually from government or from a political party because the market alone is insufficient support. In addition, the highly volatile political situations mean that the media will not easily remain divorced from political influences. It is argued that only when the economy grows and political conflict subsides can the media rely solely on market forces.

Partisanship in the Muslim world media is brought about by the need of the political elite for a spokesman. This stage is most frequent when the country is passing through a period of social transformation. The social divisions in the society tend to split the readership into camps according to political preferences. Newspaper contents are geared to appeal to a particular camp, thus securing a restricted but guaranteed readership. Periodicals often find it difficult to go beyond partisan lines because neutrality might mean a betrayal of political ideals. A government that establishes itself on firm footing after a period of intense conflict does not often wish to see itself opposed by partisan media.

As a country develops economically and becomes more stable politically, the media can emerge from partisanship into the market-oriented stage, which happened in many of the industrialized countries of the West.

The media in most Muslim countries are elitist in nature, partly from political necessity. The news published is elite-centred, in terms of nations and of people. In an elite-centred news communication system, ordinary people are given the least chance of representing themselves. Government and its high officials take up a large amount of the contents, with the government and its individual members trying to use the media to project themselves.

Periodicals generally attract the adult male urban reader. Youths, females and rural people are least represented in the contents, which may be a significant reason for poor readership among women, young people and those living in rural areas. There are several magazines for women and young people, but they, too, are urban oriented. A large majority of Muslim people are rural dwellers and young: 70 per cent of the population in Muslim countries is under thirty years of age. The exceptions are Gabon, UAE and Djibouti, where the youth population is between 55 and 66 per cent of the total population. Half the population in Muslim countries, with the exception of Kuwait and Qatar, is female.

Table 2. *Social Composition of the Muslim Population*

Countries	Rural	Urban	Male	Female	Under 30
Djibouti	x	x	49	51	60
Kuwait	12	88	60	40	68
Qatar	14	86	64	36	64
Bahrain	19	81	58	42	67
Lebanon	24	76	49	51	66
Iraq	28	72	51	49	73
UAE	28	72	72	28	59
S. Arabia	33	67	53	47	70
Algeria	34	66	50	50	73
Jordan	40	60	52	48	75
Brunei	41	59	53	47	70
Libya	46	54	53	47	72
Iran	50	50	51	49	70
Tunisia	53	47	51	49	68
Syria	53	47	51	49	75
Egypt	56	44	51	49	67
Turkey	56	44	51	49	66
Morocco	57	43	50	50	71
South Yemen	63	37	49	51	69
Gabon	64	36	49	51	55
Cameroon	66	34	50	50	69
Malaysia	66	34	50	50	69
Comoro	67	33	50	50	72
Sudan	69	31	51	49	71
Somalia	70	30	46	54	68
Pakistan	72	28	52	48	69
Senegal	75	25	50	50	71
Mauritania	76	24	49	51	72
Sierra Leone	76	24	49	51	70
Indonesia	78	22	50	50	68
Gambia	79	21	49	51	71
Maldives	79	21	53	47	74
Nigeria	80	20	49	51	69
Guinea	81	19	50	50	69
Chad	82	18	48	52	67
Mali	83	17	49	51	69
Afghanistan	84	16	52	48	71
Benin	85	15	49	51	69
Bangladesh	85	15	52	48	71
Guinea Bissau	86	14	48	52	70
Niger	86	14	49	51	73
North Yemen	90	10	47	53	69
Bourkina Fasao	92	8	50	50	71
Oman	93	7	51	49	71
Uganda	88	11	51	49	71

The Muslim media's reach to non-urban males is insignificant. Events concerning these social groups are not considered newsworthy. A survey of twenty-five Muslim periodicals in twelve countries conducted in 1986 revealed that rural events accounted for 7 per cent of the contents, female issues for 2 per cent and youth for less than 4 per cent.[1]

At present the increasing literacy rate coupled with improved transportation and communications in many Muslim countries have made it possible for the media to attract new readers. But reading habits take time to stabilize. In the formative stages if children and young people are introduced to publications that satisfy their needs and curiosity, they will become a larger periodical readership in the future.

Even though only a small minority in Muslim countries is literate in English, a large proportion of newspapers are published in English. The reasons are various: the influence of English colonialism, the need for a lingua franca in linguistically fragmented societies, prestige. In a 1982 world survey of sixty-one editors in fifty-two countries by Unesco, it was found that in varying degrees most indicated that their English-language publications enjoyed a definite advantage, prestige and influence over vernacular papers. The most important economic reason for the continued success of the English-language press in the Muslim world is its connection with advertising. Those who can read English are on an average far wealthier than those who can not. There is a strong link between elitism, Westernization and commercialism.

Information Sources

The news media in the Muslim world are dependent for their news coverage directly and indirectly on international media, including the four news giants, United Press International (UPI), Agence France-Presse (AFP), Associated Press (AP) and Reuters. Forty-two Muslim countries have their own news agencies, but they put out no more than one thousand words every twenty-four hours. In ex-French colonial Africa, which had been treated by France as an extension of the mother country, France has set up news agencies that are bound by contract with AFP to distribute automatically and immediately without omission or qualification the radio teletype service received from AFP.

There are plans to lessen the dependence of Muslim news media on Western sources. The Organization of Islamic Conference (OIC) established the International Islamic News Agency (IINA) in 1979. The general assembly of IINA consists of news agencies of all Muslim countries and claims to transmit 10,000 to 12,000 words daily. It also circulates a daily summary of news in Spanish to Latin American countries and has plans to set up its own telecommunication system.

The agency so far has failed to become an alternative to the existing foreign news agency channels. Although it has established 24-hour satellite links with the national news agencies of Indonesia and Malaysia, its ouput is hardly reflected in national newspapers. A survey conducted in 1986 found that most Arabic, English, Persian and Urdu newspapers in twelve Muslim countries used the four big Western news agencies for more than 90 per cent of their news about Muslims, whether in Muslim majority or minority countries. IINA was given an ambitious task: to consolidate and safeguard the rich cultural heritage of the Muslim world, to work for greater understanding among the Muslims, to foster closer relations among member states, to promote professional contacts and technical co-operation among news agencies of the member states, to create a full fledged news agency with its own regional centres. Unfortunately, IINA had great technical and financial difficulties.

Almost every Muslim country has its national news agency, and some have more than one.[2] In Lebanon there were twenty-six private news agencies at the end of 1984, in Turkey, seven and Pakistan, Indonesia and Bangladesh each had more than one. The oldest news agency, established in 1936, is in Iran.

Only a few news agencies maintain offices in other Muslim countries, but some have offices in such Western capitals as London or Paris. But in the Muslim press, hardly any news items on either Muslim countries or the West are attributed to Muslim countries news agencies.

The big four foreign news agencies are present in Muslim countries in a significant way. 70 per cent of the foreign press bureaus in Muslim countries belong to western news agencies. The number of Muslim countries news agencies is hardly 5 per cent of the total. The strong presence of the western news agencies make them the sole distributor of news about the Muslim world. Thus they are the main sources of information for the Muslim world media. Even the Muslim media has to rely on them for hard news.

Media in Muslim countries rely on other sources of news in addition to the various news agencies: foreign correspondents, foreign radio and television broadcasts, foreign publications such as *Time* and *Newsweek* and foreign embassies news bulletins.

In the West, the international news agencies emerged when the media began to change from party organs to mass circulation commercial enterprises. The media needed new sources of information. The high cost of news collection forced many of the papers to join together to form

Table 3.   *Foreign News Bureaus in Muslim Countries*

Agency	Countries
Reuters	27
Agence France-Presse	19
Associated Press	15
United Press International	14
Agenzia Nazionale Stampa Associatia	18
Allgemeine Deutsche Nachrichtendienst	8
Agence EFE (Spain)	10
Jiji Tsushin-Sha	2
Tsashiki (Japan)	3
TASS	23
Deutsch Presse-Agentur	6
Bulgarska Telegrafitscheka Agentzia	3
Ceskoslovenska Tiskova Kancelar	4
Polska Agencja Prasowa	7
Xinhua	9
Pan African News Agency	1
Agence de Presse Senegalaise	1
International Islamic News Agency	1
Iraqi News Agency	1
Middle Eastern News Agency	3
Saudi Press Agency	1
Syrian News Agency	2
Taiwanese News Agency	2
Prensa Latina	1
Telegrafska Agenciya Nova Jugoslavija	4
WMA (Morocco)	1
Unicom (USA)	1
Press Trust of India	1

International News Agency, 1984

news agencies, and they in turn created a world-wide news network. For instance, Baron de Reuter signed up most of the London dailies as clients for his service of foreign news before 1860.

The Muslim world has not had the financial resources to create an international wire service. Also, most national news agencies are government controlled, which means that the news agencies have to abide by strict policy guidelines that are determined by political factors. Moreover, the media in most Muslim countries have yet to acquire the characteristics of a client-oriented enterprise. As a result there is no demand on the media for better news coverage of the Muslim world; it therefore takes what is available and makes little effort to generate its own sources of information.

Table 4. *International News Agencies By Country*
N, National news agency
BF, Big four news agencies
OW, Other Western news agencies
SC, Socialist countries news agencies
TW, Third World news agencies
MC, Muslim countries news agencies

Countries	N	BF	OW	SC	TW	MC
Bahrain	1976	x	x	x	x	x
Iraq	1959	x	3	1	x	x
Kuwait	1976	3	x	2	x	x
Qatar	1975	x	x	x	x	x
S. Arabic	1970	x	x	x	x	1
UAE	1977	1	1	x	x	x
Egypt	1956	4	3	2	1	x
Jordan	1965	3	1	1	1	1
Libya	1965	1	2	1	x	x
Lebanon	1966	4	2	4	x	2
North Yemen	1970	x	x	x	x	x
South Yemen	1968	x	x	2	x	x
Syria	1965	1	3	1	x	x
Sudan	1946	1	x	1	x	3
Algeria	1961	4	2	2	x	2
Morocco	1959	3	2	x	x	x
Tunisia	1961	4	1	4	x	x
Gambia	*	2	x	1	x	1
Gabon	1961	x	x	x	x	x
Comoro	x	2	x	x	x	x
Cameroon	1960	2	x	2	x	x
Chad	1964	3	x	x	x	x
Guinea	1960	x	x	2	x	x
Mali	1961	2	x	3	x	x
Mauritania	x	1	1	x	x	x
Niger	x	3	2	x	x	x
Nigeria	1978	3	3	2	x	x
Senegal	1959	4	2	3	1	x
Sierra Leone	1980	4	x	2	x	x
Somalia	1961	x	1	x	x	x
Bourkina Fasso	1963	4	x	x	x	x
Uganda	x	2	x	x	x	x
Pakistan	1948	4	1	3	1	x
Bangladesh	1972	2	x	1	x	x
Maldives	x	x	x	x	x	x
Brunei	x	x	x	x	x	x
Indonesia	1937	4	3	1	x	x
Malaysia	1967	4	1	2	2	x
Afghanistan	1973	x	x	3	1	x
Iran	1936	1	1	2	1	x
Turkey	1953	4	2	5	1	x

Content

Although newspapers and magazines in Muslim countries appear in all subjects — politics, history, economics, film, sports, agriculture, trade, medicine, engineering, industry — not every periodical can be classified as Muslim media from an Islamic perspective. In general the media in the Muslim world is secular and nationalist in its orientation. It tries to adapt itself to the dominant core of Western journalism influenced by an international secular culture, though often without fulfilling the role of a free liberal press. Most of these periodicals are loyalist and conformist, by and large conciliatory to governments.

There are, however, publications that believe in the power of media to influence events from an Islamic perspective. *Urwatul-Wusqa*, edited by Jamaluddin Afghani, which ran for eighteen issues in Paris in the last century, set a trend that has continued to influence the Muslim media. There are now about 500 periodicals in the Muslim world which are oriented to Islam. It is sometimes argued that not many of them follow Islamic principles in presenting everyday events; nevertheless, they are essentially Muslim so far as their contents are concerned. Some are religious, others are ideological. Some have confined themselves to Muslim issues of a defined geographical boundary, whereas others address the larger *ummah*.

Muslim media are greatly influenced by the Islamic movements and organizations that emerged in the middle of this century. They fall into three major categories. A few are produced by small groups of individuals acting independently of any formal Muslim group or party. The other two categories are formally attached to an organization or party. One consists of publications from such organizations as Jamat-e-Islami, Ikhwan-ul-Muslimeen and the World Muslim League, or publications of other ad hoc groups representing Muslim organizations or movements. The third category includes publications not usually associated with any Muslim group or party, but which in general have a sympathetic attitude towards Muslim groups and parties.

Most Muslim publications lack appropriate commercial prospects. Advertising revenue and mass-circulation sales are negligible. The short supply of newsprint, printing costs, limitations on distribution through political differences and poor domestic and international transport facilities work against the magazines becoming profitable. But lack of money alone does not account for the failure of many Muslim publications. A publication still needs articles and news stories. As most Muslim periodicals lack original sources of information, they fall back on a material that is historical in nature and has no practical relevance to the present-day world.

All too often a periodical is organized and written by one or two people; their deaths, departure or disillusionment set the seal on the disappearance of the publication itself. Despite the poor record of Muslim media in a commercial sense the optimism of Muslim journalists is still high. Undeterred by their own lack of experience, Muslim media people continue to pour money into failing ventures. They seemingly insist on the most unreal calculations: 'if only 50,000 would give just a dollar a month', is their eternal prayer.

This prayer was most loudly heard in the Jakarta conference of Muslim media people where several recommendations were put forward to make the Muslim media a dynamic force in the world. It was proposed that Islamic universities should set up Islamic journalism departments, an Islamic news agency should be activated and daily, weekly and monthly publications should be brought out in the different languages from all Muslim countries. It was also recommended that an advertising firm should be established, a secretariat for Islamic media should be set up at Makkah and a supreme council for Islamic mass media should be formed.

It was assumed by Muslims that their media is mainly for a Muslim readership and if the commercial side is taken care of they would overcome all the problems they are facing. This assumption needs to be reviewed in the light of developments in the modern media world.

The effectiveness of Muslim media in the future will depend on the role that it determines for itself in the context of the world media and *ummah*. Should it always remain dependent on the existing world media or should it evolve its own sources of information? Should its appeal be confined to Muslims or should it be addressed to the world in general? At present the Muslim world media does not have any specific direction. It tries to perform an active role, but it lacks resources. The Muslim media that claims to work according to Islamic principles is so weak that it can not influence the media in the Muslim world. Unless the Muslim media take a lead in the development of alternate sources of information within an Islamic framework, and unless they show a willingness to accommodate such neglected social groups as young people, women, children and rural populations in its content, they will remain confined to a small, elitist audience without any practical relevance to Muslim people in particular and the world in general.

Such a shift in emphasis could result in the production of apolitical periodicals dedicated to specific social groups. It may also give rise to technical and educational journalism.

The Muslim media ought to contribute significantly to the development of the new information order, especially in generating alternate information sources within the Islamic framework. Such development is important not only from an Islamic perspective but from the professional perspective as well. Many of the acceptable techniques of modern journalism are repugnant from an Islamic viewpoint. Spying and seeking to confirm suspicion is forbidden in Islam, as are slander and backbiting. An information organ based on these principles can only create tension and instability.

The development of alternative sources of information is important not only to sustain an independent and dynamic news media in the Muslim world but also to break the news monopoly of the big four news agencies. No inter-governmental body can perform this function effectively: although they have tried they have so far failed to evolve a news-gathering system which can compete with existing world information systems and which can produce news in an Islamic framework. Independent structures of news gathering need to be established to improve upon the work carried out by the existing channels.

How can Muslim media develop alternative sources of information? An integrated approach is required, under which all aspects — editorial content, planning, production, advertising, marketing, distribution — should be examined. A core group of Muslim media people from various countries could serve as a media think tank, and could work in close co-operation with those who are active in other fields.

Media Resources

Studies on Muslim media are virtually non-existent. Single-country studies might be sponsored initially in those countries where there is a long media tradition. Studies on world media structure from an Islamic perspective are also important, to develop an understanding of the world media and their dynamics and to provide an Islamic critique of the mdoern media.

A reference directory of Muslim media and media people would provide a basis for world-wide or regional co-operation. An exhaustive bibliography of existing literature on Muslim world media should be compiled in different languages. Also a review of existing press laws in Muslim countries would aid the understanding of media-government relations.

As there is no single book on Islamic or Muslim media that can serve as a basic text book, these studies might be used as basic literature in universities and departments of journalism.

National Press Archives

Many Muslim periodicals have maintained for their own use a comprehensive, often exhaustive, library of clippings, documents and books, collections laboriously created and expensively maintained. Muslim periodicals might pool their resources to form a press archive at national level, the purpose of which would be to search out, collect, collate and make available primary source material on a national scale. In time, the scope of this archive could be widened to feature references from sources other than the regular channels. It might also preserve portraits, cartoons, posters, promotional puffs, sales charts and advertising rate cards.

National and International Photographic Libraries

Muslim media often lack relevant pictures of people, places and events. National and international photographic libraries would help the Muslim media, while marketing their collections to other institutions. National photographic libraries can help develop regional and international photographic libraries.

Media Courses

Long- and short-term foundation and refresher courses on media management, marketing, advertising, production and copy writing might be organized by Muslim media in co-operation with Islamic universities and departments of journalism.

International Media Monitoring Group

An international monitoring group could assess press–government relations, monitor press censorship and human rights of media people. It could also monitor the non-Muslim media's coverage of Islam. Such groups have been established in some countries, but due to the lack of adequate resources their effect is insignificant.

News and Feature Agencies

Most crucial is the formation of independent news and feature agencies. At present there are more than forty government-sponsored national agencies, but they are governed more by political than journalistic ethics. Independent news and feature agencies should be developed as complementary institutions to the already existing news agencies. Not many officials or many newspapers and magazines would be prepared to take the risk of encouraging such independence. However, without an independent news gathering and disseminating system, the Muslim media cannot develop alternate sources of information at national and international levels.

The agencies need to emphasize the coverage of Muslim minorities and non-Muslims. The Muslim minorities are neglected: little is known about Muslims in Bhutan, Nepal, Mozambique, South America and Western Europe. Similarly, not much information is available about non-Muslim societies.

Marketing and Distribution

Most Muslim periodicals have small audiences because of poor marketing and distribution systems. Air freight is expensive, returns are low and there is no guarantee that copies will reach their targeted destinations. Existing Muslim media can help develop a national and international distribution network involving Muslim organizations and youth groups.

Advertisements

No periodical can live on sales and subscriptions alone. Should the Muslim media function commercially as do similar publications in the West and sell advertising space? In such cases the periodicals are under commercial pressures; editors and journalists are encouraged to write for readers rather than for themselves. They are encouraged to watch their costs and improve their efficiency. But management may be more concerned with the profit margins than with quality. The market economics may become so significant that the original goals are lost. In the Muslim media the concept of market-based media is still in its infancy. Advertising revenue can ease the financial burden, but how can it be raised?

The circulation of Muslim journals has always remained a closely guarded secret. Without specifying the circulation, only a few advertisers will be willing to risk their money. Could the Muslim media develop a circulation audit bureau to act as liaison between advertisers and periodicals?

Organization

What sort of organizational structure would suit the Muslim media? This question is rarely discussed in depth. The common practice is for an organizational structure to be created and then for the people to be appointed to fill the various roles. An ad hoc mentality dominates the organizational pattern of most Muslim periodicals. The issue should be carefully examined.

Conclusion

There is a need to distinguish between Muslim countries or Muslim-related media and the Muslim media. The latter, rooted in religion and ideology, has the potential and enthusiasm to develop a new information order and influence media development in the Muslim world. The future planning of the Muslim media will have to take account of the overall strategy for the *ummah*.

The Muslim media world does not lack in either material or human resources. Their consolidation may improve the status, but the Muslim media must give priority to developing alternate sources of information.

At present the Muslim media is mainly elitist. Its interaction with young people, females, and the rural populace is almost non-existent. The media must diversify itself in order to evolve new styles of communication suitable to the needs of various social groups.

Little literature is available on the subject of Muslim media. There is a need to undertake single-country media studies in order to help Muslim media evolve a development strategy.

An integrated approach is required to plan the Muslim media. The existing Muslim media should come together at national and regional levels to set up institutions useful for the development of Muslim media. The co-operation in setting up news agencies, distribution networks, advertising firms, press archives and photographic libraries would ensure that Muslim people in particular and the world in general receive a better coverage of newsworthy events. The Muslim media institutions at national and international levels could work more effectively if they are guaranteed freedom from government and other official interference. The recommendations adopted at the first Islamic media conference need to be reviewed and implemented for the future development of media in the Muslim world.

Notes

1. The survey was conducted as part of the research which has been submitted to the Graduate Centre of Journalism, City University, London.
2. Gambia, Niger, Brunei and the Maldives did not have national news agencies in 1984 when the data was prepared.

Urban Grapevines
Establishing Community Newspapers

Abdul Wahid Hamid

During the past three decades large concentrations of Muslims have established roots in almost every city in the West, often in the more depressed parts. Now that they are no longer transient communities, a feeling of permanence has slowly but unmistakeably taken hold. Britain, France, Germany, Holland, Canada and the United States are each now the home of thousands, often millions, of Muslims. They are not simply the outposts for emigré workers or foreign students, but include a growing number of indigenous Muslims in every country.

Urban Muslims are affected by all the problems and pressures of high density living: urban decay, deprivation, poor housing, unemployment, underemployment, racial harassment, violence and low educational amenities and standards. Recently, a paper on Muslim Turks in Germany remarked that many live in accommodations that not even dogs will occupy. In spite of these conditions, many individuals and families, through hard work and struggle, have managed to improve their living conditions. There are signs of tremendous dynamism, both at the individual and the community levels. There is a great deal of entrepreneurial drive: a wide range of business enterprises and services are operated by Muslims, many are involved in manufacturing, an increasing number are visible in the professions (medicine, law, accountancy), a few are journalists or teachers and some are in local government and the civil services.

At the community level, there is also a great deal of activity. There are mosques and prayer places in almost every vicinity, although many still travel long distances for congregational prayers. There are evening and week-end supplementary schools for children, women's groups, youth groups and study circles. There are a number of professional associations — teachers, doctors, social scientists and, increasingly, special interest organizations concerned with such issues as human rights, Muslim aid, media monitoring and education. The activities of many of these groups are often carried on in isolation from one another, their activities often known only to a few. They could obviously benefit from knowing what is going on elsewhere and from publicizing their work regularly and effectively.

Although Muslims in urban areas usually live in close proximity to other Muslims, they are often afflicted by the isolation and alienation that goes hand-in-hand with urban industrial living. People often do not know who their neighbours are. If they live one street apart, they are like aliens to one another. The normal sources of care, support and guidance that are available in traditional societies, such as the extended family and close neighbourly ties, are not always available in urban settings. Alternative sources of support must be developed to cope with the crushing alienation that many experience.

Muslims are only now awakening to the interplay of social and political forces, realizing that they are not only at the receiving end of local or national politics but that they can actively contribute. Still, there is a great deal of ignorance and apathy; in Britain, for example, a sizeable number of Muslims have not put their names on the electoral register. This fact is of crucial significance in political constituencies where Muslims are concentrated, but especially where they are in the majority.

The Need for Effective Communication

For any community to function with a sense of cohesion and purpose, there is need for effective communication. Community growth and development are interactive processes, and effective communication between people and groups with different interests and skills is a prerequisite for co-ordinated action towards defined goals. People must be aware of the issues, the policies and the trends that affect them directly. On the basis of information and knowledge, they must then seek to influence policies, open areas of special concern, and direct trends in a way that will preserve and strengthen their institutions and make for the stable growth of their communities. These are some of the areas that a good community newspaper can be expected to support.

The existing channels of communication are woefully inadequate at best and non-existent at worst. Some mosques or community groups issue circulars and newsletters. There are some newspapers targeted to particular language groups — Arabic-speaking, Urdu and Turkish, for example, each with a particular 'ethnic' constituency. There are intellectual magazines or journals with an international and mainly political focus and with too-limited a circulation to have any major impact on the needs and direction of communities. Of course, there are other forms of communication — oral communication in the form of meetings and lectures, for example — which are effective and necessary in their own way. However, any literate society must depend on the written and printed word and newspapers in particular have an importance in urbanized, mechanized society which cannot be ignored.

Purposes and Functions of a Community Newspaper

A good community newspaper can serve a variety of purposes. It can inform the community of events, activities and developments taking place within the community, perhaps through listings of events — courses, lectures, meetings, youth-group programmes, women's activities, children's activities, madrasahs. Through profiles, interviews and reports, it can bring people leading activities closer to the general public so as to produce greater rapport between imams, leaders or activists and the general community. A community newspaper can provide information on civic and other matters of particular interest to the Muslim community: for example, what goes on in local and national government, in schools and workplaces. It can cover policies, decisions and opportunities relating to civic matters, training schemes, employment opportunities that are available but go unnoticed. Muslims are often disadvantaged because they do not know how local government operates and how they can participate. It can also provide a forum for discussing and, where necessary, campaigning for issues affecting the Muslim community in particular: the provision of amenities; facilities at schools, workplaces and hospitals; Muslim representation on education committees and boards; and a host of other areas where a Muslim presence is necessary and without which the Muslim case will definitely be lost, not by discrimination or bias, as is often assumed, but by default.

In order to avoid all the problems associated with ghetto communities, a local Muslim community newspaper must discuss and, where necessary, campaign for issues affecting the wider populace — environmental issues, problems of inner-city decay, employment, violence and falling moral standards and other social issues. This stance must come from genuine concern for the human condition, not for our own immediate community alone, but for others afflicted by harm or exposed to injustice, as well.

A local newspaper should expect to promote Muslim businesses and entrepreneurs by encouraging Muslims to buy or support their products and services. This important function of a community newspaper will help generate and keep economic wealth within the community so far as is possible and will eventually help in the provision of employment. The promotion of economic self-sufficiency in a community is crucial when considering the economic imperatives of *dawa*. The newspaper can act as a medium for advertising Muslim products and services as one of its major functions, especially since advertisements will provide a substantial part of its running costs. A community newspaper should, of course, not lose sight of the interests of the consumer and should not encourage crass materialism or conspicuous consumption.

A community newspaper can perform the function of a watchdog within the community, somewhat analogous to the functions of a muhtasib in a traditional Muslim society. Unfortunately, many within Muslim communities or who have Muslim names do not live up to Islamic ideals of behaviour and create a negative impression of Muslims that reflects on all members of the community. While not seeking 'to wash dirty linen in public', a community paper should be objective enough to give appropriate coverage to trends, developments and actions on the part of individuals or groups that are inimical to the well-being of the community. Parallel to the function of watchdog, the paper can also provide guidance and advice from an Islamic standpoint and counselling services to people who live in urban society and are desperately in need of various forms of help. Cases relating to parent-children tensions, domestic violence, racial harassment, mental illnesses — from which Muslims are not immune and, in fact, in certain areas may be particularly prone to — may come in this category.

Promoting Excellence and Training

A community newspaper is well-placed to give recognition to achievement as an encouragement to others to pursue excellence in all fields. Coverage of such activities as a group engaged in charitable work, a mother involved in neighbourhood or community outreach programmes or a student doing well at school will follow the Quranic injunction 'vie with one another in good works'. Up-to-date listings of educational and leisure activities, especially for the young — places to visit, things to do, competitions to enter, books to read — will encourage creative work and creative play. Of particular importance to growing communities will be career guidance, to the young in particular, bearing in mind the aptitudes of individuals, the opportunities available in the community and the needs and interests of the Muslim community. For example, in many parts of the urban developed world, there is a critical need for Muslims to enter the teaching profession. There are many schools where over 90 per cent of the students are Muslims. If graduates in the range of primary- and secondary-school subjects are encouraged to undertake postgraduate courses in education with a view to staffing such schools, we could have *de facto* Muslim schools in many areas. After the proper assessment of the needs of a community, newspapers should vociferously encourage persons to take up careers in critical fields.

Establishing a community newspaper will act as a training ground for young Muslim journalists — reporters, photographers, graphic artists, editors and subeditors. It is important that skills — of journalism and other communication skills, of administration, of business, of caring — be acquired by young Muslims at an early age. In fact, many a brilliant idea or scheme is bungled because of the absence of appropriate and often elementary skills. In this regard, I have always felt that any Muslim who cannot run a small office efficiently cannot be expected to run an organization, let alone complex institutions such as government departments and ministries. We need skills, as the Prophet himself often impressed upon us; for example, he offered prisoners of war taken at Badr their freedom on condition they taught Muslims to read and write.

One of the added advantages of having a network of good community newspapers is that they can provide the training ground and eventually the raw news for national and international Muslim papers. International Muslim papers do not have enough grassroot or original sources of news. They depend on the international news agencies for their coverage; much of their writing is a conjuring art which derives substance and inspiration from such secondary sources as newspaper clippings. The result is often a preoccupation with issues highlighted by others for their own benefit, while Muslim issues lose out by default, and over which few influences can be exerted.

Clearly, the function of a good community paper will not be as a purveyor of mass, inert information. It should essentially be a rallying point for concerted action, not be a case of read and be gratified or intellectually stimulated. It will be a case of read and participate, attend, advise, buy, sell, organize, study, write, travel, gather, pray, play, pay, lobby, support, co-ordinate, donate, care for, unite!

The Prerequisites of a Community Newspaper

A good community newspaper should be an independent paper, wedded to the interests of the community, not be tied to any particular organization or group. To perform its functions well, it must be financially independent, for too often the integrity of a venture is compromised by financial strings or yokes.

Because of the polyglot nature of the new Muslim communities, a good community newspaper should serve the interests of the entire community and be published in the language of the country, not in that of a section of the community. The diversity of the community should, however, be reflected in the composition of the editorial, production and marketing sectors of the paper.

A good community newspaper should not narrowly or exclusively focus on Muslim affairs. It should regard it as important, even a duty, to look at wider issues in the wider society, not with only a view to being critical but also to being supportive. It should generally promote the good and campaign against the reprehensible, for the future of these Muslim communities is closely bound up with the future of the wider society. As the stability and well-being of the wider society is a benefit to Muslims, so is the instability and decadence a threat: 'when danger threatens, it threatens all alike'.

The newspaper must guard against too much preaching in a blatant, unsophisticated way. It should not editorialize in long sermons, nor should it always assume that Muslims are being discriminated against or that Islam is under fire, though in fact that may be so. It should not adopt a strident, carping tone, for Islam is reasonable and is accessible through reason. Finally, the newspaper should carry the stamp of professionalism. Since its avowed goal is to seek excellence in the community, it should also be dedicated to the pursuit of excellence — in the balanced nature of its coverage, in the quality of its writing and design, in the soundness of its leading articles and in its business management.

Launching a Community Newspaper

The paper must first have adequate financial support, from institutions, from individual investors, from individuals establishing a foundation or from co-operative enterprises of individuals and organizations. However, no individual, group or organization must be allowed to dictate editorial policy.

There should be a proper selection and training of staff. Prospective writers, reporters and editorial staff should have a good knowledge and understanding of Islam and competent journalistic skills. Production and design people should have a grasp of state-of-the-art newspaper setting and design. Computer technology has revolutionized the newspaper industry. The easy availability and comparative cheapness of personal computers and their linking with powerful image-setters have contributed to making newspaper and magazine production easier and quicker. A professional community newspaper would employ such technology and writers and reporters who are computer-literate.

It may be necessary to organize computer courses in the pre-publication phase of the newspaper, and continuously thereafter in order to assure that staff are aware of the latest developments. In addition, there ought to be courses on maintaining archives and documentation, and on management and business skills. Most importantly, there should be courses on Islam as it relates to the goals of human life and the processes of human interaction, such as 'encouraging the good and combatting the reprehensible', and 'co-operating on the basis of righteousness and God-consciousness and not on the basis of sin and transgression'. In this case, the technical skills acquired will be wedded to the particular *adab* or style required of Islam and the direction we desire the community and society to adopt.

There must be sound and mature editorial direction and sound business practices. To be commercially viable, the newspaper should be based in an area of a potentially large readership, which is what makes the large urban concentrations of Muslims sensible targets. In today's world it is easier to produce a newspaper than to distribute it. The logistics of distribution must be properly planned. It must be decided whether subscriptions will be sold or whether, as is the case with many community papers, copies will be free. If there are enough advertisers who want to reach the large urban Muslim community, then it may be possible to publish a free paper. There is a very close relationship between the editorial content of a paper, its distribution and its capacity to attract advertising. A good Muslim community newspaper will be one that is probably produced weekly, or at least fortnightly. It will be one which all Muslim families and all members in each family, including parents and children, look forward to read, because it will cover interests and activities that appeal directly to each person of whatever age. If such content is achieved, then a good circulation will be assured, and it will follow that there will be a healthy demand for advertising space.

A successful community newspaper cannot be run on a voluntary basis, but will have a core full-time staff: an editor-in-chief, staff writers, reporters, a graphic designer, production staff, distribution staff, advertising and business managers. There will also be freelance reporters and photographers from schools, organizations and the community at large. There must be a close and effective partnership between the newspaper staff, the community and the wider society.

These suggestions for establishing community newspapers to cater for Muslim urban communities in the West have been made with the underlying assumptions that *dawa* is not only for non-Muslims but must be addressed to Muslims as well; that *dawa* cannot be effective unless Islam in its caring, compassion, justice and beauty is seen as a living reality in the daily lives of Muslims; and that if Muslims project a negative image, they will not attract but repel.

A positive image for Muslims requires a conscious effort on their part to pursue excellence, which is one of the explicit meanings of the word *ihsan* in the saying of the Prophet, 'God has prescribed *ihsan* — proficiency and excellence in [the doing of] everything'. In the creation of a positive image, effective mass communication and training is necessary and thriving community newspapers can make an important contribution to the education, well-being and solidarity of Muslims in their quest for excellence.

We should work towards, and look forward to the launching and maintaining of effective, quality community newspapers with such names as *Muslim London, Muslim New York, The Muslim Mancunian, Muslim Toronto, Frankfurter Muslimische,* and so on. These local newspapers will eventually lead to effective national and international Muslim print media with their feet on the ground and an important place in the shaping of the destiny of Muslims and of mankind.

Serving the Public
Muslim Presence on the Airwaves

Merryl Wyn Davies

This century has seen the greatest expansion in mass communication in human history. We now stand on the threshold of an information explosion that will revolutionize the airwaves. Thanks to fibre optics, satellites, microprocessors and the ever downward spiral in the cost of consumer communication hardware and software, the general public the world over will soon have multiple choice and easier access to a mammoth range of audiovisual, radio and television products. Although radio is the world's most common medium of communication for news, information and entertainment, with television fast catching up on a global scale, there has been little thought, planning or action to establish a Muslim presence in the media or consideration of how distinctively Muslim media could, or should serve the needs of the *ummah*. Without such a debate the opportunities offered by the coming audio-visual revolution will be missed, just as we have missed our chances in the past.

Muslim commentary on the media is a rhetorical extravaganza, full of sound and fury. To date it has generated little by way of Muslim media to serve Muslim audiences; nor has it made serious inroads into the task of broadcasting about Islam to a general audience. In other words, it has signified nothing. It is hard to think of one Islamic or Muslim organization that does not have as one of its objectives the counteracting of the Western media as a top priority. However, beyond reactive outbursts, and some patient, long-term, yet negatively-focused criticism — which can, incidentally, generate some positive side effects — we are a long way from thinking positively about the media.

This discussion is confined to the audio-visual media — radio, television and video. These mass communication channels of today, the broadcast media, reach the largest audiences, and radio and television take up the greatest number of hours spent in leisure activity worldwide. The audiovisual media is also the most frequent target of Muslim diatribes for its misrepresentations of Islam and the Muslims and for its general counterproductive effects on Muslim society. It is deemed a prime gateway through which decadent Western manners destabilize cherished Islamic values. The concern here is not to analyse the media as they exist today; we are deluged with words that, loosely, could be put in that category. Our objective is to try to assemble some Islamic conceptual referrants that will enable us to think constructively about the objectives, functions and ethical restraints of a distinctively Muslim media. We are seeking a frame of reference for the media of Muslim countries and communities. This framework should also give practical direction to Muslims working in the media and to those who have the means to invest in media infrastructure. Two questions are posed throughout: what role does Islam have for the media? what kind of media, in terms of organization and content, could Islam prompt us to provide for the *ummah*? Given the absence of debate, ours is a tentative, exploratory outline that we hope will initiate a more pertinent and practical debate on the Muslim media in the future.

The Basic Premises of Broadcasting

The basic premise of the Islamic framework turns out to be rather surprising. The Muslim *ummah* is charged by the Quran with an unequivocal obligation. The very definition of our community is a people enjoined to promote the good and prohibit evil (Quran 3:104, 3:110, 9:71), and to achieve this objective by making the Message of Islam available to the whole of mankind at all times and in all places. This definition has always been the basis of the discussion of *dawa*, invitation to Islam, as a basic duty of each male and female Muslim as an individual and a collective responsibility of the community through its representative organizations and institutions. The word 'broadcast' simply means to disseminate widely. The technology of the broadcast media make them the most effective means of widely disseminating information. Therefore it is not in any way far fetched to state that there should be a natural affinity between Muslims and the broadcast media. Perhaps it might be better phrased by saying the broadcast media should be an opportunity that naturally attracts Muslims because of its ability to facilitate an inescapable obligation laid upon us.

There are other basic premises, derived from the Quran, that should inform our thinking about broadcasting. The Muslim *ummah* is directed to be a knowledge-based, information-rich community. None of the objectives and purposes of the Quran are promulgated without the invocation to reflect, to think, to acquire knowledge about ourselves and the world around us so as better to comprehend and thereby fulfill the message of Islam. We know also the insistent emphasis Prophet Muhammad gave to education, the acquisition and sharing of knowledge; indeed, the Prophet placed the sharing of knowledge as the most blessed of human activities. We could further point to the Quranic verse which states that Muslims, as a community, are those whose affairs are decided by counsel among themselves (43:38). This led Caliph Umar to order all Companions of the Prophet to preach whatever they wished in the public mosque of Medina but never to allow themselves to become centres of different circles. In the Quran it is *al nas*, the people, or the nation as a whole, who are the object, the audience, as well as the arbiters of knowledge and information, the makers of decision by consensus, for in Islam the people are ultimately individually responsible before God for how they respond to the call of Islam. Without sound knowledge and information the ability to act responsibly is impaired.

Further, we should consider that the purpose of human existence is achieving submission to God, Islam, and exercising this submission through *ibadah*, acts of worship, obedience and service to God as set out in His guidance to mankind, the Quran. The process of *ibadah* involves conscious intention, knowledge and publication through action. Conscious intention is the inward, private, individual motivation; knowledge pertains both to individual accumulation of knowledge and the existence of collective provision for access to information and knowledge, while the concluding phase of *ibadah* is properly termed a publication since it is a means by which an individual intention of submission to God is made visible in the activity of an individual who can only exist as part of a community. *Ibadah* is an act of awareness that is impossible without knowledge and its instrument, information. Its effect is to broadcast through action a specific example, an instance of a total, integrative way of life and thought, the *din* of Islam. The objective of *ibadah* is that each and every act of the individual and the community should qualify as *ibadah*.

As we assemble these basic Islamic premises we begin to fill in the content and constraints which give detail to what we could call the founding principle, the broadcast nature of Islamic existence. We are also enumerating the conceptual referents of the Islamic worldview, and touching upon the concepts that have been elaborated in the deployment of that worldview in the history of Muslim civilization. Let us go back to the notion of *al nas*, the people. Along with Shariati we feel that *al nas* is a long overlooked basic premise of Islam. Shariati notes that the injunctions and invocations of the Quran are directed to *al nas*, the people.[1] We would suggest that one consequence of this conceptual proposition is that Islam conceives of itself as a mass community, a community of all mankind. We can add to this from numerous Quranic instances and the history of the establishment of the first Muslim community that Islam conceives of community not only as being mass and participatory but also as being heterogenous and diverse.[2] Indeed, the Quran states that if God had so willed He could have made all mankind one community (11:118), yet He chose to create *al nas* as different nations and tribes (49:13), with different colours and tongues (30:22). Therefore, the Islamic conception of mass participatory community includes the notion of diversity and heterogeneity within it as a purposive element whose constructive meaning it is our duty to understand and properly operate. The Quran is replete with normative values for the ways in which relations between diverse sections of *al nas* should be conducted. This extends from the clear statement that Muslims must not revile what pagans do, lest they in despite revile God (6:105), to the oft repeated phrase that *dawa*, invitation to Islam, should be conducted with wisdom and gracious argument (16:125). Furthermore, the overriding normative principle expressed in the Quran is that the objective of relations between the diverse and heterogeneous sections of *al nas* should be to fulfill one of the earthly purposes of Islam itself, that is to bring forth right action, good conduct on the part of the entire *al nas* (5:48). Could one paraphrase and say that right action and good conduct, from the moral and ethical standpoint of Islam, is achieveable as a social phenomenon even within a diverse and heterogeneous humanity where all people do not answer the call to Islam? Surely we would be correct in surmising from the Quranic referents and the example of the first Muslim community under the guidance of Prophet Muhammad and the Rightly Guided Caliphs that establishing the social infrastructure of justice and equity for all of *al nas* is not something that begins solely with or is dependent upon acceptance of Islam by all of the people. It is the inescapable duty of the believer to share the benefits of belief with all other people. Establishing the social reality of the exemplary Islamic existence was a principal means by which the Prophet himself broadcast the meaning of the Message of Islam.

It might appear that we have strayed a long way from opening a practical debate on radio and television in the modern world. Our argument is quite the reverse. So far Muslims have reacted to audio-visual broadcasting as its technology and techniques have been devised and developed in the West and imported into Muslim countries. They have often reacted emotionally merely to aspects of its content. More seriously, many attempts to define Islamic guidelines that can directly or indirectly be applied to the media in the modern world have also been reactive. They consist of stating certain propositions of the Islamic framework which can be taken to pertain to broadcasting as it exists today. Here I would cite the references to freedom of expression included in every attempt to formulate a modern Islamic constitution and specifically the section relating to the media in the model Islamic constitution drawn up by the Islamic Council of Europe.[3] Such isolates drawn from the Islamic framework undoubtedly will be applied to making policy and operating the media by Muslims. But the media remains that conventional product of Western civilization that exists today. What we have not done is to go back to the Islamic premises to examine not a few moral guidelines for amending or reforming the activity of the media as currently constituted but to recover those conceptual referents that would lead us to define what the media should be, what functions it should perform within the Islamic conception of community, what its objectives should be and those means that are best suited to enable its organization and content to fulfill these objectives and designated functions. Our argument is that only when we have such a fundamentalist debate, for want of a better word or perhaps to redeem a misappropriated one, can we develop Islamic criteria that will enable us to establish or reformulate the technology, organization and techniques of the broadcast media to suit and support the objectives of an Islamic community today.

If we take the Islamic framework or worldview to be a multidimensional, integrative source of reference, then we must acknowledge that we are dealing with a whole body of premises that are interactive, mutually defining and whose objective is to generate a balanced, harmonious system at the point of operation or the putting into practice of this worldview.[4] Therefore, we cannot take any one premise from the Islamic worldview in isolation and consider its implications and consequences for broadcasting; we need to try to understand the whole range of Islamic premises, postulates and principles in conjunction, in a systematic way, so that we can comprehend the kind of vision of broadcasting they generate and the combination of normative values they offer for the practice of broadcasting, at all levels of the process. As a corollary of this Islamic conceptual approach we cannot, therefore, take broadcasting of audiovisual media simply to mean the end products, the content of programmes that are provided for the audience. We are obliged to look at broadcasting as a process that embraces the science and technology of mass communication, the organization of the institutions that provide the technology of communication as well as employ the personnel who make the programmes, the techniques and contraints of programme-making and the means of distribution of these programmes to the end users, the audience, *al nas*.

The Provision of Broadcasting

Describing radio and television as mass media has caused many people to overlook a basic fact. Broadcasting is a mass medium only at the point of delivery, in terms of the number of people it can reach simultaneously. In its infrastructure and production, broadcasting has always been a restricted — many would argue restrictive — elitist medium. Few people own and can operate the technology that makes programmes and few people can operate and control the production process of the programmes that reaches the mass audience.[5] Despite the sophistry of the arguments about giving people what they want, the power to make choices and determine what people hear and see resides in very few hands. This distinction will become even more complicated with the advent of new technology and its proliferation of channels. It has been argued that more channels will mean greater public access to production of broadcast products, thus changing the existing balance of power. The evidence available so far suggests this rationale is illusory. The realities of financing broadcasting with new technology mean active and concerned citizens can and do make their own locally-based programmes. However, they are largely broadcasting to themselves and their supporters. From an Islamic perspective, such public access is effectively creating separate circles, not ending them, while giving some people a false sense of broadcasting power. Indeed, the whole trend of new technology could be described as a switch to 'narrow casting', concentrating on selected special-interest audiences by fragmenting the mass nature of the audience. Therefore, within the Islamic frame of reference, we urgently need a debate focused not on the content of broadcasting but on the ethical regulatory and legal context in which the organization and provision for the right to broadcast operates.

The means of broadcasting are expensive. Without an infrastructure of transmitters — and in the case of television, an electricity supply — there is no broadcasting.[6] In this the new technology is no different from the old: the cost of laying cable, either above or below ground, is enormous and the cost of putting a satellite into orbit can be more than the total annual budget of many Muslim countries. Should this part of the resource question concern us when virtually all countries in the world now have some infrastructure for broadcasting? Yes, precisely because there is a link between the manner in which this infrastructure is provided and the culture of broadcasting that develops. Our focus of concern should, therefore, be to create a framework of legislation and ethical practice that covers how the existing infrastructure operates and how new infrastructure is developed and made available.

Broadcasting is a duty of the *ummah*, and it serves the multiple needs of the *ummah*. Therefore, we suggest that resources to fulfill this public duty and service should themselves be public funds, that the technology of broadcasting should be publicly accountable. The justification for allocating large amounts of scarce resources to broadcasting must be public utility, and in Muslim civilization it is the community, in the broadest sense of *al nas*, that is ultimately the arbiter of *istislah*, public welfare. In the vast majority of developing countries, and this includes the bulk of Muslim countries, the infrastructure of broadcasting is state owned; indeed, the broadcasting services are also completely state run. However, here we come upon a significant distinction in Muslim history, where the state is not coterminus with the community, and communal provision of services has never been exclusively the province of the state. The example of *waqqaf*, trusts, which were privately endowed for public purposes is the obvious example. Education, undisputably a communal obligation, was largely financed by *waqqaf* throughout Muslim history so that education was available to all but not dependent upon the state. This historical model gave to education and the intellectuals a necessary independence. In the same way we believe that broadcasting needs a guaranteed independence which is not possible while it is exclusively state owned and run.

There are two points here. First, there can be multiple sources of finance for broadcasting in the Muslim community, but once the infrastructure is created these should become public resources. This would allow for collaborative financing of provision, within and between Muslim communities; those with the resources can fund them, indeed would have an obligation to help provide them for those who lack the necessary resources. Secondly, whoever finances the provision of broadcasting on behalf of the community, there must be a system for establishing public accountability in the way the resources are applied and for setting the regulatory measures that govern their operation. Only when there is a common framework, by which we mean an internationally accepted convention, of regulation and legislation can we be confident about the development of the new technologies, particularly satellites, which have the capacity to broadcast across national boundaries. A regulatory legislative framework common to all aspects of the broadcasting process is essential to harnessing the best potential of an integrated service for the public welfare and to determining how to deal with the diversification of channels new technology can offer. The prime consideration of *istislah*, public welfare, rules out leaving broadcasting either purely to state control or commerical undertakings, whose responsibility is to return a profit on their operations. The commercial system has been tried: an analysis of broadcasting in the United States can be taken as clear evidence that market forces, even within a regulatory context, do not serve the public interest. By its very nature such a system must end up reinforcing the materialist commercial interests they represent.

The Technology of Broadcasting

Accepting broadcasting as a duty and a service to the *ummah* does not imply that the technology of broadcasting that exists has to be accepted wholesale, and imported as it stands. Broadcasting in Muslim communities can be a positive aid to public welfare, but achieving that end requires careful selection and adaptation of technology. Broadcasting needs research and development, which can be done by a specialized centre of excellence funded by Muslim countries collectively, or by an independent non-governmental organization on a *waqf* basis. A Muslim broadcasting research and development agency should assess the available technologies according to an Islamic perspective, undertake its own innovative research and make available its findings for Muslim communities to use. The range of issues would include the cost effectiveness of technology according to a distinctive Islamic definition of values, how well different kinds of broadcasting equipment respond under different climatic conditions, and the environmental impact of broadcast technologies.

Proposing a Muslim broadcasting research and development agency that undertakes Islamic technology assessment is a matter of seeking self-reliance and self-sufficiency for the Muslim community, two necessary Islamic objectives. The aim will be to end the dependency on imported technology. A fundamental failure in thinking about broad-casting is to think its infrastructure is a separate issue from the messages carried on the channels of communication. Only when we begin to subject the technology to the same frame of reference as the messages carried will we stand a chance of creating a genuinely Muslim culture of broadcasting. Without our own technology assessment capacity the overwhelming pressure is to believe that the way things work elsewhere is the way they must operate everywhere.

The Danger of Imitative Inertia

We suffer from a number of impediments to generating our own integrative culture of broadcasting. Imitative inertia is a mind-set that Muslim civilization has itself imposed upon Islam for some centuries. Impairing the capacity to explore the changing world rigorously from the conceptual standpoint of Islam, it seeks to deal with the extant form of things by an imitative imposition of age-old, borrowed judgements, the *taqlidic* approach. Imitative inertia is also a product of fascination with the West of the worst and most self-abnegating kind. It is the product of hero worship at the throne of technical marvels we do not have the capacity to produce ourselves and the naive, and thoroughly misguided belief, that by appropriating the objects we acquire their power. The worst and most pernicious stage of imitative inertia is to believe that the power of machines and the means of utilizing them lie in the way of the thinking that produced them and, hence, continues the dependency upon Western scientific thinking and social practice. This again is a misguided blind alley, for the way of thought that leads to the practice of science and technology and broadcasting is merely a conven-tion, one possible but not the only potential way of structuring ques-tions. This convention is subject to a particular set of constraints per-ceived according to and deriving from an implicit set of values. It is a particular culture in history and its set of values operated by a particular set of people that leads the questions of science, technology and broad-casting to be structured and practised as they are. Overthrowing imitative inertia, through a technology assessment capacity that answers to a different load of values, culture and history is the only way to discover the potential of existing technology and new ways of using it and to become aware of the consequences this technology will have on our own communities. With such awareness a rational choice can be made whether the cost of these consequences is acceptable, tolerable or unsustainable. Where an existing technology is unacceptable, such an assessment process of itself should highlight alternative means of answering our own self-defined objectives; in other words, the assessment process is a stimulation to independent innovation. With imitative inertia we have no choices at all, but can only complain at something we have neither the means nor the wit to improve.

The Duty To Provide Receivers

The infrastructure of broadcasting is normally confined to the means of transmission, leaving the provision of reception out of the discussion. From an Islamic standpoint this is obviously unacceptable. We take broadcasting, mass dissemination, to be a duty because it is a prerequisite of another overriding Islamic duty, that of aiding mass participation, through knowledge and information, in the affairs of the community. It is no good enjoining the duty to public welfare upon the transmission end of the broadcasting equation and subjecting them to public accountability if only an elite few have means of access to receive the broadcasting output. Much of the content of broadcasting in the West, that is programme-making and its whole culture of ideas and attitudes, arose precisely because it began as an elitist medium restricted to those who could pay for receivers; the whole Western broadcasting industry has never overcome attitudes inculcated under those conditions. When the commercial provision for broadcasting reception is considered, we can see that it has done nothing to alter the elitist structure of ownership and control in programme-making; yet, the drive to attract maximum audience numbers drove down standards of programme content to the lowest common denominators of sensationalism and over-simplification, the elitists' arrogance and contempt towards the common people.

Our argument is that for Muslim communities there is an equal and binding duty for ensuring at least a minimum of provision of broadcasting receivers: radios, televisions and video recorders, as a public duty in each community. Without such basic provision the Islamic objective of mass communication for public welfare cannot be achieved: to refer back to Caliph Umar, separate circles are inevitably created within communities. We are not necessarily talking of a radio, television and video recorder in every home, but that these pieces of hardware are essential to the communal objective. Making provision to schools, mosques or centres where the community has access to them throughout the hours of broadcasting is more in line with our conception of basic provision. It is common for *dawa* organizations to provide funds to buy books or to produce books which they distribute. We would simply make the point that, given the incidence of illiteracy in the Muslim world, they might be well advised to switch to purchasing and distributing broadcasting receivers which are less restrictive in their potential use and are essential in helping to prepare the way for a Muslim public service broadcasting system to be put in place.

The Islamic Ethics of Broadcasting

The consequence of the Islamic frame of reference for broadcasting is the existence of a unitary moral and ethical code for all levels of the process, from setting the terms of regulatory legislation to the day-to-day decision-making of programme production. The corollary is that each stage in the process is publicly accountable for responsibly implementing this unitary framework. For example, those who provide the infrastructure have a responsibility for the nature of the messages carried on their equipment. The owners or operators of the infrastructure of broadcasting cannot simply make their facilities available to anyone, any broadcaster, the highest bidder, or favour any special interest group irrespective of the programme content. Making such a unitary framework viable requires compatible structures for the financing and provision of infrastructure, from transmitters to the organizations that make the programmes.

Public Consultation

The prime duty of broadcasting must be to serve the needs of the community, because those priorities are determined by public consultation. It has long been the case that broadcasting has been producer-driven, the limited few who make the programmes give the audience what they, the broadcasters, want to give them or what they, the broadcasters, think the audience wants. Even where broadcasters have been charged with a responsibility for public service broadcasting no corresponding duty to demonstrate that they have engaged in public consultation to determine the nature and priorities of that public service has been included. We are suggesting a new kind of institutional arrangement for public consultation as an essential feature in the operation of Muslim broadcasting services. There will no doubt be many ways in which this obligation to discover the priorities of public needs can be carried out; the details must be left to each country or community to determine for itself according to what is most appropriate for its individual circumstances.

The common principle is that accountability to the audience for meeting its perceived needs in the overall balance of programming through consultative procedures should be enshrined in the legislative framework of broadcasting. Determining the utility of what is broadcast cannot be left to the redundant argument of ratings, when the audience has no means of expressing preferences for programmes they are not offered.

As it is quite likely that professional broadcasters would cringe at the notion of public consultation about programming priorities and since this is something of a new concept, some elaboration is required. What one is trying to guard against is the arrogance of broadcasters who invariably argue that they know best, when what they mean is they have the monopoly of decision-making. We are trying to distinguish two aspects of the decision process broadcasters normally confuse. It is the professional duty of broadcasters to know how to translate publicly determined priorities into the widest range of the most imaginative and effective programmes. That is not the same thing as broadcasters being the best fitted to determine the overall priorities of what the broadcasting service should provide. We are not seeking to tip the balance in the other direction, to a vast bureaucracy of interminable public debate that generates the most boring compromises in programming, or to public representatives who determine the fine print of what appears on each programme: such arrangements are not too far from the present state-run media in many Muslim countries. It merely amounts to substituting one monopoly for another, with an equal degree of arrogance. The usual state monopoly is exercised without benefit of professional expertise and stifles initiative, creativity or imagination on the part of those who work in broadcasting.

It would be foolhardy not to recognize that the public is often not sufficiently informed to be articulate in selecting alternatives that can be made available in programme content or even in imagining the kind of content that might be possible. Consultation is aimed at determining the overall objectives in allocation of broadcasting talent and financing to specific areas of need, such as educational programmes, public-participation programmes, locally-produced programming, provision of programmes for children, programmes on agriculture, health or other special interests. Such consultation should be broad-based, participatory and should include more than the government or elected representatives of a community, who in themselves form a special-interest group well capable of manipulating broadcasting for their own purposes. Consultation is part of institutionalizing responsibility to the public welfare within the structures of broadcasting, the attitudes of broadcasters and the expectations of the audience as a mutual process. Ideally, consultation would provoke broadcasters to be more imaginative in serving the public interest. Ultimately, broadcasters must be responsible and be given the freedom to translate publicly-determined objectives into the most creative programming possible: we cannot legislate creativity, but can only try to establish an appropriate environment that will nurture its development. Broadcasters should be aware that if public consultation is part of the environment that nurtures their creativity, then they have a strong case to argue for the funding necessary to fulfill the demands of the public. It is not uncommon for the audience to have vociferous demands for what they want to see and hear, usually competing, often quite contradictory, and all costing far more than a particular broadcasting service can afford or is capable of providing. Publicly determined priorities are no impediment to high quality and creative programme-making: in quite the reverse, the public should demand only the best and the requisite resources to supply the best. We are proposing that broadcasters should not be alone in making decisions, not proposing that good broadcasting be submerged by the systems regulating its existence.

Consultation must be an on-going process, a permanent fixture of the distinct culture of public-service broadcasting we envision. The public is often unable to articulate its preferences without viewing a number of alternatives, and public tastes and preferences are likely to change with changes in circumstances. Priorities will, therefore, become clearer over time through feedback and audience response through consultation. It is easier for the public to criticize what they get and to express general aspirations than to formulate new options. The environment of consultation should heighten respect for broadcasters, who are those with professional expertise and the imagination to generate new ideas that meet public needs. It is not an environment that denies broadcasters the right to try, to experiment or even to fail. It is merely the creation of a new kind of institutional framework which defines more clearly the values that would guide their efforts and their accountability to the whole of the audience, rather than vociferous, organized and articulate sections of the audience.

But one cautionary tale about the audience. In Britain, Muslims are uniformly critical of the lack of service they receive from the media. One often repeated complaint is that broadcasters do not even announce the sighting of the moon that signals the start of Ramadan. This, in broadcasting terms, is a simple request to accommodate, and on public service grounds and public relations considerations would probably be entertained. However, the same Muslim public that is so critical of broadcasters has never been able to articulate this preference to the broadcasting authorities. Furthermore, the Muslim community in Britain fails to acknowledge even to itself that it is unable to agree among itself on a common procedure for acknowledging the sighting of the moon. British Muslims regularly observe three different dates for these important communal events. The broadcasters make an excellent scapegoat; complaint at someone else is an excellent substitute for the difficulty of tackling a more deep-seated problem that the mere provision of broadcasting facilities could not resolve. Creating a climate of consultation between broadcasters and the public can do much to demystify the alleged power of broadcasting and enable a better public service to result. But responsibility to the public is no recipe for making that public an ideal community or for generating perfect broadcasting.

The Duty To Provide Educational Broadcasting

One function of broadcasting that must be a basic statutory duty, where consultation is a matter of determining what aspects are the greatest priority, is education. The first pillar of Muslim public service broadcasting must be educational broadcasting. We must emphasize that the term educational is not restrictive and must not be taken in a narrow sense of meaning airtime for schools programmes. Certainly audiovisual media have a great role to play in supporting existing schools and higher education, but its potential is far wider than that: community education for all sections of the community, all ages and interests is the kind of duty we mean. To fulfill the obligation to educational broadcasting, a whole range of formats can be employed in broadcasting the widest range of issues and concerns. One British example illustrates how far the educational remit can extend. One of the longest-running radio programmes is a daily saga of country folk called *The Archers*, consciously devised in the years following the Second World War to encourage farmers to adopt new techniques to increase food production. A basic resource in writing the scripts were Ministry of Agriculture circulars, so that amid dramatization of village life there was talk of the best sheep dip, rotation of crops and other such issues. The programme has always been as popular with non-rural audiences as with the farming community.

The duty to educational broadcasting is only partially tapped by Muslim countries at present because the culture of broadcasting they have imported is not atuned to the needs of their communities. Illiteracy is a major scourge in Muslim society and most pernicious among women. Television and video cassettes are one of the best means of extending literacy programmes, particularly to women. Indeed, the video cassette, a pre-recorded programme that can be played on a television receiver time and again is a vast unexplored field for disseminating educational material: it is probably the best means of providing schools broadcasting. The medium can supplement the scarce trained personnel that are a major constraint on all mass educational projects. It is also an effective supplement in the provision of teaching aids. The visual medium of television and video is obviously less exclusive than written material, offering no instant handicap to the illiterate. The other great advantage of broadcasting media is that they can personify and humanize education, whether it be health education, agricultural improvement or community development work. They can express the advantages of new ideas through the experience of ordinary people who can be seen and heard talking for themselves. With imaginative application, existing broadcasting technology and programme formats can be made interactive, a channel for feedback on ideas. Instead of centrally devised wisdom being disseminated without regard to local problems, the wisdom from afar can be adapted to local circumstances and included in the programmes. By such means, broadcasting can help communities participate in policy-making by providing planners with information about how their projects actually work in practice. Nicaragua has used the most basic resources to develop community radio, the cheapest and most accessible of the broadcast media, to serve this kind of community development. At the other end of the spectrum Britain has the Open University, catering for those who want a second chance at higher education, that operates through television.

The Duty To Inform

The duty to educate should go hand-in-hand with the duty to inform. Information is essential to creating the awareness which enables people to participate responsibly in mutual consultation, a prime Islamic objective. The Islamic worldview guarantees freedom of expression, opinion and belief. It regards diversity of opinion as a blessing for the community to be widely broadcast, making it available to everyone so that factionalism is challenged and fragmentation avoided. There are further guidelines for respecting the beliefs of others and discussing with wisdom and gracious argument. The Islamic moral and ethical code for broadcasting information then could be stated as a basic duty to provide information, to represent all diverse points of view with balance and equity, within the confines of respect for which mutual understanding is a prerequisite. Further, Islam argues for equality of opportunity for all members of a community, which would extend to having individual views represented in the broadcasting media.

We view the Islamic moral and ethical framework for broadcasting information as unequivocal. It relies upon the development of conceptual principles long held, elaborated, and often practised by Muslim civilization. It is signally absent in the practice of broadcasting in Muslim society today, and in every other system of broadcasting as well. However, it should be pointed out that some non-Muslim broadcasters get closer to this ideal, even within their limitations, because they at least pay it lip service. We cannot underestimate the real difficulties of establishing this Islamic principle within the culture of Muslim public-service broadcasting in the real world: it strikes at too many vested interests of those who actually operate broadcasting systems. Muslim society is riven by factionalism and sectarianism; vast sections of our populations feel marginalized, excluded and under threat. Our societies swing from one extreme to another and the most difficult path we can conceive of is the middle path of moderation, toleration and mutual understanding, without which there can never be mutual consultation and consensual agreement. It is the Islamic ethic which is the panacea for these ills, not broadcasting; yet we argue that broadcasting according to clearly delineated Islamic ethics can assist our societies in achieving a more balanced and stable existence.

Public-service Broadcasting

It would be naive not to acknowledge that the practice of Muslims, their non-adherence to Islam in the name of Islam, is a real impediment to the kind of Muslim public-service broadcasting ethic for which we are arguing. Far too often Muslims themselves, in their ardent desire to reinstitute Islam as the guiding principle of Muslim society, are in the forefront of intolerance, seeking to suppress those ideas with which they do not agree and which they consider contrary to their conception of Islam. Nowhere in the Muslim media today can we find a balanced and respectful debate among Muslims on diverse opinions about Islam and the contemporary meaning and implication of the Islamic worldview. Such programmes would be the most contentious and most difficult to get broadcast. We thereby delimit any programme-making about Islam to the lowest common denominator of agreed, historically accepted pious statements principally concerned with private morality — the very minimal Islam. While maintaining a core of cultural identity, it perplexes a mass of Muslims and totally confuses non-Muslims who try to understand how an entire communal system can be derived from such minimal propositions. We thereby rigorously avoid any of the delicate questions essential to establishing policy and programmes that will implement Islamic social action and achieve justice and equity. We have no debate on Islamic environmental ethics, medical ethics, economic and consumer issues and a whole range of other topics. Or perhaps it would be more correct to say we have no such debates that reach the mass of Muslims. Our intellectuals inhabit remote enclaves of the conference circuit where they regularly converse among themselves and where even their best and most practical ideas have difficulty percolating down to the level of the ordinary citizen who stands in greatest need. Our populations are therefore vastly uninformed or underinformed about Islam and contemporary Islamic thinking, yet their strong Islamic sentiment makes them the demonstration fodder of Islamic sloganizing that is minimal in its practical content. Worse still, for lack of an informed community, Muslim society is caught on the hook of conniving in the translation of the *ulama* into a clergy, a restricted body of authoritative experts whose own knowledge, essential to the existence of Muslim civilization, is disseminated as isolated pronouncements, not explanatory arguments. Irrespective of problems relating to the education and training of the *ulama*, they are an essential storehouse of knowledge for the community and neither the *ulama* nor the intellectuals nor the organizations of our society make concerted effort to share this fund of knowledge with the Muslim people. In this dilemma Muslim public-service broadcasting must have a constructive role to play, if Muslims will let it develop.

Islamic premises are by no means self-evident as practices of broadcasting, and cannot vaguely be identified with the highest rhetoric of public-service broadcasting as established by Western television stations. In the United States television stations are governed by the Fairness Doctrine enforced by the regulatory agency of the Federal Communications Commission; in Britain, the duty to balance is part of the charters of the British Broadcasting Corporation and Independent Broadcasting Authority, the regulatory body for commercial television. Similar instances can be found elsewhere, since Britain and the United States, the innovators and initiators of broadcasting, form the two basic models. However, fairness and balance are routinely interpreted to mean countering one view of a topic with an opposing view, not reflecting fairly and accurately a range of diverse views. In fact, the culture of broadcasting that has developed in the West is adversarial television, where complex issues are reduced to simplistic oppositions: the opinion is either this or that, and the function of opposite views is to argue and deny the validity of the opposing view. The very conception of this kind of 'balance' or 'fairness' arises from long-established philosophic ideas deeply ingrained in Western culture; the legal system, for example, is entirely based on the adversarial principle. One could even trace it back to judicial combat, where right must inevitably triumph through might, which was a common inheritance from mediaeval Christendom. Indeed, it is hard not to view much modern television as exactly this kind of gladiatorial combat, often complete with a baying audience out for blood. Watch any American 'infotainment' chat show and no other conclusion is possible.[7] We argue that this state is totally contrary to the Islamic notions of equality of opportunity, freedom of expression and mutual consultation.

The overriding objective for Muslims is to foster mutual understanding and consultation in which all people can participate. Essentially it is access, balance and freedom of expression, promoting conciliation and highlighting areas of mutual agreement that contribute to the creation of consensus. This distinctive obligation must be enacted through the structuring of programmes and the grammar of broadcasting. The purpose is not to demonstrate that A and B can never agree or that their different approaches to life must be accepted, one to the exclusion of the other; rather it brings together differing viewpoints and, while acknowledging irreducible differences, asks on what can they all mutually agree for the public welfare and what consensus is there even if the points of view remain distinct. It is an approach to balance that is directed towards harmony, an equitable and responsible mode of debate that instead of being reductive can take account of and foster a better understanding of complexity within its aim of identifying consensus. It is a mode of discussion that places the need for beneficial action at the centre of debate and assumes some kind of consensus to that end is possible. In other words, it is a practical example of the Islamic ideal of unity through diversity. It is an attainable broadcasting ethic and practice, the kind of broadcasting practice that audiences in the West have been longing for years.

Public Accountability

The duty to inform, from an Islamic standpoint, is not an absolute, but is tempered by an equal duty to understand. Broadcasters must earn their right to broadcast by demonstrating that they operate to their utmost according to ethical guidelines. It is easy for arrogance to settle into the fabric of a broadcasting organization. Broadcasters' public accountability for fulfilling the broadcasting needs of a community must be matched by public accountability for discharging their obligation to fairness and equity. It must be possible to call broadcasters to account for misrepresenting particular groups of people or for broadcasting opinions that through misrepresentation have opened people to public ridicule or have contributed to ill feeling between people or groups within, or even between, communities or countries. What this points to is the need for independent regulatory bodies that can arbitrate matters of dispute between broadcasters and those who appear in their broadcasts and between the public at large and the broadcasters. Such independent monitors should have powers to direct broadcasters to make redress, to secure access to broadcasting time for those who have a substantiated complaint. The regulatory body must also be charged with an equivalent duty of defending and upholding the rights of broadcasters, to make it clear to the public where broadcasters have fulfilled their remit to the best of their abilities. They should also regard it as their duty to stand as a public rallying point against pressure aimed at suborning broadcasting towards or on behalf of any vested interest, no matter whether political, commercial or communal. A culture of broadcasting is not the creation of broadcasting professionals alone; it is the work of an entire community of people and their collective commitment to common values. There must be other voices in the community urging and supporting the ethics of broadcasting, its independence and freedom to broadcast according to publicly-determined priorities to warrant the name of a mass participatory medium.

Taste, Decency and Decorum

There are a whole range of issues that derive from moral and ethical precepts but manifest themselves as issues of taste, decency and decorum, where in practice there can be many grey areas. We do not accept the common Western view that because these are often difficult matters they are best left to the professionals, and where such regulation as exists has little power, practically or morally, to restrain the practice of broadcasters. We begin from the premise that freedom of expression is not an absolute, it is a right that is always balanced by obligations and duties. The Muslim broadcasters' duty to inform is therefore balanced by their obligation to demonstrate they have made every reasonable and responsible effort to inform themselves on any matter included in their programmes, and they can be held accountable to demonstrate what efforts they have made. The Muslim broadcasters are bound by the same moral and ethical code that is upheld as the ideal by the community they serve. This, however, is not any guarantee that broadcasters and the community agree what this means on questions of taste, decency and decorum, especially where the broadcasters are also charged with equitably reflecting diversity within the community. Furthermore, an inalienable part of the ethical code of broadcasting, because it is part of the fabric of Islam itself, is the duty to uphold truth, in so far as they are able. The truth may well include the existence and persistence of indecency, outrage and lack of decorum. It is here that the regulation of broadcasting meets some of the most difficult and complex issues.

Upholding Truth

There are some issues relating to upholding truth where most people can easily arrive at a consensus that broadcasters have both a right and a duty to the public welfare to perform. If we take the example of the Islamic Council of Europe's model Islamic constitution, it clearly indicates a right and duty for broadcasters to undertake what is conventionally termed investigative journalism: 'to expose and protest against oppression, injustice and tyranny regardless of whomever is guilty of such acts'. Who would argue that programmes detailing the persistence of apartheid and exposing its consequences, or the disenfranchising and injustice meted out to the Palestinian people would qualify? Nor would there be much argument that exposing fraudulent activities by business or public agencies would be exemplary activities for broadcasters fearlessly to carry out. Would there be quite such a unanimous agreement that broadcasters should expose the existence of prostitution, child abuse, child slavery, deviant sexual practices, the abuse of women, rape, drug addiction? It is not so much a question of lack of consensus that broadcasters should 'protest' against these things; rather it is a question of whether the Muslim community is ready to acknowledge the existence of such things in their midst, and to agree that to 'protest' against them the broadcasters may have to show their existence. There is no doubt that all of the above mentioned abuses do exist in many Muslim societies. Does the argument for taste and decency, along with the powerful protection of privacy of the person and home, granted by

Islam, mean that it can be argued justifiably that such matters should not only not be shown but should not even be discussed? There is a long-standing and well-attested, though far from proven, argument that by broadcasting such matters, even if they exist in reality and are dealt with solely in factual terms, programmes are giving aid and succour to the very practices they are supposed to be protesting against.

A familiar argument often applied to news coverage purports that by showing violence, it encourages violence. The argument extends to the dramatic representation of violence, even when there is a serious, responsible moral purpose. The news reporter, the responsible morally-aware dramatist and the makers of popular 'cops and robbers' series all can, and do, argue that what they reflect is reality, the truth as operated by society. New York, Los Angeles and Chicago are only marginally less blood-soaked than an average episode of *Starsky and Hutch*. Is it the responsibility of broadcasters, in whatever genre they work, artificially to recreate society for the audience on some abstract notion of taste and decency, or better truthfully to represent what society is and does? Drama, it is argued can use fiction to penetrate the truth, and especially the complexity of truth, which is not instantly ammenable to other forms of factual communication. There is clearly a wide scope for balance and the concept of responsibility to public welfare to be introduced into this debate. We have no confidence whatsoever in the sophistry of self-justification put forward by Western broadcasters on this issue. However, there remains a point at which the question cannot be wished away by any kind of balance or notion of responsibility. There must conceivably be a point when responsibility to the public welfare requires making the public aware of the nature and consequences of violence, indecency and a host of abuses because they are part and parcel of the world in which we live.

When we reach a point where an unwelcome or ugly truth is broadcast, then the question of objectives, intentions and the means that are used become crucial. Quite clearly, an ethical framework for Muslim broadcasting would set out that voyeurism, dwelling on details of blood and gore, or sensationalizing such details must be avoided. Perhaps the clearest argument on this point has been stimulated by the coverage of human disasters, when there is often acute human suffering which is true and whose representation often provokes a positive and natural human compassion and concern to assist on the part of the audience which might not have been so forthcoming without some visible evidence of the suffering. The fact is that television as a visual medium is best at conveying emotional impact, producing a direct communication between people in a particular predicament and the audience. The power of the image and the difficulty of regulating the emotional response is an ongoing problematic conundrum for television. The taste, decency and decorum faculties of the broadcasters must be developed by their training in moral and ethical guidelines as part of their entry into the profession. Broadcasters will always be making decisions on such questions: how to convey truth on behalf of an audience must be responsibility to and utility for the public welfare in justifying what they present and not voyeurism and sensationalism. Broadcasters must be aware that since they will routinely encounter these questions more often than the ordinary member of the public they need to be sensitive to public response. We must accept the argument that too much recourse to explicit coverage of violence or any other kind of deviant practice or the sensationalizing of their effects and the details of human suffering can contribute eventually to devaluation of compassion by blunting sensitivities. But the point of tact is not easy to decree, or even with hindsight to agree upon. Tolerance in a Muslim community must include, sometimes, tolerance of the fallibility of broadcasters, even when they work within a regulated ethical framework. Such a framework will make the broadcaster no more perfect than any other member of society and the maturity of the Muslim community will be judged by the kind of public debate and acceptance they have to offer when broadcasters do err. If we too rigorously close off options for decision-making by Muslim broadcasters we will be denying them the freedom to inform their communities and uphold truth. We will also be condemning ourselves to continue the overriding modern characteristic of Muslims as people who seek to uphold Islam by myth-making about ourselves and the real world through our flight from reality.

Personally I feel most uncomfortable with the phrasing chosen by the Islamic Council of Europe when they state 'regardless of whomever is guilty of such acts' in stating the obligations of broadcasters to protest and uphold the truth. In one sense this can be taken to mean no matter who, or how powerful, or of what high repute the persons involved might be. This is of course in line with the Quranic injunction to uphold truth by giving witness even if it is against ourselves or even our parents. That is a clear imperative and cannot be shirked. Yet the Quran talks of giving witness against, not attributing guilt, which is a rather different matter. Trial by television, even responsible, publicly-accountable broadcasting is not the place for attributing guilt, for it is open to abuse and error by broadcasters. The obligation of broadcasters is to substantiate the cases they present, without fear or favour, to the best of their abilities in a spirit of fairness and equity, even to those they investigate; to make the facts of oppression, injustice or tyranny as they know them known to the public so that appropriate action may be taken by the community, which would include prosecution and the establishment of guilt by legal authorities.

The Privileged Position of Broadcasters

Our argument for an Islamic vision of broadcasting would circumscribe the privileged position of broadcasters. From a definition of their objectives and functions within the community they serve, there would be communal obligations that professional broadcasters might be called upon to exercise in a privileged way on behalf of the community. It is worth noting here the famous dictum which is the basis of absolute privilege for the coverage of legal proceedings granted by Parliament to the media in Britain 'that justice should not only be done but be seen to be done'. Therefore, journalists have a right to be present in courts of law and in Parliament, can report anything that is placed in the public domain there and their very presence is taken as evidence that the proceedings are public. The duty to ensure that the community is informed should give definite rights of access to broadcasters and other media personnel, such as journalists, as representatives of the public at large. There will always be an obligation upon Muslim public-service broadcasting to operate as a medium of record; that is, to cover those occasions when the traditions and rituals of communal identity and incorporation are expressed and to keep records of the performance of public duties, the occurrence of events, the course of ideas and activities of persons that are of note and moment to the community. To be a channel of record for the community would of course mean of all the diverse sections, ethnic or other groupings that are part of the community.

Monitoring Public-service Broadcasting

If there is a public-welfare function to the community inherent in Muslim public-service broadcasting, then it is incumbent upon the institutions of the Muslim community, and especially the ulama and Islamic organizations to put their weight of authority behind the exercise of such public-service broadcasting. In the all too-real world in which we live, the kind of public-service broadcasting we have been discussing is in all honesty a pipe dream, one more easily achievable today by Muslim minority communities existing in the West than in many Muslim countries. In the future, even if we take a firm Islamic ethical basis for the development of Muslim public-service broadcasting, there will still be a need for its rights to be protected by and on behalf of the community by all who champion the commitment to Islam. Independent bodies that make it their business to monitor the media already exist; indeed, they are ubiquitous. They have a positive role to play in supporting, acclaiming and endorsing the exercise of good public-service practice wherever it occurs, so that the direction to genuine Muslim public-service broadcasting can be made clear and Muslim broadcasters can be encouraged to develop accordingly. A community will eventually get the broadcasting it is prepared to tolerate, even if it tolerates with distaste for lack of any alternative. Developing an alternative requires positive efforts on many fronts, not least the independent formation within the community of a nascent monitoring body prepared to stand up for the rights of responsible broadcasters long before a distinctive Muslim public-service broadcasting system with all its full panoply has come into being.

Promoting Cultural Heritage through Broadcasting

Broadcasting today is principally a tool of entertainment. Is there any place for entertainment in Muslim public-service broadcasting? I would argue that Muslim broadcasting has a duty towards the cultural well being and aesthetic development of the community, which includes entertainment. At present there is a great deal that the media in Muslim countries could do to maintain, support and revive the indigenous cultural heritage that it is palpably not doing. Most Muslim countries still have strong traditions of oral culture: the traditional story tellers, village festivals and pageants, poetry, music, arts and crafts. All of these can be and should be reflected and encouraged through broadcasting. Radio is probably the world's most material-hungry medium, and what better medium is there for keeping alive the traditions of story telling or poetry? What better gift is there to the makers and schedulers of radio ˀrogrammes who, instead of paying fees for endless replaying of popular music, have a resource of great public benefit on their very doorsteps? This use of radio should not be considered as a museum item, a recording of an art form destined to wither. Story telling is a staple of the universal grammar of radio, something the medium does better than any other. Because of its immediacy and instant access, radio excludes neither the illiterate nor those too lazy or lacking the time to read; after all, we can listen while performing other work. Radio also gives best service to the imaginative communication between author or story-teller and listeners. Traditional story tellers draw upon an indigenous cultural matrix and its values; they can set the pace for the development of new writers and create a constituency, an informed audience, that is attuned to and demands literary products reflecting their own culture and values.

Muslim public-service broadcasting has a duty to the cultural traditions and products of its community, to reflect their diversity and promote their production. Television stations the world over have adopted the conventions of Western television in set design, use of cameras in studio, the way images are presented. Virtually no experimentation has taken place in introducing an indigenous aesthetic into the presentation of this visual medium. We cannot tell whether introducing indigenous traditions would work or what it would look like until someone tries it. We can say that at present audiences in Muslim countries are being weaned to the idea that only Western-style television is television because of the lack of imagination and inventiveness by Muslim broadcasters. In style and content across the range of broadcasting output today, we confront once again the pernicious phenomena of imitative inertia.

The Training of Muslim Broadcasters

The radical departures from Western conventions of broadcasting heretofore proposed, which define ways in which new kinds of programming can develop, require trained Muslim broadcasters to fulfill the vision. This training should incorporate both the ethical premises of public-service broadcasting and the skills of the medium in which they are to work. Pious commitment without developing the requisite skills is, after all, a denial of the framework of *ibadah*. Training must encourage confidence in their own indigenous way of thought as a source of creativity and imagination that can be applied to operating the grammar of broadcasting in new ways to generate new kinds of programming and fresh uses of established formats. Just as the establishment of a centre of excellence for Islamic broadcasting technology assessment is essential, so is the need for regional centres of excellence for the training of broadcasters. We need a number of centres, distributed around the Muslim world and for Muslims in Western countries, to glean the best of available talent. The training centres should also regard it as part of their function to generate links with existing broadcasting services. They, too, can benefit from the dialogue of the ethos of broadcasting promoted by the centres, promote, as well as providing job opportunities for those who are trained at the centres.

Training centres for broadcasting excellence must incorporate the full range of skills necessary for the production of good programmes. They should include the training of the whole range of technical and engineering personnel, such as sound engineers, camera operators, editors, reporters, researchers, writers, directors, producers, graphic designers and costume designers. Broadcasting, and especially television, is more than anything else a collaborative medium which works to its full potential only when there is a proper respect for the talents of each contributor to the final product. The best idea in the world can be turned into the worst programme when some part of the production process is lacking in requisite training or when creativity and encouragement to contribute to the process of creativity that is programme-making is violated. These training centres should be magnets for people with a wide range of interests and talents; the purpose of training should be to increase knowledge and awareness across a host of disciplines that are often encouraged to distance themselves from one another. In short, the polymathism that has traditionally been a product of the Muslim world-view and educational system is a prime requirement for the success of such centres.

The training centres will be the ideal places to encourage experimentation in broadcasting techniques. They should be the proving grounds for developing distinctive Muslim public-service broadcasting. They should be the obvious places to experiment with new aesthetics, and by mutual stimulation and cross fertilization to discover the potential of the broadcasting medium. But there is one characteristic prevalent in the film schools of the Western world such centres should guard against; there should be no place here for inbreeding a culture of elitism or the manufacturing of an artistic elite that becomes the arbitrator of culture for the community in isolation from the community. The training is for a mass participatory medium, broadcasting, that has a responsibility to the public through consultation with the public. However much students are taught to become creative and imaginative, they must if they are to break out of the imitative inertia achieve that creativity within a distinct Islamic framework. Creativity and imaginative excellence can breed elitism where the culture of arrogance exists, but elitism can also creep into any organization or human undertaking where a clear ethos stressing the ethics of equality, access, tolerance and mutual understanding are insufficiently prominent.

The Quality of Broadcasting

No amount of legislation and regulation for Muslim public-service broadcasting can make the idea a reality without the trained personnel capable of realizing the vision. Given the culture of broadcasting that exists around the world today no such personnel will be available without determined constructive efforts to train Muslims in a new convention of broadcasting. For too long the whole tenor of Muslim discussion of the media has been complaints unmatched by constructive proposals for action. Who or what do the armchair Muslim critics think can redeem television? At present it seems they expect broadcasters, whom they traduce as ignorant, antipathetic, secularist and anti-religious, somehow to achieve the miraculous transformation. It is nothing new for Muslims to look outside themselves, their communities and worldview in expectant anticipation that others will resolve our problems on our behalf. The contemporary predicament of the Muslim *ummah* is potent evidence that this will not and cannot happen and that only exertion characterized by self-sufficiency and self-reliance can answer our present and future needs.

Soap Operas

A staple of television output the world over are soap operas, ongoing melodramas of quasi-ordinary life, or escapist fantasy life. It is the television ouput most often decried and yet most avidly watched. The loyalty of the audience testifies that this wide spectrum of drama serial is a strength of television, something it does superbly well; it is a genuine television form. So, before we sweep it away as trivial, counter-productive and not conducive to the high moral tone and educative function of a new kind of broadcasting, as many commentators and critics of broadcasting would seem to advocate, it would be advisable to ask a basic question. Can the form be utilized to serve a different moral and ethical purpose for the public welfare? I am not alone in arguing that there definitely is a great deal soap operas can do for social awareness and responsibility. Socially responsible drama, dramatization of complex social issues with a moral and educative purpose, whether as single dramas or regular serials, point to the possibilities. The trouble is that fulfilling the possibilities means taking the genre seriously, getting the best writers, actors and programme-makers. A glance at any audience research or sociology study of audience response to this common fodder of television reveals that the mass audience likes such programmes and claims them to be educative, because they give examples of how real people respond to common human life crises.

The defence of soap opera is a defence of the potential of the form, not the content of all soap operas as they exist today. It is a counter to the dreadful elitism of those who criticize any mass entertainment, where a major factor in the criticism is precisely the mass attraction of the entertainment provided. There is no necessary contradiction between entertainment and high purpose. All prophets have taught through parable, containing high messages in dramatizations of scenes familiar to ordinary people. In a far less august realm, the soap operas of today are following an age-old technique. There is no reason why moral purpose should be boring and worthy, rather than entertaining and engaging to a mass audience. Throughout I have argued that broadcasting is a mass participatory service; shunning those things that engage mass attention is hardly a recipe for fulfilling this brief. The focus of attention should be on how to infuse the content of mass audience-pleasing genres with the objectives of educating, informing and strengthening self reliance and respect for indigenous cultural integrity. The evidence of the past thirty years is that audiences will watch even bad television, not just because it is there but because it is an easily accessible form of diversion. The onus then is on making the best possible television using the best wit and talent available and not decrying the very mass appeal that makes television so compatible with Islamic purposes.

The Influence of Television

Today television has become an easy scapegoat for problems that are much more profound. If one looks at the statistics of advertising, the use of television most geared to direct manipulation of public behaviour through visual imagery, then it becomes apparent that television advertising campaigns can fail as often as they succeed. Television does not displace nor override individual decision-making nor substitute remote-control dictation for communal responsibility. Television is merely one among a host of influences on a community. Muslims are particularly fond of using television as a scapegoat for the introduction of alien manners and mores into their societies. We would do well to remember that if a staple of television in Muslim countries are imported Western soap operas, these merely portray a lifestyle that is assiduously aped by the elites and is the logical end product of the entire thrust of development policies selected by many Muslim countries. If television stands accused, then others should be arraigned on the same charge and share responsibility with television. No study has yet been able satisfactorily to substantiate a direct causal relationship between television and the development of any kind of anti-social behaviour. What studies do suggest is the need for moral responsibility and quality control in the content and use of television.

The idea that television is a passive medium is illusory, for we know that television can and does prompt people to action, to become involved in community campaigns and action. Television is a conduit for stimulating interest and involvement with a whole range of issues. It has been argued that television kills conversation and the reading habit, yet discussing television is a staple part of the talk of many people with their workmates, friends and neighbours; sales of novels soar when they are dramatized on television. The whole of modern technology, including television, probably does lead to a differing kind of relationship with literary forms; these relationships have changed many times in the past while communication has remained the basis of communal existence. The relevant question is not about what means of communication or literacy (oral, written, graphic or visual) predominate, but whether a community develops skills and sophistication in accumulating, manipulating, evaluating and discriminating information in the generation of knowledge.

The Quality the Audience Requires

Broadcasting is a medium of communication. Our concern is with the quality of its output, the quality of the messages it carries, their objectives and intentions. We can define such objectives and intentions. We can refine the ethos and system of regulation within which broadcasting operates. What we cannot do is legislate for the impact the messages have on the audience. If we highlight instances where television has positive impact, then it is important to remember, which few people seem to do, that this effect is caused because the message elicits this response by the choice and decision of the members of the audience. Even high-purpose broadcasting can only have the effects upon a community a community is willing and able to generate, and there will no doubt still be irate viewers and listeners who find the whole thing objectionable, morally degrading, banal or plain boring, whatever one does.

Since we envisage a broadcasting service that has wide-ranging and diversified content, bought-in or imported programmes from Western or Eastern television stations will still have a place and a function. They can be provided to keep the audience abreast of diversity of ideas and opinions and to promote mutual understanding. The bone of contention at present is the nature of the programmes that are imported for Muslim audiences and the proportion they form of total output, not the princi-ple. According to our criteria, there is no reason why public-service programming cannot be produced by non-Muslim stations; indeed, at present, the nearest approximations to it are made by Western stations.

The Financing of Broadcasting

The crucial question for securing the freedom and independence of Muslim public-service broadcasting to fulfill its remit from the commu-nity is the financing of on-going programme-making. Without getting this aspect of the process right, those who operate the service will be subject to the real pressures to fill the airtime with whatever is available. I believe a public levy or licence fee is essential as a basic source of income for broadcasting and is the logical consequence of the framework we have been outlining — mass contribution to secure mass provision, public accountability for a service for which the public pays. Funding through public levy is a means to insulate broadcasting from the pres-sures of commercialism and to throw a cordon of secure finance around a service that may well have to compete with other channels that are commercially funded.

Public-levy financing does not mean that other sources of income for programme production should not be available. Indeed, I am firmly convinced that one of the best ways to get from the present situation to the development of genuine Muslim public-service broadcasting is investment by a whole range of organizations and institutions in inde-pendent programme production. Without financial exertion no amount of thinking about and planning for an ideal broadcasting service will bring it into existence. Subscription services, sponsorship of individual programmes or just general contributions from organizations are all possible supplementary sources, as is the willingness of banks or busi-nesses to allocate money to television production, either in sponsorship or through joint-venture loans based on the subsequent sale of pro-grammes to other television stations or the sale of video cassettes. What-ever the supplementary sources of finance the objectives and ethical framework, editorial control and context of programme-making is set by the regulatory environment of Muslim public-service broadcasting. I am not envisioning state-owned and operated broadcasting; however, since education and information are a high priority in programming, then it would be sensible to expect various government departments to allocate funds to the independent broadcasting services for the production of programmes within their areas of interest. The important point is that once a secure, independent general source of funding exists, broadcasting does not then become beholden and subject to unwarranted pressure from other sources of supplementary finance. Television production is an expensive business and a range of sources of finance will always be needed if quality output is to be made available.

There is no reason why funding for programme-making cannot be sought through joint ventures with Western broadcasting stations, given the range of co-production financing that is becoming an increasingly important aspect of the television production worldwide. As a corollary, it would be essential in fulfilling the remit of the public service we hope to see develop that it makes programmes directed towards a general audience in the Western or Eastern block. Mutual understanding is a two-way channel and at present there is a complete absence of balance in coverage of Islam or Muslim issues. The only constructive way to create such a balance is for programmes to be made from a Muslim perspective to the highest professional and editorial standards, and entered into the range of Western and Eastern broadcasting output.

Independent professional Muslim broadcasters able and anxious to make programmes do exist. The current problem is absence of financing for such ventures. There also exists a general climate in which those who might be prepared and are certainly able to finance programme-making want a degree of control and influence on content which is a denial of the very ethics of broadcasting we are trying to encourage. The absence of a general debate on the potential of the media for serving Islamic principles and public welfare contributes to the persistence of attitudes that continue to inhibit general financing. What gets produced at present are *dawa* efforts which lack professional production values, concentrate on limited sets of agreed content heavily weighted to minimal Islam, lack imagination and creativity in presentation and misuse the opportunities of the very medium they utilize. Such ventures into the audiovisual field compare unfavourably with the standard and grammar of broadcasting the Muslim audience is already familiar with and attuned to, and have no attraction at all for non-Muslim audiences. The broadcast products currently available whose overt intention is to serve Islamic *dawa* testify volumes to Islamic commitment; sadly, they also speak volumes for the mind-set of Muslims. We are not prepared to meet the real needs of the *ummah* or demonstrate an equal command of knowledge, skill and talent in broadcasting to match commitment by ability. Adequate financing within an agreed framework of broadcasting objectives is an absolute essential to overcome the present impasse. We need far more than programmes about an abstract ideal Islam removed from the real world, or the endless succession of programmes that seek to explain or portray Islam only in the context of its past history. History is important to any civilization, but the integrity of Muslim civilization is also its vision of an Islamic future. There is a desperate need for programmes about contemporary Islamic thinking and ideas that can clarify the relationships between Muslims and Islam today. We need programmes that use broadcasting to build bridges of mutual understanding, not compound mutual incomprehension. Most of all our current predicament requires a diversity of programme-making efforts that cover a wide range of approaches, formats and programme content to meet urgent needs of the *ummah* and a general audience, not monotonal, repetitive expositions of the Five Pillars. People get the broadcasting they are prepared to pay for. Finance is a major key to our current broadcasting needs; adequate finance will put us on the road to the Muslim public-broadcasting service of the future.

Notes

1. See Ali Shariati, *On the Sociology of Islam*. Berkeley: Mizan, 1979, pp. 49–57.
2. For example, one could examine M. Hamidullah, *The First Written Constitution in the World*. Lahore: Ashraf, 1975.
3. See, for example, Maulana Maududi's *The Islamic Law and Constitution* (Lahore: Islamic Publications, 1980), which includes a discussion of a constitution proposed in Pakistan. The Islamic Council of Europe drew up a model constitution which includes a whole section devoted to the media:

Article 80
The mass media and publications have full freedom of expression and presentation of information so long as they respect and adhere to facts and to the norms and values of Islam. The freedom to publish newspapers and journals shall be permitted within these limits and the closing or censoring of the news media shall be through judicial procedure, except in times of war.

Article 81
The mass media and publications are obliged to:

a. Expose and protest against oppression, injustice and tyranny, regardless of whomever is guilty of such acts.

b. Respect the privacy of individuals and refrain from prying into their personal affairs.

c. Refrain from inventing and circulating slander, calumny and rumour.

d. Express the truth and scrupulously avoid spreading falsehood or mixing the truth with falsehood or knowingly concealing the truth or distorting it.

e. Use decent and dignified language.

f. Promote the right conduct and ethical values in society.

g. Strictly refrain from the dissemination of indecency, obscenity and immorality.

h. Avoid condoning or glorifying crimes or acts repugnant to Islam.

i. Refrain from suppressing evidence except in so far as it might cause harm to the interests of society.

j. Avoid becoming instruments of corruption of any kind.

Article 82
The executive organs of the State shall have no authority to take any administrative action against or to penalize the media or publications in any way except to prosecute violations in a court of law. Similarly, media and publications' personnel are protected in the performance of their professional duties.

4. For an elaboration of these points, see my *Knowing One Another: Shaping an Islamic Anthropology*. London: Mansell, 1988, chapter 5.
5. For an overview of the media today, see Everett M. Rogers and Francis Balle (eds.), *The Media Revolution in America and Western Europe*. New Jersey: Ablex, 1985.
6. One is forced to add here that television has often reached remote areas before provision of electrical supply, or other 'modern' services such as health care and education. One can find rural villages complete with television aerials where the sets are run off car batteries! It is proof of the inventiveness and innovative capacity of people that often leaves highly trained experts lagging in their wake.
7. 'Infotainment' is a term applied to programming that strives to make information into a parlour game. The staple of such programmes is the discussion of human interest stories, often through a chat-show format. The most famous examples of confrontational chat shows are the American programmes *Geraldo* and *Donovan*.

Epilogue
Dawa: Planning Beyond Disasters

Abdullah Omar Naseef

The activity of planning requires a vision of the future, a defined objective towards which we can harness and direct our efforts. Planning for the Muslim *ummah* is founded on the concept of *dawa*, the endeavour to secure a future based on the activation and operation of the principles, concepts and guidance of the Quran and Sunnah in all aspects of the lives of individuals, communities and the *ummah* as a whole. *Dawa* is the collective term for the means by which Muslims live up to the call of Islam; it summons them to witness to the truth and implement the enjoining of what is good and the forbidding of what is evil so that by their examples they can invite all people to the Straight Path. Planning on the basis of *dawa* requires concrete policies and programmes to be enacted in the present within the conditions that currently exist. Planning allows Muslims to achieve moral, material and spiritual betterment, to secure justice and equity in the relationships of human existence — between us and our Creator, between the various peoples of the earth and between us and the earth upon which we depend, which includes all the flora and fauna, the waters and air, the very stones and muck of this planet.

Planning defines a course along which we wish to proceed, in practical terms of policies and programmes that can be undertaken. Planning must detail the route and means of travel, which are determined by the destination we wish to reach and the condition in which we intend to be when we reach that destination. The success of planning therefore

201

depends upon our plans being rooted in the same value system, the same conceptual orientation as our desired destination. Unless we travel in a manner appropriate to our objective there is little hope our policies and programmes can magically transmute the means into the end; the means and the end must be harmonious. The activity of planning is a training, a preparation to make us ready to cope with the fruits of our success. Unless we prepare ourselves in the exercise of justice and equity to create a future characterized by justice and equity we will have little skill in operating a world in which justice and equity determine daily life. Perhaps Utopia has always remained an unattained ideal because this essential link between means and ends has never been rigorously carried through. Achieving Utopia has usually meant sweeping away the world that exists by any means possible. Attaining Utopia has been a justification for every kind of brutality and duplicity in a naked power-struggle where conviction in a right end has obviated the need to convince others of this rightness. Once the end is imposed then the rightness of the causes will miraculously take care of any qualms that were expressed along the way. The planning to set in place an ideal world has so often violated the values of the ideal, in people's anxiety to get to the end by any means rather than the right means, that it is little wonder that the legacy of achieving power deforms the longed for Utopia. The history of mankind is littered with good intentions and wonderful dreams, all of which have stumbled at the hurdle of implementation.

In planning for *dawa*, the future begins today. The future is contained in both our present and our past, but neither past, present nor future can be separated from the need for a worldview, a source of guidance and insight that renders them both comprehensible and subject to moral and ethical analysis and regulation. Past, present and future are not separate entities but interconnected, interactive parts of an on-going process in an on-going system. The threads of continuity and change, the means of getting from one phase to another are just as much part of past, present and future as any characteristic used to define each of these conditions. So continuity and change, the means of policy and planning, the programmes and schemes to get from here to anywhere must also be subject, subservient and submissive to the worldview, the values and concepts by which we know of the past, seek to live in the present and towards which we strive in the future.

The greatest hurdle is the first hurdle; it is the hurdle of Islamization that seeks to integrate and operate our worldview, the *din* of Islam, within the reality of the problems and predicaments that confront us. Our worldview should make the problems of the *ummah* scream out at us; it is our worldview, the *din* of Islam that demands of us commitment to change things, to make the path of Islam walkable for all Muslims and for all mankind. When we focus our vision on the past, present and future through the lens of Islam we are most likely to see the opportunities to proceed Islamically to redress the predicaments of the present, arising as they do out of our past, which are impediments to a better Islamic future.

The Muslim *ummah* is beset by disasters. In recent years Muslim peoples have experienced widespread drought and floods, famine, massive dislocation of population in a flood tide of refugees, which must be added to the ongoing, ever present toll of premature death from preventable causes, poverty, endemic ill-health, illiteracy, increasing tensions resulting from mal-development and mis-development, wars and the rumours of war, increasing violence and turmoil in the supposed progress of organized community and social life. These are all human disasters that run contrary to the message of Islam. These are all human disasters that make the call to Islam harder. These are all human disasters that *dawa* must strive to eradicate to be worthy of the name. Unless *dawa* activity is planned in a coherent and concerted manner to surmount the disasters confronting the *ummah*, then today's Muslims are not answering the call of Islam and are committing the greatest hypocrisy by insulating themselves in pious hopes for an Islamically better future. The only means to wish and pray for a better more self-sufficient, self-reliant and self-sustaining Islamic future is to act now to tackle the problems, the human disasters that beset the route to that future.

Disaster seems to lurk at every turn in human activity, an accepted part of human fate, a feature of the natural world. In the last decade there have been significant international studies of disasters, with plans for crisis management to be used at the onset of the next potential disaster. Muslims have been absent from these deliberations; whether in the fields of relief or planning, they have been slow to respond for a variety of reasons. Yet now we find there is a stirring among Muslims around the world. There is an acceptance that the obligation of *dawa* should mean our practical engagement with all the humanitarian issues. The resurgent consciousness of *dawa* makes us keen to be seen to be doing our part. Therefore, it is timely for Muslims to reflect and plan how they should practise *dawa* in the context of disaster. Before we accept the notion that disasters exist and by virtue of their existence demand that we follow along with the remedial measures already established by others, we should subject disasters to an Islamic analysis. We must determine how to understand a disaster within the conceptual framework of Islam if we are to plan appropriate *dawa* policies that will bring Islamic solutions for a better future. This call for analysis and reflection is not an invitation to procrastination; we have already offered too much of that. It is an invitation to be clear and precise about the distinctive contribution we can and must bring to resolving the perplexity of the human condition in today's world.

One place to begin reflection and analysis is to consider the distinctions and relationship between a disaster and a hurdle. A hurdle is an impediment in one's path, a blockage preventing easy passage along a route. However, a hurdle is also a surmountable obstacle; we can train horses to steeplechase and athletes to hurdle. The world record for the 100-metres hurdles is a matter of a few seconds, a few blinkings of the eye, more than the record for an unimpeded 100 metres. We can train ourselves to master the hurdles so that our advance along a given course can become effortless, appropriate and accommodated to the terrain we must cross.

Disasters seem to be another matter altogether, but the operative word is 'seem'. We think a disaster is more than a hurdle, that it is not a manageable and normal obstacle in the natural course of events. People who go round looking for disaster are morose pessimists, the kind of people we would rather avoid. Let us at least make the best of things while they are going well, be optimistic and look on the bright side, after all it may never happen. And when disaster does strike then it is the will of God and we must again make the best of it, pick up the pieces as best we may and proceed along amid the wreckage of disaster. What else can people do?

The argument I wish to present is that there is a great deal we can do. And the first thing is to gain a better understanding of how patience, forbearance and reliance upon God should be activated. The Prophet Muhammad advised that we should say our prayers and tie our camel. The moral lesson is clear. We as sentient beings endowed with the capacity to accumulate knowledge, called upon to exercise our reason to study and understand the processes of the natural world and to exert every effort to employ our God-given talents in the best possible way according to the limits set by God's guidance, must do our part. We must tie our camel. Prayer is part of doing our utmost, not the sum total of what can be done, especially since practical action in pursuit of right ends to earn God's pleasure is itself prayer, worship. Only when we have done as much as is humanly possible can we take strength in forbearance, fortitude and the concept of the will of God. To substitute reliance on the will of God for imaginative and creative human action is negligence and dereliction of our clear duty. Indeed, to summon up the will of God to explain the occurrence or calamity of preventable, avoidable or man-induced events seems to be both presumptuous and potentially blasphemous.

Instead of finding convenient explanations for disaster in the awesomeness of the Divine that is far beyond our understanding, we need to exercise the reason and understanding granted us by the Divine to study and make sensible connections between the causes of what we call disasters, the ways they occur and the effects they have on the course of our lives. I would say we almost invariably make a disaster of a hurdle, and we do so from sloppy thinking, inertia and a host of reprehensible and surmountable traits of human inadequacy. So the second hurdle we confront is to properly understand what we call disasters and how they originate. When we have looked at them through the clarifying lens of Islam, I venture to suggest we will find an improved set of values and sense of direction to make what were disasters into hurdles we can neither abolish nor ignore, but that we can train ourselves to master by techniques that render them less devastating. If we discover the right approach, we can make these hurdles a normal part of our path towards a sustainable life of justice and equity, in adversity as well as in plenty.

Disaster Mentality

The Canadian geographer Hewitt has written a tremendously challenging critique of the dominant Western paradigm of disaster, the disaster being an event occurring in the natural world outside the parameters of normality. He writes convincingly of the *un* syndrome, where disasters are *un*natural events, *un*predictable, *un*expected. Western science has worked to master the laws of nature to achieve dominance over the natural world, to establish order and control. The disaster stands outside this normal course of events; it is the surrounding chaos that threatens to engulf us, the implacable hostility of the forces of nature as yet still outside the ambit of human control through science.

The response of science is therefore to study the operation of natural forces. The disaster is made manageable and subject to normal science by remote sensing by satellite or by seismic detectors planted underground. Disaster is a function of the natural world, especially prevalent in particular parts of the world — the disaster world being largely the Third World. Large amounts of money are spent on the theoretical understanding of natural forces as a means to understand the *un*natural upsurge of *un*natural occurrences.

Closer to the human consequences of calamity, a different perception has begun to emerge in recent years: the understanding that human action often contributes to the genesis of human devastation in natural disasters. Take the prime example of supposed disaster famine, either prompted by drought, flood or crop failure through pestilence. In studying the social history of these disasters, researchers have pointed out that famine is never an absolute absence of food in a so-called disaster-stricken country. Usually a whole region may be affected, not a whole country. In all the great famines when hundreds of thousands, even millions, have died of starvation, food has still been available in the country. In many of the most notorious famines, countries have continued to export food while the starving perished. Famine is the social fact of inability to command the available food resources. What causes people to starve is not natural forces beyond human control, but the eminently human and controllable condition of poverty.

While drought or flood are natural-enough events, not man-created, their occurrence and impact can get considerable assistance from human action. Over exploitation of land, removal of ground cover, over concentration of particular herding-grazing animals, especially goats, the failure to build or maintain flood embankments, and many more human actions increase the severity of devastation when *un*natural events occur. Do we need to be reminded that annual inundation has become annual disaster in Bangladesh, where disaster is not some uncontainable worsening of natural forces? It is a consequence of the strengthening of natural forces by the systematic deforestation of the Himalayas, beyond the national boundaries and jurisdiction of Bangladesh itself. Poverty is a major contributory factor to the deforestation process, as it is to other cycles of action that increase the ferocity of natural forces. Poor people lack the resources to be prudent and the existence of poverty gives a licence to unscrupulous so-called 'development' projects.

However, the most important point about the consequences of disaster that is now coming to be appreciated is the human social organization that goes into the making of calamity. If the process of setting a famine in chain can be detected early enough, remedial action can protect a population from drought and famine can be made a thing of the past. The resources always exist to achieve this end; what is usually lacking is the human ingenuity to devise the techniques of monitoring, the willingness to commit the resources both to monitoring and relief and, most of all, the awareness that what is called a disaster is most often a surmountable hurdle. While this trend in disaster research is instructive, it still must battle against the received wisdom that disasters are not hurdles but something wild and uncontrollable, until after the fact, the event, the occurrence.

Disasters — the Islamic Perspective

It is integral to an Islamic perspective that risk is inherent in every human activity. Risk is an acknowledgement that mankind does not have perfect knowledge, absolute control. The foundation of the Islamic approach, as seen in the arrangements of Islamic economics, is the equitable sharing of risk between all parties. What cannot be eradicated must not be made an unfair burden, especially upon those least able to cope with the consequences.

While risk is always with us, the Prophet's dictum of tying one's camel indicates we cannot resign ourselves passively to risk. The *shariah* injunctions in economics demonstrate the need for a creative strategy both to accept the existence of risk and to operate to delimit its consequences, to make them containable within the ordinary course of ongoing social organization. I take this to be the model for an Islamic perspective upon disasters that converts our mental conception of them into hurdles. When a disaster becomes a hurdle it becomes surmountable, something for which we can plan, something we can encounter without devastation, dearth, distress or death.

There is nothing new in this approach; it has been available to us since the revelation of Islam more than 1400 years ago. We should also realize it has been part of the strategy of traditional communities since time immemorial. A great measure of the decay and waning of great civilizations can perhaps be attributed to the waning of what can be called on-going disaster management, the ignoring of prudent living. Traditional life styles, the supposedly backward societies of the world, demonstrate a sophisticated awareness of the natural environment, far more sensitive than modern scientific rationalized activity in the same areas. Traditional man knows the risks and incorporates the costs of the bad years in the activities in the good years, husbands resources and organizes his life style against need to come. The arrogant triumphalism of Western economics and science believes in its dominance and the satisfaction of immediate needs; the generation of immediate gains, husbanding, conserving nurturing the environment against need to come is not their ideology nor value orientation. It is this dominant and dominating outlook that has so often made hurdles into full blown disasters, and the process of recovery in the aftermath of disaster into a tortuous hurdle of its own.

The outlook of risk assessment needs to be part of the planning of Muslims in a wide ranging and inclusive way. Our risk assessment is about looking at the costs of economic, industrial and productive activity for the hazards it holds; about looking to human health, welfare and betterment in material, moral and spiritual terms; and about looking at the hazards human activity holds for the natural world, for the flora and fauna and for the interdependent systems of the biosphere.

Effecting the paradigm shift from disasters to hurdles, so that we can learn to cope with the risks and surmount the hurdles effortlessly, is not confined to just a few kinds of activity or a limited number of occurrences. It is part of thinking about every human activity, since every human activity has the potential to engender long-term consequences. The devastation being caused by acid rain today comes from generations of profligacy in the use of hydro-carbon fuels without adequate study of the effects. The effects of human activity may appear utilitarian, an advance at the outset; but future generations who have to live without forests, with acid rivers and lakes, can have little cause to thank us for the advances that have bequeathed them an unsustainable environment.

Risk assessment is the implementation of the duties and obligations of the *khilafah*, the action of the prudent steward. It is the operation of the central teachings of Islam in the conditions and opportunities of the modern world. It is not merely a turning of backs on the get-rich-quick rewards; it is a question of whether those who can be wealthier in resources and material standards can sustain their life styles by stealing the opportunities and potential of future generations. The assessment of risk and the sensitivity to hurdles that can create problems for the future means we must study both the phenomena of the natural world, the fruits of human ingenuity in employment of the earth's resources and the system of social organization within which ingenuity and production operates. A sustainable mode of production and technology can effect disaster because of a faulty social system of human organization; the great famines of the world have taught us this lesson. If we would make disasters into surmountable hurdles then we must bring the dynamics of human relationships within our field of risk assessment.

The Message of Islam offers success in this world and the next to those who follow its concepts, values and principles with diligence, effort, exertion and conscientiousness. It is the worldview of Islam that enables us to take a fresh look at our current predicaments and begin sensing the disasters we can make into hurdles and the means by which we can overcome these hurdles. The overriding objective of planning practical *dawa* on the basis of Islamic risk assessment is to acknowledge a simple truth: the best time to prevent a disaster is before it happens. The best moment to act to promote regeneration of natural systems is before you engender their degradation. The objective of *dawa* is a gradual reformation of society, a continual transformation of people and communities to bring them closer to the Straight Path and maintain them along this Straight Path. Islamic risk assessment as part of every activity is the mental awareness necessary for this inescapable task.

There is one other consequence of Islamic risk assessment we would do well to keep firmly in mind. It is a consequence entirely consistent with *dawa*; indeed, it is merely another way of stating something essential about *dawa*. Islamic risk assessment means working to change our priorities, planning for different and more preferable ends than those currently available, by employing means that are more appropriate than those on offer today. We stand at the end of four development decades. If we were to undertake a full cost analysis of all the activities undertaken in the name of development, then trace their credits and debits we would have a mass of data to support the informed and intuitive conclusion that development has not been value for anyone's money. Today there are more poor and they are comparatively poorer than at the onset of the development decades. The environment in the Third World is more degraded, impoverished and fragile today than before the administration of a battery of scientific means used to increase its yield. Despite advances in strains of wheat and grain which have increased yields, more countries have a food debt than before. Despite advances in medical science, death and chronic ill-health from preventable causes is as prevalent as ever. An unjust world economic order that now wallows in the debt trap of ever-higher interest rates, choking off economic enterprise, is more entrenched and further from amendment than ever. The ethos of development as we have experienced it in the last four decades has encouraged dependency at all levels of our societies. The fruits of development have destabilized cherished traditional values, overturned traditional systems of mutual support and left millions newly pauperized and without substitute means of aid.

Most significant of all, the development decades have clearly demonstrated the interrelated nature of human existence. No one can claim with any credibility that we can have 'development' of any kind that does not affect social order, economic justice, equity and environmental well-being, any more than we can have 'development' in one nation that does not at the same time have consequences for other countries. The question then becomes not one of 'development, yes or no', but what kind of development, according to what priorities, implemented in what way and with what kind of accounting for inherent, ever present risks, and, neither least nor last, with what vision of benefit and human betterment as an objective?

Islam requires the Muslim to take an holistic view of existence, a view that is material, moral and spiritual and sees these not as separate domains but as integrated aspects of each and every instance. The Islamic framework fits us to make the kind of assessment of current problems and plan future remedies in the way the world urgently requires. It is the Islamic worldview that uniquely calls upon us to resolve human predicaments, prevent disasters and surmount hurdles in individual, social, economic, political, intellectual, material, moral and spiritual life in a coherent balance. In modern terminology it is the full cost assessment *par excellence* that focuses our full attention on evaluation of priorities, examination of consequences, selection of the route of greatest public benefit in the broadest possible definition, and the shunning of narrow gains at the expense of hardship to others.

The worldview, ethos and the mental outlook of Islam has never been more fitted for the task that faces mankind. The objectives set by Islam of attaining self-sufficient, self-reliant, self-sustaining, homeostatic, balanced and harmonious growth of the individual, community, society and mankind as a whole have never been more needed, nor more under threat from human profligacy. But without planning we cannot bring the benefits of Islam to anyone. Without making Islam operative as practical *dawa* we remain Utopians, idealists, mere talkers. The only way to witness Islam in the modern world is to articulate its concepts in constructive, reformative action that engages with the problems that confront people today. Our task is not to idealize with some history-bound vision of how Islam has been and should be in an ideal world. The task of practical, planned *dawa* by Muslims must be to reformulate our understanding of the eternal message of Islam, its concepts and principles in the context of the predicament of contemporary reality to deliver well-researched, carefully thought out, suitably-resourced practicable solutions that improve the lot of humanity in accordance with the clearly defined and unchanging values and priorities of Islam. *Dawa* today is about planning to change things, to transmute the potential and real disasters of our times into surmountable hurdles. It is the only training available to Muslims to prepare ourselves to inhabit a viable Islamic future.

Index

The index includes references to subjects, authors, publications and organizations discussed in the text, but the notes at the ends of the chapters have not been indexed. References have been arranged in word-by-word alphabetical order, and page numbers of diagrams in the text have been given in *italic*.

211

Muslims 16–17, 19, 38,
175–6, 191
women
attitudes towards 25–6
community development 64, 110
education 6, 105–18, 181
Islamic organizations 117
media 7, 146, 153, 157
poverty 102, 104
Women's Home Islamic Literacy
Programme 115
World Assembly of Muslim Youth
(WAMY) Conference,
Riyadh (1976) 140
World Conference on Muslim
Education, 1st, Makkah

al-Mukarramah (1977) 62
World Council of Churches
Commission 27
World Muslim League 140, 152
World Vision 126
worldview 9, 83
and broadcasting 181, 182
and *dawa* 29–32, 202–3
and disasters 208, 210
and wellbeing of *ummah* 7

young people 64, 157

zakat 99
Zen 19